MAX THE BUTCHER
by Max Block
with Ron Kenner

Lyle Stuart Inc.   Secaucus, N.J.

Queries regarding rights and permissions
should be addressed to: Lyle Stuart Inc.,
120 Enterprise Ave., Secaucus, N.J. 07094.

Published by Lyle Stuart Inc.
Published simultaneously in Canada by
Musson Book Company
A division of General Publishing Co. Limited
Don Mills, Ontario

Manufactured in the United States of America

Library of Congress Cataloging in Publication Data

Block, Max, 1909-
  Max the butcher.
  1. Block, Max, 1909-   . 2. Trade-
unions—United States—Officials and employees
—Biography.   3. Butchers—United States—
Biography.   4. Amalgamated Meat Cutters and
Butcher Workmen of North America.   I. Kenner,
Ron.   II. Title.
HD6509.B55A35   331.88′16490281′0924   [B]   81-18478
ISBN 0-8184-0322-5   AACR2

To Lil

1 What we went through building the unions in America—the terrible conditions, the bloodshed and fear and pain, the growth, and later the pussy-footing—it's like you had two schools of people: the old-time union leaders, the ones that came up from the bottom like I did, and you fought your way often at the threat of your life; and the others, the ones that got in on the gravy train.

It was easy to see the difference. Over the past fifty years or so, I knew most of them—the names you hear, Reuther, Hoffa, Meany, Fitzsimmons. And the politicians, Joe Kennedy, John, Bobby, Teddy, Dewey, Eisenhower. I knew the fighters —Barney Ross, Dempsey, Tunney, Marciano. I met the entertainers and the Las Vegas crowd—Dean Martin, Wilbur Clark, Howard Hughes. Also I knew many of the people in the mob —Frank Costello, Meyer Lansky, Carlo Gambino and the others who directed the syndicates in Chicago, New York, Miami . . .

Gambino, the godfather, was a friend going back forty years, though for a long time I didn't know who he was. I'll have more to say about Gambino, the mob, the guys from Murder, Incorporated. But the mob is not the biggest problem with the unions today, and neither is the corruption in the big unions. The biggest problem is sitting around, not **organizing**

—while millions of workers, unorganized, or in phony unions, still lack decent conditions.

I remember Walter Reuther. He was a dynamo, always raring to go organize. So was Jimmy Hoffa. Today you don't have those, the Hoffas, the Reuthers, the Blocks. . . . You got them hanging around just to collect, one way or another. Some of the old-timers—they're still there. They're still alive. They didn't retire like I did, but mostly they just drag it on. And the new ones come in and know nothing. They're reading a book, how they can do it legally. But that way, you're not organized, because there was nothing there—no members. When the unions were built, the bosses hired the cops and the tough guys. If you want to talk about "legally," then nothing would have got done.

Maybe there's less violence now. Maybe it is more legal. But the mob is still around. And you still get knocked off if you don't go along. So there's always corruption—that's part of human nature. During the 1950s, in the McClellan hearings, I was their star witness. They had me on the stand for days. asking about union corruption. But you have to look at all of it —not just what makes headlines so someone can get elected.

Today, for example, the independent unions in the United States are very big. And they're all controlled by the mobs. Nothing is legitimate. Everything is illegitimate. But nobody touches it, because it wouldn't be in the headlines. It's a small union and not a national thing, not a large international union. The workers in many of these small unions don't get any meetings. There's no elections, no sick pay, no job security— nothing! So it didn't change.

I know. I've been through it. In Connecticut, when I was about sixteen, my family was all in the cattle business, slaugh- tering. And many cattle—when you opened the stomach, looked cancerous, or had measles, and we were afraid we'd get poisoned. So we used to put on rubber gloves and pull the skin, with the pus pimples, down. We were afraid that regular gloves would get the juice. That's the way it is all over the country. The only thing, if it's not federally inspected, you cannot ship meat or meat products out of state. Inside there's no federal supervision, and you can sell poison, any shit.

Of course there's no guarantee you wouldn't ship. You can

go over the state line with a truck. It's no big deal. I've seen it. And in state, you can still sell and slaughter without federal inspection. So we'd put on rubber gloves and pull off the skin with the infection and then sell the meat to the butchers, and they'd sell it to the customers. And that's the way the thing goes to this day. Today, high prices encourage this stuff more and more. Cattle are being rustled, taken to places where you knock them off under a tree with a block and tackle, like we used to years ago. We didn't give a damn then, and it's the same now. That's the way it's done in every state, because that's the law.

For years I was president of the Amalgamated Meat Cutters. We organized thousands of butchers and cutters and the workers in the packing houses all over the country. I was living in it. I'd been dealing with meat and poultry and food all my life, so I know what goes into the food you eat, including a lot of things you don't see on the labels.

Since the 1930s, my brother Louie and I organized all the butchers and boners in the wholesale and slaughtering houses and rendering plants in New York and New Jersey. In Local 640 of the Amalgamated Meat Cutters, we organized the plants where they render the fat and bones.

I was head of the Butcher District Council in New York and New Jersey and president of Local 342 of the Amalgamated, covering all the butchers in New York and at the time the biggest retail local for all the butchers and markets in the whole country. I was also vice-president of the international—the Amalgamated Meat Cutters International and Butcher Workmen of North America A.F.L.–C.I.O.

So I had connections with the renderers, and one Friday night this guy came to see me from the Sage Rendering Plant. Sage had been picking up fat, bones, and skin in Pennsylvania. Then the son, Bob Sage, began picking up the stuff in New York, and this fellow John was his manager and salesman in the area. So John came to see me and stayed over the weekend with my family. But it turned out he was on special assignment from another company. It was a very big company that makes gelatin, the biggest, Kine and Knox. And that weekend John explained to me about bones.

The renderers were picking up the bones for one cent a pound in the butcher shops and slaughterhouses, and from restaurants from the garbage, where they keep the bones and fat in separate cans. So because I was well-connected, this company told John to offer me five cents a pound for bones if I could help them get a million pounds or more a month.

I asked him, "Why do they have to give me five cents? They can buy 'em for one and a half cents from you, the renderers." This is after other people in the restaurants get through chewing on them. But still our bones are cleaner and healthier than some others.

"No," he said. "We can't give 'em a million pounds a month for any price." And this is because the renderers need the bones. They make bone meal. They make food. They need the phosphorus for fertilizer, and some of the calcium is used to put in the cow feed, because every time a cow gives birth she has to be fed extra calcium.

"So they're short, at any price, and they need it," he told me.

"Well," I asked him. "Where do they get the bones now, and where have they been getting them all the years gone by?"

"They're getting them," he said, "from places like Latin America, India, and the African jungles—and they find them lying around or they sort it out of the garbage and then they pulverize those bones. And that's how we get the bones, and that's how they make their gelatin."

"How come," I asked, "our federal government lets 'em get away with that stuff? You're talking about rat bones, mice bones, and all other sick and diseased animals that you find in the jungle. In India you got cows in the street that have been laying there for days, in the heat, with the flies and bugs and who knows what else. . . ."

"As long as they pulverize the bones," he said, "they let 'em get away with it."

"You mean all these colorful gelatin packages you see on the counter, that's it?"

"Definitely," he said. "That's how we get the bones. We're running short. All these years we've been bringing them in by boat."

So that's how they operate. The big companies put the gelatin recipes on the boxes and they tell you how to make all the gelatin with the different flavors: raspberry, cherry, lemon, lime, strawberry, orange, peach, apricot, and so on. It all sounds good, but you can't make gelatin without bones—it won't gel.

The gelatin is supposed to harden your nails. And maybe it does. But they're still bringing in all those bones by the boatload from the jungles and India and places like that.

Once I pressured the poultry industry to get federal inspections. The chickens get certain sicknesses, and in the plant they cleaned and processed them after they were dead already. And I handled these chickens. I know. I went to the plants. Maybe five, ten percent died there. But nobody cared. So instead of throwing them out, the feet and all the other offal and bones from the sick chickens, they still sold it to the soup companies like Campbell's. Today they're federally inspected, but it's not that clean. They don't buy chickens to make soup. They buy the heads and feet. The feet are one thing, but you know the head consists of eyes, brains, junk you can imagine.

I saw how chickens have a habit, they peck on each other. If a chicken has a sore, the other chickens begin to eat at it until they kill it. But if the chicken lasts a day or so the sore gets infected. When the infected chickens are slaughtered their heads and feet are thrown in with the others. One of the large poultry producers I knew would sell the feet, heads and guts to Campbell's and another large soup company. They'd cook this into soup.

I visited and organized many of the boning places of the cattle meat. You get the meat in quarters. Then you bone it out. The better cuts, filets, eye of rib, shoulder, are sold to restaurants and supermarkets, along with the better part of the chuck. The rest of the forequarters and hindquarters is chopped up for the hamburger you get in the butcher shops and places like McDonald's, Burger King, Carl's, all the chains—whoever will buy it. And where you fabricate and bone, you use the carcasses of the poorer grades of the cow.

You can't take a good steer and bone it out because it'd be too fat, too expensive. So you use lean cows and bulls. Now the tripe, from the belly, they freeze this and after it's frozen solid they pulverize it very fine. And then there's the spleen. This gives a red color to the meat because it's a bloody thing. Same with the hearts. They also used to use the lungs for the same purpose, all frozen and pulverized and chopped up, very fine, and that's added to the chopped meat, and this is part of the hamburgers we eat. Basically we're paying for pure beef, what they advertise as pure beef. But what we're eating includes the insides of the cattle, which isn't so good at all.

Now to give you an idea about legality, the hamburger is supposed to be eighty percent protein and twenty percent fat —and that's how it shows up, because all the offal and junk they put in is all protein. So the inspector can't do anything because it's legal that way. And the chain-store operators that buy this stuff, maybe in patties—some of them are rolled, with a fancy name and a fancy package—these chains, they're selling this at a high price. They're making millions of dollars on that crap. And all they do is add a little water and the junk they buy for five cents a pound. Campbell's, McDonald's, whatever—it's no different. People buy gelatin, hamburger, soup, they think they got something. It's nothing!

In Harlem, and in places like the poorer areas of Brooklyn, you find big sales in pet food. They don't have that many dogs. They don't have cats. But still pet food is a big seller in these areas, because it's cheaper and the people are eating it. The truth is the pet foods are better than some of the junk we get. You shouldn't have to eat that junk today.

I remember Poland in the 1920s when people were starving, going around with bloated bellies, and you didn't have that much choice. Or before that, when I was a kid and we used to have to hide the potatos or the bread so others wouldn't know we had food. But even then the stuff had less chemicals than today and probably was healthier to eat.

My father came from Poland and lived in Connecticut with his family, and they were in the cattle business. They would buy cattle and slaughter them and sell the carcasses to butchers. I slaughtered too. I did it under a tree with tackle blocks, and by hand. They also traded cattle, in different towns. So we'd go out and buy cattle—two or three or ten, or whatever —and then we drove them home. Those days we had to walk with them without trucks.

Before I was born, my father went to visit his folks in Vilna, Russia. Now that area is Poland. He met my mother, who must have been about eighteen. They got married over there, and then the First World War broke out and they couldn't leave, so they wound up staying and having six children. And one boy died.

My father married my mother about 1907. I was the oldest son. I was born in 1909. My older sister was born in 1908. So we remained there, though my father had tried to get us out when he realized the war was coming. He became a butcher in Poland, too, because my mother's family was all in the business.

The Germans attacked Romania in 1914. Toward the end, the Germans were losing and ended up displaced for a couple of years. So we used to get a lot of food from them. My father's butcher shop was at one end of the town, and he did a lot of business with these soldiers—he got stuff like corn flour, jams, like that. I really don't know what business he did with these soldiers, but I know they were friends of his. They would bring stuff, and maybe he used to pay them off in cash. I can't say exactly how he exchanged with them, but I know that's what was happening, and so my father would keep the food in the barn, in a big hole underneath the manure. You had to hide it or people would just grab it.

Then my father got a kidney infection. There was no doctor available. He didn't have any medicine. So that was it. My father died. Soon our stored stuff was used up and we were hungry. We were starving. Everybody was starving. People were falling apart in the streets. So I would take my brother Louie and go out to the potato fields and we'd dig for what we could find that had been left behind. Some of the potatos were discolored, a little green, but we used to come back with about ten, twelve pounds, so we had enough food. We were luckier than some.

I must have been about ten, eleven years old, and Louie was about nine or ten. My mother used to have flour buried, and she'd mix this with the potatos and bake certain breads, late at night. Not too big, though, because it takes too long to bake and people would smell, at midnight even, and you were afraid of that. So my mother was a good business lady and somehow she used to get a certain amount of meat for sale.

I began to go to certain farmers with her. We'd walk five, ten miles to farmers that had owed my father money. They were rich farmers, and sometimes we'd bring back a calf. So we'd slaughter it, and we had meat. We also brought back corn, and occasionally they gave us someone to walk back with for safety. Times were rough. Very rough.

My grandmother lived with us too. My mother's mother used to beg my mother to take the children to America. And of couse, my father had told my mother about America too. So after the war we got ready to go. They wouldn't allow all of us out; the quota didn't call for it—my grandmother couldn't go. We didn't want to leave without her, but she kept insisting. So finally my mother took us, and we left my grandmother with her stepson.

We left some money behind, because my father had left money, American money. You couldn't get things without money. You couldn't buy bread. People walked around blown up like balloons from hunger. They used to drink water, I guess, and blow up and die. There were so many funerals there weren't enough vehicles to cart the bodies. There were no longer horses because there was no food for them. Food was needed for people. So a lot of the horses died from hunger too, and some were killed for horsemeat.

Years later, horsemeat and kangaroo meat were passed off on tens of thousands of innocent consumers in the United States. Only this time it was not because of a food shortage, but because a few people wanted to make a lot of money.

2

We came to this country in 1923. My brother and I went to New Jersey, and the rest of the family settled in New York. My mother and two of my sisters went to live in the Greenpoint section in Brooklyn with my mother's younger sister, whose husband was a baker, and my oldest sister, Fanny, was set up with another retired uncle in the Bronx, Uncle Solney. So Fanny lived and went to school in the Bronx, and Sonya and Helen went to school in Brooklyn. Louie stayed with an uncle in Madison, and I stayed with an uncle in Morristown, where the school was.

Eventually we all got together. My mother bought a grocery and delicatessen in the New Lots section of Brooklyn. It had been an old swamp, but they built a tremendous housing section there. So my mother took a five-room apartment; then called me up to give me the address and tell me she wanted me to come home. I did. We were five children. We were so happy we could be together again. We were not used to being separated.

In Brooklyn, at above five o'clock in the morning I'd deliver rolls from our grocery to customers. Then after a while my brother Louie handled that and I got a job as a butcher in New Jersey. I was about sixteen. It was a good wage, but I had to live in New Jersey away from my family, because of the distance and the hours. We were working day and night! Twenty-five dollars a week, with board—room and food. My boss would knock on my door at any hour. He wanted me to sleep over in his house so he could wake me early. We'd get dressed, eat breakfast—I was a good eater, and I was young— and then we'd go to the shop and work.

I knew the butcher's trade since I was a kid in Russia. I could handle a knife and everything else by that time.

We cut the bones by handsaw. It took a couple of hours. Mostly I did this, and then there was cleaning up the store, and delivering. It was rough work. The boss would wake me at maybe three o'clock in the morning, and we used to come home again about seven, eight o'clock at night. Saturday we worked until midnight, or later, and Sunday was a half day.

On Sunday at one o'clock I'd go visit my mother in East New York, and then wake up very early Monday morning.

I think the boss was Polish. At least, he spoke a couple of Polish words I recognized, and the operation was kosher style.

One Sunday, a guy came in and asked for a piece of meat. I put it on the scale. I told him it was seventy cents or whatever. And he said, "You Jew son of a bitch! You're selling meat on Sunday." And he started being abusive in front of the other customers.

Finally I said, "Let's go outside," on account of his being a wise guy. He was a stubborn Polack, about twice my size and maybe twice my age. I'm about sixteen. He's maybe thirty or thirty-two. So as we're going out, he's alongside me. I kept my apron on. I didn't take it off. Then while he was taking off his coat, he couldn't move his arms freely. He was wide open and I belted him in the mouth, hard. It knocked his teeth out, and down he went. I figured I needed the edge, but that taught me to go to the gym to learn how to fight.

I was a tough street fighter even before that. I remember, the early ones at the Speedwell Avenue Public School in Morristown. Miss Mercent, the principal, was a beautiful lady, a fine lady. She had white hair, but she wasn't all soft. She knew I was tough because I'd gotten into fights, usually because I was a Jew and a foreigner.

She understood me pretty good. A lot of kids tried picking on me. All of a sudden, I beat this one tough guy. And she was a very smart woman. She knew I didn't pick fights, but that I could fight good. So she matched me with bullies, with gloves, in the playground.

I used to beat them up pretty bad. It taught the bullies a lesson, and I got more confidence. I was thirteen or fourteen. I was tough, because I had to survive.

Later, when I was about seventeen, I began to box. I had moved to Connecticut to see my father's side of the family that was in the cattle business in Derby, and I began to train.

There was this guy Chappy, a six-footer, about nineteen or twenty. He was supposed to be my buddy. He was about my build, a little stocky, but taller. He used to help me go out and drive the cattle, and he and I became friends. So I didn't want to hit him. But we got talked into a match in back of this candy store, in a large room by the potbelly stove.

Chappy beat the shit out of me. I didn't feel like hitting him—I considered him my friend. But Frank de Martino, this butcher, initiated the fight. After Chappy beat me so badly, we arranged for a rematch a week later, same place, in the back of this stationery-and-candy store. Peppy, a little guy, a Polack, a little older, he was betting all his money on me. And de Martino, he was betting on Chappy.

Chappy was like a bull. Strong. But I must have been stronger. This time I gave him an unmerciful beating. He couldn't work for two weeks. I hit him one shot and he ran with his head into the potbelly stove and burned his head.

The shop was owned by Joe Levitez, who had graduated from Yale and then bought the place. He was having a problem with this guy Mike, who had the bowling alley and used to pick on him. Levitez said to him, "Mike don't do that; I'll knock you out." But the guy didn't stop, so Levitez hit him and he went flying into the middle of the street, into the car tracks, and that took care of Mike. He behaved after that. This was on Main Street in Derby, a tough, cold place, just over the bridge from Shelton.

When I moved back to Brooklyn, I worked out every night for a year in Willie Beech's gym in East New York, Brooklyn. Then I met this guy Ferky in the gym; he got me an amateur card, and took me to fight in Canarsie. They used to run fights there every week. Those days it was a four-man class, all in the same division. The winners of the first fight would fight in the finals on the same night.

The first one I fought was Eric Lawson. Lawson later became known as a challenger for the world light-heavyweight championship, yet even on my first fight I beat him pretty good. He was a good boxer, with more experience, but I was tougher. And I kept getting him on the inside when he'd try to jab me. In the end I overpowered him. I won the three-round decision.

I put on my robe and sat with my brother watching the next match because I knew I'd have to fight the winner. It turned out he weighed 168 pounds against my 150 pounds. His name was Rudy Berger. He was German, a muscular guy, and he was fighting a guy that was very short. And this little guy, when the bell rang, he came out and threw maybe thirty or forty punches into Rudy. But it didn't faze him. Rudy came up with one left hook and knocked the little guy out.

Now this is my opponent for the next fight. It made me a little nervous, but I had confidence because I had worked hard in the gym for a year. I kept thinking how I ought to handle myself. I hoped I'd come out all right and not make a bad show of it. Also, I knew I was very good against someone that threw good left hooks, and this guy was a good left hooker.

The fight started. Before the round was over, I had kept up pretty good. Then Rudy hit me one left hook in the mouth —it jarred my head and I thought I'd go flying out of the ring. It just about knocked my teeth loose. I took it okay, but my teeth shook for six months after that. So I got back. Before long, the opportunity came. I beat a left hook and crossed a right to his mouth. The impact on him was terrific. He went down to his knees, to the count of eight. I hoped he'd stay down.

The whole thing was played at ten o'clock at night. Those days, we didn't have mouthpieces fitted like today. When you got hit in the mouth, you really felt it. Now Rudy's lips looked like they'd been chopped up with a knife. He was bleeding. There was blood all over him, and me, too.

The place was in an uproar. Finally, he got up. But pretty soon he threw the same punch, the same left hook. I crossed, tearing into him—he went down again. There's another count. This time the bell saved him.

The next round, he went through the same moves—he was predictable. I hit him again, the same right cross. Now the referee stepped in. He took one look at Rudy and stopped the fight. He asked me to help carry Rudy to the corner, which I did. It was my first TKO.

I was very sore from the two fights and the whole routine. I took hot baths with epsom salts, to heal—I'd dump in a whole box—and I didn't go near the gym for a month. I didn't want to get punchy or have cauliflower ears. I had no intention of staying with boxing. Besides, I had a job. But still, I was thrilled—I never expected to beat Rudy like that.

I continued to fight in the ring, now and then. I kept winning, usually by knockouts. Then they brought in some fighters from Chicago, and they needed a middleweight. This was at the Knights of Columbus in Rockaway, a well-to-do section of Atlantic Beach, and I was supposed to fill out the ticket.

So I went against a guy named John. I get into the ring and I see the assistant in his corner is a blonde girl. She turns out to be his sister. So this fellow is about six-feet, and thin. I didn't think he'd be a good puncher. But when we start, every time he hits me with his left hand it was like a shot going through me.

I was amazed at his punching power. Before the first round was over he hit me with a right hand over the bridge of my nose, and I bled like a pig and everything turned dark. I realized the round was almost over, and he was very tall. I kept bobbing and weaving, very low, to last out the round, and I did. They watered me off, pasted together the bridge of my nose.

The referee came over to my corner. "Kid," he said. "I'll have to stop this fight. You're not getting a million dollars for this. It's not worth it."

"Please," I said. "Let me go out for the second round. I'll knock him out."

"I like your courage," he told me. "But if he opens up the area and the bleeding starts again, I'll stop it anyhow."

"Okay. But please let me go out."

The bell rang. I came out and we sparred off. Pretty soon there was an opening. I hit the guy a left hook on the chin. The next thing, he's lying on his back—wiped out. Then his sister is screaming from the corner, "Johnny! Johnny! Get up! The Jew can't fight!" So everybody in the place is laughing.

Because he's on his back, and it's me who can't fight. He couldn't even get up. The referee motioned me to help him pick the guy up and take him to the corner, which I did.

In my second fight the same night, the other boxer was Jimmy McLoughlin. He was considered old, about twenty-five. We were all under twenty. They were supposed to award prizes, but the real payoff was cash under the table. Maybe twenty dollars. Anyway, Jimmy was real rough. He used to knock everybody out. Then I'm fighting him, and he was hitting at my nose, so it opened up and started bleeding. The other guy had busted it. But now the bleeding got pretty heavy, so the referee stopped the fight. They awarded Jimmy a TKO.

"I got to get a return match against Jimmy, because I know I can beat him," I told my man Ferky, my manager, "because he knocks out everybody, but he didn't knock *me* out. And my nose, that was the other guy."

So a number of weeks went by because I had to get my nose cleaned up and healed. Finally, I went to fight again at the Knights of Columbus, in Far Rockaway, where Jimmy was the big favorite, knocking all the kids dead over there.

Louie was down in the dressing room with our friend while I watched the next fight. Then somebody ran up to tell me Jimmy McLoughlin was beating up my brother in the dressing room. Jimmy said a friend should have got a decision, but Louie said the judge's decision was fair so Jimmy hit Louie. Jimmy should have known better. He's twenty-five or twenty-six, and Louie was only about sixteen.

I got there. They had stopped the fight, and Louie was hurt. Now I was ready to pound Jimmy, but his manager came between us. "You want to fight," he said, "you get paid. You want to fight Jimmy, you get paid. Fight next week."

I said, "Okay." We arranged to fight the following Friday in the same place. So on Friday we took a lot of guys with us, because now it was a grudge fight. Jimmy was a sore loser, I knew. Most likely he would bring most of his friends from Ozone Park. So we decided to bring some of our friends, about three or four cars, in case of trouble.

Jimmy and I were the final bout, and we each would have only one fight that night. I got into the ring, a clean-looking kid. He looked like a gorilla. The bell rang, and he rushed across the ring. I had just stood up, but I crossed my right and I hit him in the head and he went down to his knees—took the eight-count. After this, I didn't want to knock him out so early. I wanted to give him a beating. I was mad, because he had broken Louie's nose. So I gave Jimmy a terrible beating. He was bleeding from his ears, from every part of his head. And I was afraid to hit him on the chin because I didn't want to knock him out.

They called me Jackie. In the corner, my man said, "What are you fooling around for, Jackie? Knock him out. Because he can come back."

"I'm not worried," I said. "I'm gonna chop him to ribbons." Which I did.

We came out for the third round. Jimmy kept spitting on me. "You Jew son of a bitch!" he said. "Why don't you fight?"

"Jimmy," I said, "don't talk—fight!" And Jimmy made his move at me, and I tore into him—practically knocked his chin off—and he hit the canvas. Fell flat on his face. Out. No count, even.

The referee motioned to me to help pick Jimmy up, but I wouldn't do it. It was a grudge fight. Anyway, that night there was no trouble with Jimmy's friends. They saw we were pretty tough kids.

On the way home, Louie told me how during the fight he was sitting next to two ladies with white hats. When Jimmy walked into the ring they said, "Oh, wow!" Then they saw me, looking like a nice kid, and they said, "We're sorry for him!" But the fight started, and Jimmy ran across the ring to me and they saw me hit him—I really stiffed him almost— and one lady said to the other, "That kid can fight."

So Louie told me how he looked at them and said, "That's my brother."

So now they were half-rooting for me too. But he said he was nervous. His teeth were shaking. "I knew you were gonna beat him," Louie said, but he was so nervous his jaw was shaking. Anyway, I felt good about it.

3 I was working in the butcher shop in Jersey City on Ocean Avenue, and one day I met a fellow by the name of Krasnapovsky. He said to me, "Max, you're a good worker." But he advised me to join the union instead of working day and night in New Jersey. That sounded pretty good, and so he talked to me some more, and he asked me what day could I be free. I told him I could meet him on Monday.

On Monday, I had my brother Louie with me, because we always did everything together. So Krasnapovsky took us to East Ninety-eighth Street in Brooklyn. We met a fellow on the corner, and Krasnapovsky said this was the organizer of the Food Workers' Industrial Union, and we were talking and they were telling us about the right-wing union of the A.F. of L. that had an injunction against them.

The Food Workers, maybe eight or nine hundred members, was the union that covered everything in the food industry, everyone that worked in a supermarket, the butcher, grocer, produce people, the restaurant worker. The others, maybe an equal number of workers, were the straight union, the A.F. of L., and these were called the right-wingers. But the Food Workers was the left—I didn't know the difference between left and right. And so these guys from the Food Workers were telling us that everywhere they'd go to organize, the A.F. of L. would come around with an injunction and get them locked up.

While they were telling me this, some guy came by and he yelled out, real loud, "Here comes the revolution."

"Who is this guy?" I asked.

They tell me he's one of the fellows they're talking about. And the organizer, he says, "Hit the rat!"

So I said to my brother Louie, "Take a poke at him."

But the man began to scream, "Gangsters! Gangsters!" And he started to run.

I got mad. I started chasing him. He was running down East Ninety-eighth Street, and you had all these shops with the big plate-glass windows. He was yelling, "Police! Police!"

I kept after him. I chased him almost two blocks before I got to him. Then, while he was still running, I swung around and crashed my fist into the side of his face. Hard. He was running so fast—now he went flying, through the plate glass window. He went right through. And it was amazing—instead of shattering the glass, it made only a round hole, and he landed on the floor in the store. He went through like a bird but didn't really get hurt or cut.

Meanwhile the women shoppers were screaming. Louie joined me and we just walked away, leaving the guy laying there. We went around the corner to a delicatessen. Then after about twenty minutes or so I see the guy walking around with the cops, looking for us. But we stayed and had lunch and sat there a while, minding our own business.

That night, we went to a meeting of this same group from the Food Workers' Industrial Union in New York on Fourteenth Street. We went up to the second floor, where we were invited, especially now they saw we could fight like that— good kids, with no police records. While the meeting went on, the police came. Detectives. We knew they were cops because they showed up with this guy, Heller, who I had sent through the window. They had a wagon downstairs. I was a little nervous, expecting the guy to point me out, but I didn't do anything, because I figured maybe he wouldn't recognize Louie or me. But then, what this guy did, he pointed out three *other* guys that were supposed to have hit him. Not my brother and not me.

I was sitting there. He saw me. But he was afraid to point me out. I'm too tough to mess with. He knew. And so did all the others—about three hundred people there.

So we're initiated into the union. That was the start of it. And now I had a reputation, from my activity. They gave me this job as a butcher, in the co-op, the cooperative apartments, a big complex across from the park on Allerton Avenue in the Bronx. That was the hangout where all the students stayed— that whole section, about six blocks down and a couple of blocks across.

I left the butcher shop in New Jersey and started as a butcher in the co-op market, and I took a small apartment there with Louie, who was given a job in the dairy. Because of all my training since I was a kid, I'm the best butcher in cuts. So I worked as a butcher, and we also made sandwiches, which we sold for the benefit of the union, for the workers. Those days it wasn't like now, with computer checkouts. They had a cash register in every department, and you just took the cash. You either put the money in the register or in your pocket. But I wouldn't take anything, because I was honest. Anyhow, the average wage was maybe forty dollars a week, and I was getting about fifty-five. I was well-liked. And I appreciated the fact that now I got an hour for lunch.

So that's how I began to be sold on the union—because before, I used to *always* be working, and now I see the difference between the union shop and the nonunion shop, and it's like the difference between day and night.

When I took a day off, they replaced me, and I didn't lose any pay. But mostly they took me around on days off to fight. They began to use me on some tough strikes—different things. As a worker I was just working in the shop, but every time they needed me for something they called me, and I went and did it.

Now I had time to go up to the gymnasium, and I continued boxing in the amateurs. I was winning every fight, knocking out my opponents. But I only did that to learn how to fight. Now the issue came up that the Food Workers wanted to organize Union Avenue in the Bronx. Big shops. Butcher shops, dairy, grocery, produce. All big. So they began to tell the story about Mr. Miller on the corner. There was a large produce shop that employed sixteen people and was owned by Mr. Miller and his wife, a young couple. I was appointed to hand the contract to Mr. Miller.

This was the summer of 1929. The deal was supposed to have been set up already, and it was all one way—our way. I didn't figure there'd be any problem, and I didn't think much about it. I went with a few guys. And there was this Conrad Kaye. He was a handsome guy, very handsome, always telling jokes, a good guy to be with, but he was a Communist, something I found out later. He was supposed to go along to help us, and he was being sent by the union to keep an eye on us.

There was myself, and Harry Davidson—we called him the Monkey—another guy by the name of Harry, a tall, thin fellow about six-foot-one, and a fellow by the name of Jackie from the Bronx, who came into the group the night before. All three worked in produce, in a different shop at the co-op. Jackie was not tall. He was about my height or shorter, maybe five-seven, five-eight. The Monkey was about the same size as me, a little huskier. Jackie, about twenty, was a bachelor, and the tall guy, Harry, about twenty-five, was also single. He grew up in Coney Island. The Monkey, a little older, had a wife and kid in Brooklyn. His uncle was a rich man, very big in supplying restaurants in Washington Market and New York with produce, cheese, and stuff. So they were all good, clean kids. None had boxed like Louie or me, but they could handle themselves. They didn't know anything about politics, but they believed in what they were doing, in improving conditions for working people the way I did.

Four of us showed up, that's all. Louie didn't come. And there were fourteen workers, and Mr. and Mrs. Miller, maybe in their thirties.

I had the contract on me. Before we walked in I told the Monkey and the other Harry and Jackie, "I think that's all there is to it." Because I had already given the instructions. The guys with me carried single-edged Gem razor blades.

There were two doors. I went in the front door to talk to Mr. Miller. The other fellows walked in the side door, and went behind the counter with the blades. The thing is, you cut the strings of the aprons. That means they're like out on strike, even though they haven't really joined the union yet. So you cut the apron strings with these blades. If the worker resists, if he wants to put up a fight, you cut the face. That was the order and that was the movement. Those were the instructions. So I walked in, and the others walked in.

I go up to Mr. Miller, a kind of chunky looking redheaded guy.

"I'm from the Food Workers' Industrial Union," I said. "I'd like to talk to you about signing a contract." I go to hand him the contract. But right away he started yelling at me, getting excited. Instead of reaching for the contract, he grabbed his hatchet.

Produce people use a certain hatchet, like a hammer, but lined with steel. The moment he pulled out the hatchet I gave him a hard left hook to the belly and a shot over the head, and down he goes. And as he goes down, he pulls the sleeve completely off my new coat.

At the same time, the Monkey jumped over, cut Miller right across the forehead, with his razor blade. Then Miller's wife started coming at me with something. She looked vicious. I hit her. She just went flying, like a bird, right over the fruit stand. She banged into something and she was out, or she wasn't getting up. It happened so fast, none of the other workers had made any moves.

Now we go to leave, but we take the others with us, the fourteen workers from behind the counter. They didn't want to go, but we forced them out. They knew we had the blades. So they go along by subway to the union office. They had to travel with the Monkey, and Jackie, and this other Harry from the Bronx to Seventeenth Street, about an hour and a half ride. The workers outnumbered us, but they didn't cause any trouble—they knew we could always come back.

I didn't go by subway. I know I clobbered Mr. and Mrs. Miller, and I wasn't going to get arrested if I could help it. I had a new Chevy. So I headed down to the office, and the others went by subway.

I didn't want to use the strong-arm tactics, like forcing the workers down to the union with blades—I didn't like that unless you had to, unless it was in self-defense. But the *main* fight—first of all you were fighting the worker, the guys you were out to help, because the worker was the toughest person to organize. For one thing, he was scared. Because things had been tried and tried and failed, and the guy that's joining the union or out on the street trying to help organize, who wants

24

the union, he's blackballed—and he can't ever get a job again. These were tough times. Plenty of people were out of work, hungry. So they were afraid of that.

At the office, I saw Conrad Kaye, who instigated the whole thing. Then the others arrived. I asked Kaye, "Where've you been, you son of a bitch? What happened?"

"I stopped off to get a shoe shine," he said.

But he was the one that gave the instructions.

"You son of a bitch! You yellow bastard!" the Monkey said. "You stopped off to get a shine? You instigated the fight. You started the situation. So while we were under fire, you got lost."

Kaye didn't answer. What could he say?

That afternoon, the same afternoon, we went back to Miller's place with a picket line. The workers we brought to the office didn't want to picket. They were afraid. So we took our own people, and we went back, but we still didn't get anything signed. We didn't confront the Millers, and they didn't come out. They knew better.

We put our people out on strike, and that was it. We picketed that same afternoon. We had blank signs in the office, lots of them—they were part of the union equipment—and we filled out Miller's name with a crayon, and we were yelling and singing, "Miller's on strike! Miller's on strike!" So then this was to be an example in the Bronx, because it was one of the more important shops on Union Avenue, an important area with lots of markets we wanted to organize. And this was to be the first.

We kept up the strike. Some customers didn't go in. Miller wasn't doing much business, but we figured he may have been helped along with money by the area businessmen, because once he would sign up with the union, then everybody else would have to sign up too.

It became an issue. There were incidents. Before long, while we were picketing every day, Miller hired some tough guys to get us killed or out of action. A common practice of the bosses—and they bought the cops, too. This was years before you had the National Labor Relations Board and all that. It was just a question of who was going to win the fight—like when you go to war. There was no rule and no law and order. The cops were all on the side of the employer, who paid them off, and that's how things went. We couldn't carry weapons to protect ourselves, because the cops used to search us. And they beat up some guys. But they didn't search the tough guys. So you had some bloody fights. Before it was over, a few people got stabbed—it wasn't baby games.

Miller must have hired these tough guys, mobsters. One day, after we'd been picketing Miller every day for a week, I was standing by a shoemaker's shop, right around the corner from the open stand. I saw Louie running, and he wasn't chasing anybody so I figured somebody was chasing him. Then I saw two guys coming with big, long butcher knives. They didn't recognize me, because they were too busy chasing Louie. So I had my back against the shoemaker's shop, and I leaned over and grabbed a hammer off the counter.

First Louie went by, then the guy after him. Now the second guy was coming. I raised my hand with the hammer. As he went by, I bopped him one, a good crack in the head —just battered his head and dropped him. The guy in front, chasing Louie, he didn't see anything. Neither did Louie, still running. But I knew the guy'd never catch Louie, because he must have been about thirty-five, and Louie was seventeen, and too fast.

The guy I hit was finally taken away in an ambulance. I didn't know what happened to him. Maybe he died or wound up in a hospital for a long time, because he had his head busted. They didn't report things like nowadays. I immediately walked away. The cops had been all over before; now you couldn't find any. They must have been paid off to take a walk before the guys came out with the knives.

So there was a lot of violence. Sometimes it got bloody. It was a rough deal. It wasn't a question of people wanting to join the union. The conditions were still bad—people worked like slaves. And if you didn't like it, there was always someone to replace you.

So someone had to organize, and we brought in more people from the outside, and the violence continued. It wasn't something you wanted, but you knew it was always coming, and you learned to take care of yourself. As for the cops, they'd get paid off to chase us and use their clubs, and they defended the mob that the bosses hired.

The left-wing union didn't hire anyone from the mob then.

We were on our own. We used our own kids, our own young fellows. But we were plenty tough. When we had to, we used knives, guns, clubs, anything—a lot of rough work. But the employers still hired the mob; and the mob and the police worked against us.

So Miller had the support of the other shop owners, and the Food Workers had the backing of the people in the cooperative. And it became a big issue. On Saturday night, the Food Workers had arranged a mass picket in the Bronx—that whole area on Union Avenue. You had lots of immigrants: Jewish, Italian, Polish, Irish, German. Well over a thousand people showed up.

It was a heavy shopping section, all stores, fruit, dairy, produce, butchers. The whole street was crowded. Later we learned the Communist party was behind the demonstration, along with the left-wingers and the Communists from the co-op. We walked with the crowd in the street, in the demonstration, moving along, and some others were picketing by Miller's place nearby, and the only things we carried were knives—well, blackjacks, too, a few of them. Then we realized there were some detectives in front of us—a lot of cops around —plainclothesmen you couldn't recognize at first, until suddenly they began to crack heads with blackjacks, hard—women, kids, people carrying the picket signs. The cops gave no warning. Nothing. And there was no provocation. Noises. That's all. People screaming and yelling, "Miller's on strike! Miller's on strike!" Stuff like that.

The cops had no business hitting. So we were behind them, and a couple guys and myself we began to stab them a little bit. Not many. Maybe four or five. Mostly in the ass. But that was an example of my activity, the way I was sold on the idea of unionism. So we stabbed a few cops, and then they began to shoot. They shot Steve Katovis, one of the demonstrators, and also another fellow, Jimmy, a truck driver. Jimmy got shot in the leg, but Steve got shot in the back and it went through his guts, and he died in a couple of days. It was in all the papers. It would become a Communist party cause, because Steve was a party member. And this was tremendous' publicity for them. These were hard times. People were angry. And it was momentous. Lots of people got hurt. Hundreds. You could hardly move in the street.

After Jimmy got shot in the leg, I took him to a doctor we knew two blocks away from the co-op, and the police were looking for the guy that got shot, because they wanted to arrest him. The doctor didn't make out any report, but he said he couldn't take out the bullet, because of the way it lodged itself, so it remained for a long time. But Jimmy was lucky. The bullet went all through Katovis' insides, and they took out all his guts and they still couldn't save him.

I didn't know Katovis except by sight, but I went to the mass funeral. After that shooting there were thousands that showed up, and there was some rioting.

The Miller strike went on for months. There were more incidents as Miller kept bringing in tough guys, gorillas to be after us. So it went on. It was a big shop, but with the business down the way it was, we knew he had to be supported by the area businessmen. And the cops kept harassing us—but we were prepared to strike until doomsday. After a while, as you take sides, the positions harden. The determination to win overrides everything else.

4 Before I knew it, I had
fought eighteen amateur bouts and won sixteen, mostly by
knockout, and one was a draw. But I only did that to learn
how to fight, to handle myself okay. Louie had some fights
too. He followed everything I did, and he was pretty successful but not as active in the ring as I was.

After a while somebody introduced me to Sammy Goldman.
He managed Tony Canzoneri, a widely-known fighter who
held three titles. Sammy got me a professional card, and the
next thing I knew I was in the ring again, this time in the old
Madison Square Garden. So now I became a professional.

I was too young to fight ten rounds. You had to be twenty-
one. So six rounds was my limit. But I didn't need six. I won
by a knockout in the third. The guy was a classy fighter, but
he'd go to jab me and he'd leave himself open—so I plowed
into him. The guy's name was Tony Bendak.

Mostly I would remember my second professional fight, in
Ebbets Field, where the Dodgers played in Brooklyn. They
gave me a tough boxer, and we were on the same card as
Jack Delaney, the light-heavyweight world champion who was
fighting Nando Tassy, the heavyweight champion in Italy.

I get into the ring. I don't remember my opponent's name,
but he was from the college crowd. I got a good price, about

three hundred dollars, but I wasn't in it for the money. The guy, a student from Columbia University, brought his band and cheering section. He was a pretty good fighter, and every time he touched me with a left jab, the band would play. But before long I chopped him up very bad. He was a good boxer, but I'd catch him on the inside—I cut his whole face up.

After about the third round, the guy's manager must have told him to move in and fight, instead of running. But I'm powerful. He had to feel my punch. And I know where to hit, because in my trade, cutting up meat, I know the body, every muscle, like a surgeon. Every time I hit him he must have felt sick. But still, after the bell, he comes out, and he doesn't run from me. He fights. He's perfect for me, because I would never swing. Not even on the street, since I learned how to fight. When a guy made his move, left or right, that's the time I countered, right or left, and boom, he's gone. So I wouldn't throw a punch unless someone made his move at me, and if a guy was smart enough not to swing at me, I was smart enough not to swing at him either. I waited. I got time. So I didn't lose fights.

Now the guy comes at me. The opening is there. I hit him in the stomach and he goes down, curls up like a ball and just stays that way. Again the referee calls me to help carry the guy to the corner. I do. It took them twenty minutes to bring him around, but I didn't hear the band when he was out. I felt sorry. He was a nice gentleman, a good boxer, and I guessed he wanted to earn a few dollars to continue school. Those days you didn't get any loans from the government, the city, or anybody else. You had to earn your own hard way, and that's how it was.

After a while the Food Workers needed me in another butcher shop, in the Bay Parkway area of Brooklyn. The Food Workers had all the butcher shops in the area signed up. But Local 234 of the A.F. of L. kept coming around, trying to take away shops under the Food Workers' jurisdiction. So the Food Workers took me out of the meat market in the co-op by Allerton Avenue, and they put me in Brooklyn on Sixty-fifth and Bay Parkway.

I was glad. It was closer to my mother's house. The other way, if I traveled to my mother's house from the co-op in the

Bronx, it took maybe two hours from one end of the subway to the other, stopping at every stop. I always enjoyed going over. I'd relax. My mother would make a nice meal and she had a good sense of humor. When I'd leave she'd say, "Max always travels light. He just takes his fifty-three pieces with him."

So then you ask, "What are the fifty-three pieces?"

And she says, "A deck of cards and a tie."

On Bay Parkway the boss's name was Poker. He was given a contract with the Food Workers, and I was sent there to help protect the neighborhood from the A.F. of L. taking away the shops. One day this guy by the name of Leff, from the A.F. of L., shows up. He had two of his members, and he began talking to me about leaving the Food Workers and coming to his union. He talked to the boss about signing an agreement with him.

"How can I do it?" Poker asked him. "I got a contract with the Food Workers."

"Take a walk," I told Leff and his buddies. "We got a contract here."

So they argued with me, and they offered deals.

"What do you want to stay with these Communists for?" Leff asked me. "Come with us."

"What do you want me to do?" I said, "I'm a member here."

Again I asked him to go. He wouldn't. So I asked him outside. Then, as we're walking out, I hit him—boom! And he goes down, right in front of the store.

Now the other two came at me. I got one cornered into the wall. I shot him a few points in his stomach, and he went down—crumbled.

Suddenly I got hit in the head—the lid of the garbage can. It shook me, but I turned to the guy and I blasted him, flattened him, too. So I knocked them all out, and the three of them were just lying there on the sidewalk.

These were big, husky guys, but they meant nothing to me; they weren't trained. I went back in and left them there. Poker didn't say anything to me, but while he was behind the counter he must have seen the other customers watching.

One customer, a middle-aged woman, said, "Oh, you must be from Pitkin Avenue. I didn't know you could fight." It was like a compliment, but it was true. Pitkin was my area, the

31

main street with all the shops, restaurants, markets, big shopping stores, clothing stores, furniture, everything, a whole shopping area. And off Pitkin Avenue, you had the little side streets. Some pretty tough kids lived there, because we had to be tough. I was strong. And I had plenty of guts to hit a guy or break his head or kill him or whatever.

When you're involved, you don't think about getting arrested. Or what's going to happen. Or even about what's happening at the time. You worry about that later, and you try to take care of yourself for the moment. Now I could feel the lump on my head; the side of my face where I got bashed with the lid of the garbage can. But it wasn't bad. Meanwhile, the three guys finally got up and left, because they knew they didn't have a chance. And I stayed on at Poker's place.

Louie was still working at Allerton Avenue in the co-op dairy in the Bronx, and I stayed on at the Bay Parkway in Brooklyn, because they needed me to help protect the area. And so sometimes you didn't know, maybe you wonder if you're coming back. The competition between the Food Workers' Industrial Union and the A.F. of L. got very heavy. So you could get yourself killed. You never knew. But I was too young to think about those things. Or maybe I did and just didn't worry about it, because that's part of life, and who the hell knows what you're doing—you just got to handle whatever comes along.

There was a bad case some while back that got a lot of notoriety in the papers. A couple guys from the A.F. of L. Local 234 got in a fight with a fellow from the Furriers, the same union, with the same left-wing and Communist leadership as the Food Workers. The A.F. of L. guys, challenging the jurisdiction, approached a butcher shop in the Bronx, the way Leff came to Poker's place in Brooklyn.

The furrier, Shifrin, was outside protecting the shop. Then Shifrin got into an argument with these other two, from the A.F. of L. One of them, Silver, pulled out a butcher knife. But Shifrin also had a knife, and he knew how to handle himself. He kept himself against the wall—his back protected. The other guy, Phillip Borris, made a move—maybe to grab the knife away.

Borris got cut badly, by Shifrin. It left a gash the full length of Borris' arm, from the shoulder down past the elbow.

Now Silver lunged at Shifrin, leaving himself open. Shifrin stabbed him in the chest—right through the heart.

The blood started spurting out, through Silver's chest, like from a faucet. So Shifrin takes off, just races away. But amazingly, Silver started running after him. Clutching the knife with one hand, his chest with the other, Silver chased Shifrin for almost a block—finally, Silver collapsed on the sidewalk, died there at the scene.

Later Shifrin would stand trial. But eventually he beat the case, claiming self defense. Some guy reading meters testified on behalf of Shifrin. The fellow said he was across the street and saw the two fighting with Shifrin, and that Silver had a knife. So Shifrin won in court, but the A.F. of L. guys were still furious—they put the blame on the Communists.

Butchers work with knives all the time. They know how to handle them. A normal guy, he'll cut himself or hurt himself with a sharp knife, but a butcher knows how to use it. Then some butchers carry tools to and from work, so a butcher might be carrying his knife with him. They got a little box, including a knife, a steel (a boning knife)—a couple different knives. And so, because of the tools they carry, if you have one butcher against another, you have problems.

Certain guys would use knives, and others wouldn't. It depends on the individual. But the guy that stabbed Silver was a furrier. The A.F. of L. guys felt Shifrin came for that reason, bringing a knife over from the fur market. He didn't belong there. He came to help out the Food Workers' Industrial Union. So you had a lot of animosity between the groups. And there was that hatred of the Communists. But Louie and I weren't Communists, and we didn't see ourselves as Communists.

A few blocks down the road from where I worked on Bay Parkway was a butcher by the name of Lox. He'd been talking and bragging. "The union members," he said, "both sides will spill their blood right here in front of the store." He meant his store, and he was saying this to everybody. He was going to get us to fight one another.

He went ahead and signed up. First with us, then with the A.F. of L. group. He didn't care which—he just figured we'd knock each other out, and he thought it was funny. But no one needed any incentive, because long after Silver got killed, the membership of the A.F. of L., especially, was hot, mad, ready to fight. And there were a number of fights. I had a couple of bad ones.

And then there were larger fights with more people involved. Whenever one person would see someone from the other side, there was a good chance of a battle.

But Mr. Lox, who thought both sides would spill their blood right in front of his store—four o'clock in the morning one day, when he had to go to the market to buy provisions, the meat and chickens and so on, he got hit in the head. That took care of him. And nobody spilled any blood there, except his blood was there. He got hit pretty good, with a blackjack. He needed twenty-three stitches, and his head was in bandages for weeks.

After this thing with Lox, and some other incidents and bad fights, the A.F. of L. didn't come around. And the three guys I laid out in front of the shop, they never showed up again either. If they did, the bosses were afraid to talk to them anyway. So as the butchers were being organized, there was a lot of fear all the way around.

I always tried to keep in good shape. Jack Burstein was my buddy. He was a couple inches taller and a pretty fast runner. I remember when he came to work out with me when I was doing road work.

"I'd go out about four, five o'clock in the morning to get in a couple hours before going to work. Usually I'd run in the park, around the track, trotting. But Jack got excited. He thought I was running too slow, so he was going to pace me some.

"Fine," I said. And we started running. But pretty soon Jack stopped dead. Once around the track and he's all tired out. Meanwhile I was in good shape, from the steady road-work, so I just continued.

A few days later, Jack was in the gym. Apparently he had done a little boxing. He had a different style, and he decided to give me a few pointers.

"If you want to teach me something," I told him, "put on some trunks, a pair of gloves, get in the ring and show me."

"Fine," he said. So we get into the ring.

34

Right away, I shot him a couple hooks to the face. It started bleeding a little. He said, "Don't hit me here."

Okay. Fine. Then I hit him a few times in the chest. Pretty soon, he asks me not to hit him in the chest.

Meanwhile I'm trying to go easy on him. I hit him a light punch in the stomach. Now he says, "It's okay. You can hit me here—I can take it here." So fine. Then I hit him in the stomach, and it knocked him out.

After that, we brought him to. I looked at him and I asked him, "where can you take it, in the ass?"

I had begun seeing more of a relation of mine, Jean. Her real name was Zelda. We were somehow related. Like third cousins. She was a beautiful girl, but so far I had never dated her, and she had a couple of boyfriends from high school, in Brooklyn somewhere. Instead of going to high school, I had started working. I never actually finished grammar school. I was the best speller and very good in other subjects but instead I continued with my trade.

The teacher said, "Max, you're such a good student." But I told her I had to quit school and go to work. And I cried. So they didn't have much control in those days, and I left school.

Meanwhile, I'd see Jean once in a while. And although I had never dated Jean and didn't see very much of her, people used to tell her all the time that she was going to marry Max anyhow.

Suppose she had a sweet-sixteen party. I'd come with Louie, because we were relatives and we were invited—but then on the way out, all the time she'd jump up and give me a hug and a kiss. She didn't kiss Louie. Things like this. Louie asked me what was going on. I told him, nothing was going on. But some people knew, apparently. They felt it.

Then one day Jean asked if I'd take her for the holiday weekend to her uncle's place in Colchester, Connecticut. Because I had a little car, a Chrysler now. I said yes. Her mother sent along her brother as a chaperon. So we got up there and we slept over and then the next morning we're laying outside, getting sun, while her uncle is plowing the ground.

"You know," she said, "I had a funny dream last night."

"What did you dream about?"

She told me she dreamed that she had a baby from me, or something to that effect, Which was unusual, because I hadn't made any advances or anything like that. I had respect for her. I wouldn't touch her because we were related somehow, and the family was close.

Later, we took a walk in the woods, and then she said, "Turn around." I turned, and saw her brother following. So I found a place that we called the swimming hole, and we used to go there. We had our bathing suits and we swam and we washed and we did this and that, and her brother hung around all the time. But that night already we were getting closer, in the hammock, fooling around and all that.

The next day we left, and on the way back we stopped off at my cousin Joe's house where he had a farm in Huntington, Connecticut. We visited with him, and then he was going somewhere to pick up some cattle with the truck and I told him to take Jean's brother with him, which he did. Jean and I were sitting under the apple tree, and that's where I proposed to her. And we came home that night or the next day and I slept over in their home.

I slept with her brother and she slept in her room, and the next morning when I passed by her room she said, "Good morning!" So I walked in her bedroom and I stayed there, talking to her. She said, "I wouldn't bite you, you know." I figured she must have meant I should give her a kiss. So I bent over, gave her a kiss, and I left.

I went to my mother's, about seven or eight blocks away, and I was away maybe a half hour or more. When I come back I find her mother sweeping the sidewalk and she says Zelda is not here: "She went away, looking for you."

I said, "Oh, where's she looking? I told her I'd come back."

That's how it happened. I'm sitting there on the stoop waiting, and suddenly she comes running over. She gives me a big hug and a kiss, and she says, "Funny, the moment you walked out of the house I couldn't be in the house. I had to get dressed and run after you." So that was the real thing.

A few months later, my sister got married—my older sister, Fanny—and Jean was invited to the wedding, of course, because we were all related.

On the way to the wedding, Jean says, "You know, I was to

another wedding a while back and they announced an engagement, and that was very nice."

I said, "But I don't have a ring. You should have told me about it a couple of days ago. I'd buy a ring."

So she says, "Why don't you borrow the engagement ring from your sister who's getting married?" And I did.

At the wedding, I came up to my sister Fay, and I said, "Lend me your ring."

"Oh," she says, "You're going to get engaged to Jean."

"Yeah, to Zelda."

Then one of my cousins got up, and the music played and they announced our engagement. We stood up, and I put the ring on her finger, gave her a kiss, and that was the beginning. Jean was a doll. She had beautiful green eyes. Long, thick, flowing hair. She had so much life in her, and I thought she was the most gorgeous woman I ever met.

5

Louie and I would go to the Food Workers' meetings, and a lot of the complaints made sense, because the working conditions in many shops were so terrible. In the late twenties, you had a lot of Communists involved in the union leadership. Of course, many union members were just supporting what they thought was a good cause. They didn't know from politics that much. I was not a Communist. I didn't know what it meant. I knew what Communists were, but they just called it a left-wing union. And when we had the picket lines, I was working.

So we had a tough situation going, and I had to do some tough work. They used to call on me and my brother, and we'd go over there, wherever we were needed. We were tough kids, and we fought in situations that they instigated.

I used to ask, "What do they call us Communists for?"

And I was told, "Oh, I don't know. Anyone who's progressive is called Communistic."

Later, some fellow was sent as a special organizer to work with me. They told me that he used to be an organizer in Pittsburgh with the steel workers and that his name was Korn. He was a little guy, medium height but slender, with sharp, piercing eyes and dark hair. He was maybe thirty-five. He kind of latched on to me, made it his business to be friendly with me.

One day, we were sitting at a meeting in the cooperative, and he started telling me about how bad things were, and how they needed to be changed, and that you didn't need a majority to do it. All you needed, he said, was a united minority, and to weaken the police and the power structure that holds you down. So he was telling me this stuff, and I was just listening, but it began to sound funny.

It was true. These were hard times. It was bad. The workers had bad conditions and were working all hours. Others were starving. Friends I knew. Hundreds, thousands were out of work. And it didn't seem like it was getting any better. But still I didn't see that this guy Korn was interested in establishing any more jobs. It was like he was on a soap box. I felt he was more busy publicizing some campaign of his. It didn't sound like he was interested in businesses doing well and giving you more money to earn a living. From what he was telling me, he was more interested to destroy the shop, the businesses—even the social structure.

Still, I didn't argue with Korn. I was just listening. But then he said to me, "Max, you're ready for a book."

"I got a book," I said, talking about my union book.

But he said, "I don't mean this book—I mean the party."

"The party—what party?" I showed him my union card.

But he just said, "No, the party!"

And so now it dawned on me that he was talking about the Communist party. But to be sure, I asked, "You mean the Communist party?"

He said, "Yes."

I realized then that the Communist party was controlling the Food Workers' Industrial Union, because it was Korn that got friendly with me, and then after a couple of meetings he tries this on me—and it was the leadership of the Food Workers that introduced him to me, and they backed him.

Now I just looked at the guy, and I told him, "Forget it!"

So that's how it went through the depression and the early thirties, with the left-wing outfits. The Communist groups, the leadership, did not actually work to get very good conditions for the workers. They were constantly fighting the boss, and at the same time they'd keep the strike going to keep the workers hungry and militant so they'd join the party and fight their cause.

There were a number of other organizations that, like the Food Workers, were known as left wing, or Communist. And I saw that they were strictly controlled, because every business agent and every union official appeared to be Communist.

Conrad Kaye, who later would fight against Franco in the Spanish Civil war, was all Communist, and then he came back as an official of the Food Workers. No problem. He was a good bullshit artist and a good instigator.

Jackie and the Monkey, and some of the others, they were not really Communists—they were just dopes like me. They explained that everyone progressive was being called Communist, I believed it. I saw they were doing good for me, because I had better conditions than when there was no union. But I also realized that the Food Workers were not trying to better conditions for the worker—because the worker would get fat and complacent and wouldn't want to become Communists. So you fight the boss all the time, and they keep the workers hungry on the picket line.

After the meeting I got hold of Louie, and I said, "Louie, these bums—they're Communists!"

I was twenty years old. I realized I had lived with these monkeys from when I was seventeen. They never stopped trying to convince the people that they're God's gift to mankind and that everybody else's system is no good and that they know all the tricks of the game, and they're using them all the time.

They used me, too. I could have gotten killed twenty times. I might have killed or hurt many people. That night I said to Louie, "Those cocksuckers, those Communist bastards!" And so we left them. I was twenty years old. An old man already.

The stock market had collapsed. We were in a depression. But I wasn't worried about leaving my job at the co-op. I was young. I was a good butcher. I'd make a living anyhow. All the time I was with the Food Workers they always watched out for me, because even though I didn't know it, they were always building up to that point when they would make me a member of the Communist party. So Louie and I had the best jobs all the time.

Meanwhile my mother had the grocery store in Brooklyn. She was doing fine. She didn't need any help. She had my older sister Fanny with her. Sonya was in school all the time. Also I had been making extra money in the ring, and saved a little. So Louie and I, we were young kids, good workers. We didn't worry about a living.

I had about fourteen professional fights and scored knockouts in most of them. I won all except two. Once I was knocked out. Not really knocked out—I didn't hear the count. I was on my knees, wating for the count. Everyone in the crowd was yelling, "Stay down!" "Get up!" "Stay down!" Meanwhile I was just trying to hear, but I couldn't make out the count, so I didn't get up in time.

But most were knockouts. That's how it went.

I knocked out some guys in the gym, too. One guy they called Joe the Iceman. He probably worked in the wagon carrying those big chunks of ice, because he was so big, over six feet, and more than two hundred pounds. He had decided to become a heavyweight, and he was making a lot of progress. Nobody wanted to work out with him, because he was so rough. They asked if I would and I'd get paid so much for every round, about fifteen dollars, and those days that was a lot of money.

I was about one hundred fifty pounds, my usual fighting weight. He had over fifty pounds on me. They'd never match me to fight him in the ring. Of course, he could hit just as hard in the gym. But so could I. I was fighting pros now— getting pretty good. Also, I was a stablemate of Tony Canzoneri. We had the same trainer, Sammy Goldman. Canzoneri was a great fighter, and I watched his style, and I thought I could use that style against Joe the Iceman. So I said, "Yeah. Okay."

I wouldn't always fight the same. I tried to figure out a strategy, depending on who I was fighting, because you had to be dumb to fight the same way all the time. So now I copied Canzoneri.

I get into the ring with Joe the Iceman. I start fighting sort of keeping my hands down, leaving my guard open some. I thought it might work. The guy was very tall and big. In my mind I figured that if I tried to fight his way, I'm at a disadvantage. And this way I'd get the guy to swing at me, and I'd counter, and I'd tire him out. After a couple of rounds, I had him a little worn out. I was a lot faster, and I began to really throw it on. Then I countered with a good one. A solid punch to the head. I knocked him out.

Later, I found out that after that match, the guy quit fighting. He got hurt a little. Somebody told me he said, "If I can get knocked out by a welterweight, I don't belong in the ring." In those days you really had to be good. He didn't realize how hard I could hit, or that you don't have to be a heavyweight, or even a middleweight, to be a good puncher. Some of the toughest fighters were middleweights. A lot could punch just as hard as the heavyweights, sometimes harder, and they'd throw more punches and they had more speed.

So size could be misleading. Mickey Walker was the welterweight champ, but later on Walker fought Jack Sharkey for the light heavyweight title, and Sharkey could also fight heavyweight. Rocky Marciano wasn't too big, and not too heavy, but he could take them on a lot bigger than he was. He could have been a light-heavyweight, but he fought heavyweight because there was more money in it. Rocky was pretty fast against guys that weighed two hundred or more. And Rocky could hit, too. So he could fight them any size.

Jackie Fields used to be the welterweight champ. He was a great fighter, and I liked his style. He was a counterpuncher, like me. I sat and watched him in Stillman's gym for a long time, timed him until I had him down perfect. Meanwhile, Ray Arcel, a well-known trainer, was handling Jackie Fields. And if you fought the champ, you'd get paid so much per round. So Sammy, my trainer, arranged that I should box Jackie a couple of rounds. Sammy was in one corner, and Ray in the other, and Jackie and I got in the ring.

Jackie used to fool all the other fighters. It looked like he was making a move but he really wasn't. So he'd get the others to swing at him, and then he'd counter, because he was such a good counterpuncher. They'd move into his punch, and he'd really lay into them.

But I was a good counterpuncher, too. I saw what Jackie was doing. Now he made his moves, but I knew how to deal with him.

I hit him. Boom! Boom! I countered straight. Left. And I

was giving it to him. He got hurt. It was in the middle of the first round—he backed off.

"Take this son of a bitch out of here," he told his manager. "I'm tired of him. Take him the hell out of here."

They stopped it. He didn't want to fight me. But I got paid for the two rounds anyway.

So I was doing okay, and I kept winning in the ring, and then one day Sammy Goldman, my manager, says to me, "Max, next year you'll be middleweight champion."

He planned to take me right to the top, but I wasn't interested. I liked a guy to be able to handle himself, but I was against professional boxing for various reasons. You fight too often, and it does things to your brain. It's dangerous to be constantly banged up. So after a fight, I'd usually keep away from the ring at least a month. Maybe two. I didn't want to stay with it because a man can get crippled. Also, the mob was involved. So I said to Sammy, because I never told him before, "Next year I'll be married, and that's it. I won't fight no more."

Jean knew I wasn't going to be a professional fighter forever. But still she said to me. "You're a nice fellow. You're going to be a businessman. What do you need it for?" She was right, and I agreed with her.

Jean never saw me fight in the ring, but her father and mother did. And they were thrilled. They saw me in my first professional fight, with Tony Bendack, that big Polack from New Jersey. He had very light skin, like milk. He was a blond fellow, and they told me I had put marks all the way around his body. You could see the marks, because he was so light. Before I knocked him out I had hit him a lot to the body, but he hit me solid in the ear. After that my ear was standing out swollen for weeks. When I slept, I put Omego oil on my ear, and I slept that way every night until my ear got into shape.

Later, I fought a guy, Joe Salina, a good middleweight. He had about ten pounds on me. I was a welterweight, about one hundred and fifty pounds, but most of my opponents were middleweight. I fought Salina at 135th Street in Harlem. Tony Canzoneri was fighting Kid Chocolate in the main bout, and Canzoneri was the champ in the featherweight, light-weight, and light-welterweight divisions.

So I fought Salina. It was a rough fight. We mixed it up pretty good. I knocked him out in the sixth round. I still couldn't fight more than six because I was under twenty-one. But Joe Salina was supposed to fight me again, because the people were going crazy. So they announced there'd be a rematch in about three weeks. Then Salina wouldn't go ahead with it. I saw him one day a few weeks later walking down Broadway.

He had a little briefcase with him. He was selling something, and he was all dressed up. He was from Italy. His accent was still thick. I said, "Joe, we announced we were going to fight. Why did you back out? Why didn't you fight?"

"You think I'm crazy?" he said. "Every time you hit me, I thought I got hit in the head with a hammer." So he wouldn't fight me again because I kept right on him, and I kept hitting him in the head. And then I had knocked him out when I hit him on the chin.

The public thinks if you have a match and you're the winner that you come out clean. But it doesn't work like that. Salina had a certain punch. His right hand used to catch me by the hip, and it was painful. Later I went to the ocean and I spent some time in the salt water, and it went away, but that hip was sore for weeks. When we met on Broadway, I told Salina, and maybe that made him feel better.

The guy you're fighting, you might have seen him around, in the gym or somewhere. But usually the fight doesn't affect how you get along with someone, you look at it as a job: If the guy hits you, that's what he's supposed to do. So you're not going to get mad at him. But that doesn't mean you forget about it, because you can carry the bruises for weeks. That much I knew. I had learned the hard way, despite my wins.

Jean and I got married in May, 1931. Meanwhile I went to work for my father-in-law. He had one butcher shop, then he bought another one, and I was paying it off. I didn't join or go organize for any other union. I just worked and it went on like that for some time.

I continued to work out at the gymnasium on Broadway in Brooklyn about once a week. After a while, a fellow, Jimmy Clark, who owned the gym, asked me about taking a fight in Staten Island. I didn't want to because I'd have to go ten rounds and I hadn't fought a match in months. But still I had been working out a little, and he said, "Listen, you don't smoke and drink, you live a clean life. All you need to do is hit the guy." That's the way he told me.

I was married, but I liked the game. He didn't have to twist my arm. So I said, "Okay."

In Staten Island, they didn't use my name. I asked Jimmy not to, because I didn't want anyone to know I'm a fighter. I'm respectable. I have the butcher shop. But then I get there and I see the posters—I'm supposed to be fighting as Georgie Levine, a contender for the welterweight champion-ship. Now Jimmy didn't tell me I was substituting for this guy, so I didn't want to fight. My opponent was too tough, too classy, a powerful black guy named Snowflakes. It was the same guy I'd fought once before, when I couldn't hear the count. Now Snowflakes had a string of fourteen straight knock-outs behind him. He had come in from the Coast. He had a flashy purple robe, and when he took off his robe there was nothing but bulging muscle underneath. But I didn't back out. I went ahead with the fight.

In the first round I got him down twice, and in bad shape, but when I got back to the corner Jimmy said, "Take it easy." Because I had to go ten rounds. But I told Jimmy I couldn't go ten rounds. I could feel it. I said, "I got to knock him out as fast as I can."

I came out in the second round and he made a move at me. I countered—*bam!* Right into his chin. And I knocked him out.

The fight paid three hundred seventy-five dollars, a lot of money at the time. I was glad just to get out of there. It took me three days to get the money, which was unusual. We got paid the same stake, win or lose. The advantage in winning is you can come back again. And you don't get killed.

In May, 1932, after I was married a year, my father-in-law died of a heart attack. He was only forty-three. We were very close, and he called for me when it happened. Now I handled his butcher shop for the family, plus my own. So things went along that way. Then one day in July, I went to buy some meat at a slaughterhouse in Brooklyn on Johnson Avenue. It was to be an important day in my life.

My mother-in-law had three small kids, so when I bought meat for my shop I took care of the buying for her shop, too.

I'd buy the meat, and then usually I'd go on weekends to the country and bring back my mother-in-law from Mount Freedom, New Jersey, because her three kids were spending the summer there. And then I used to stay on the weekends with Jean.

That Friday Louie wanted me to wake him early so he could go along to the slaughterhouse. But I knew how he liked to sleep, and he didn't know that much about buying meat anyway, so I didn't wake him.

In the morning I left very early so we could get out right away for the country. I went first to one of the slaughterhouses on Johnson Avenue. There was a whole string of them. Mike Nagel, who had sold his New Jersey plant to Cudahy, later showed me the first million-dollar check I ever saw. He was the owner of the first place I stopped at.

I wanted beef and veal. I bought my beef from Mike Nagel and then I went across the street to Aaron Brothers, where they used to slaughter veal and lamb.

I was in a hurry. I looked around quickly, but I didn't see anything I liked. I didn't want to buy any lamb, and I figured I'd leave. But then Mike Aaron, one of the brothers that owned the slaughterhouse, he comes up to me: "Hey, Max. Where you going?"

"I have to go to the country," I said. "I haven't got time."

"Here, I'll give you a good buy on the lamb," he said. So he urged me to buy it, and he gave me a good price, and I made a deal with him. Then he gave me tags, with hooks and numbers on them. And as the lambs come off the killing floor, freshly slaughtered, I would pick the ones I wanted. I put the tags with my number on the hooks, and meanwhile the hooks with the carcasses hanging, they go on tracks, pushed in different directions to the refrigerator.

The old building is large, maybe fifty feet across in each direction for this one room where the calves are hanging. The calves are all worked and clean, a little wet, dripping blood, ready to go into storage or to be pushed into the cooler. At night, after they're chilled, they're moved on the hooks into the trucks at the loading dock.

I went to the car to get my stamp with my address to stamp it on my meat. When I got back, something had happened. I recognized the meat I'd selected. I had a very good eye for that. But there were different tags on the lambs, different numbers. So I looked down. My tags were on the floor. Somebody had pulled my tags off, and put on his. So I did the same thing. I dropped his tags, picked mine up and put them on and started stamping. I was doing this, stamping, and suddenly out of nowhere someone slammed a fist into my mouth.

I didn't know what was happening, but I turned and saw the guy. He was about five-eight, stocky. I took a fast measure and blasted him on the chin. He went flying, landed on the floor. Somebody ran over and grabbed me, but I could see that the guy holding me was a friend, Harry, a shipping clerk.

"Max. What'd you do?"

"What do you *want* me to do?" I said. "Kiss him? I'm bleeding here."

My lip was busted. And while we're talking, and Harry was holding me by the arms, the other guy got up off the floor.

He had a hook in his hand, a very sharp hook, and I saw it was too late to stop his swing. There was a flash of movement and he ripped me across the face. It could take my eyes out, I knew. But before I could feel anything, it sliced across the bridge of my nose, just under my eyes, from eyes to eye. I felt the sting. Then it sliced across again, almost the same way.

I was cut bad, I knew. I threw Harry off, to free myself. My sight was blurry. I jammed my fist into the guy's jaw, barreling into him. I felt the impact. He went down, hard—it made sort of a thud.

All this came out of nowhere. The guy was still down. I could see I might have hurt him bad, but I figured he asked for it. I could tell he was knocked out. He wasn't getting up. So I left. I never expected anything like this to happen.

I go to the car, look in the mirror. Except for the blurring, I could see, but I didn't know how bad it was. You don't feel it right away when you get cut. But now it was beginning to burn like hell. I was bleeding like a pig, the blood coming down over my face.

I took off in the car to go to a barber shop. They "fixed things" in the barbershop then, and I was all ripped up. So I traveled five, six miles to the barber, my steady barber, so he could clean me up.

Somehow, I got there. He looked startled. "What happened, Max?"

I told him, "I had a fight."

I didn't know what happened. I knocked a guy out. I knocked out a lot of people in my life, because many times when I hit someone I knocked him out.

The barber fixed me up. He put a hot towel on me. He put on powder, alcohol. He used Witch Hazel, so it wouldn't burn. Then I had to get shaved because I was going to the country that afternoon with my wife to meet my mother-in-law and the three children.

I had a feeling it might be bad, with the other guy. I wanted to know if the cops were at my place. And I wanted to prepare Jean and Louie. After the barber cleaned me up and shaved me, I called home. I recalled how Louie wanted to go to the slaughterhouse. If I'd gotten him up and he'd gone along, I thought, maybe it wouldn't have happened.

I got Jean on the phone and asked where Louie was. She said, "Asleep." Then she said, "Three people were here looking for you. Two looked like police. The other was a butcher. They said they had an appointment, and they asked where you were. I told them I didn't know."

I wanted to talk to Louie, so she woke him up.

"Louie," I said, "I had a fight. The cops are looking for me." Then I told him to take the car, with luggage, and meet me at the entrance to an elevated train station in Brooklyn.

Louie took one look. He could see I had two big cuts on my face, across the nose and over the cheekbones, from eye to eye, and my lower lip was busted.

"Let's go get the son of a bitch!" he said.

"If he survives," I said. "I'll heal."

Then I called the slaughterhouse and asked for a friend, Lou Glick, a cutter. He came on the phone. I asked how is the guy I hit. Glick told me they brought the guy to, but he was complaining about his head. Then he walked into the cooler. Later, they found him, unconscious. Glick thought maybe the guy died, but he didn't know.

When he told me this, a jolt went through me—who expected a thing like this? I came from a good family. I had a clean record. I wasn't a hoodlum or anything.

So it happened. But I didn't change my routine. I told Louie, "Pick up Jean. We'll go to Mount Freedom in your car, and you take my car."

When Jean saw me she asked, "What did you do to the other guy?"

She knew me. She knew I wasn't going to take getting cut across the face like that and let him get away. She knows me since we were kids.

"Nothing," I said. "I knocked him out."

Jean looked at me, worried. We headed out to Mount Freedom, to the hotel we always went to. I tried to reassure her, that I was all right. Actually, it would take seven years for the scars across my face to go away.

On the way out, nobody stopped us. That was Friday.

Saturday, seven in the morning, I get a call from my brother-in-law. A putz.

"Hello, Max. The guy's dead. Run away. The cops are looking for you."

It was a blow. Meanwhile, Jean was reading my face. I didn't want to go into details, with her alongside. I didn't want her to know yet, until I could prepare her. I was also hoping the guy was wrong. I wasn't so sure he knew what he was talking about, because I thought it dumb of him to call me like that.

"Where you calling from?" I said, finally. "Don't use my name."

"The house."

"Don't call me," I said. "I'll get back in touch with you." And I hung up.

From the way it sounded, the cops were on the way. If they didn't know where I was before, they might now. In a couple minutes, I was dressed. Jean sees me rushing, and so right away she's dressed, too.

"What happened? The guy died?"

"No," I told her. "He's in bad shape."

"I'm going with you."

"No, darling."

"I don't care where you're going," she answered. "If you're going to the Sahara desert, I'm going with you."

"Okay," I said. We went to Madison, New Jersey. I had an aunt and uncle there, where I stayed when I went to school as a boy. They had the store and house on the highway, on the way to Morristown. The place was off the highway, and I knew I could hide the car in the back of the house.

So Jean and I drive up, and nobody's there. I climbed in through a window and let Jean in. Then I made a telephone call from a phone booth nearby.

I reach Louie. "I got a call from my putz brother-in-law," I told him. "He says the guy's dead, but maybe it isn't so. Go and make sure. Meet me tonight at Raymond's store in Newark." And I told Louie where I was at, mentioning my aunt's place by the school but without naming the place. And Louie knew I was talking about Raymond Black's butcher shop.

I went back to the house to wait. I was still hoping the guy was alive. You wish the problem would disappear. I knew I had to keep calm, but my feelings outran my thoughts. It was difficult to grasp. This was something I was never involved with, even though I had been around death all my life since I was maybe five years old and first saw a calf slaughtered.

I could remember, when I lived at my aunt and uncle's place there at Madison. They called it the City of Roses. I was going to school in Morristown, and before and after school I worked in the poultry shop, where I used to slaughter the chickens.

You take a perfectly healthy chicken and you chop her head off. Everything else in the chicken is still working, especially the heart, and it pumps the blood until the blood runs out. You chop off the head—you can't use the brain no more, I imagine. It's such a shock. For a while, the heart is still alive, because it keeps pumping. But the head is dead. I never saw the head move, after I chopped it off. However, the chickens moved all over the place. They don't make any noise, not with the heads cut off, but the blood shoots out and the wings flutter and the chickens bounce around maybe a minute and a half from side to side in the barrel. So they could still be alive. But the head is no longer connected to the body, so there couldn't be any awareness of sensation.

The head goes into a different barrel than the body. Then the heads are taken away, sold to the places where they make the soup. The head, feet, sometimes the neck, though sometimes the neck stays with the body. Today, it's different.

They don't fool around, killing the chicken. Not the way we used to do it. It took maybe a half minute to kill a chicken, when you had to do it all by yourself. Now the chicken goes by on a conveyer belt hanging on one foot, and you have a constant line. The conveyer belt stops briefly. It's specialized. One man kills the chicken. Then another is involved with the plucking. Stuff like that. They use hot-water sprays. When the chicken's skin gets hot, the feathers come off easy. They have machines, you don't pluck by hand no more and it's a lot faster. So in an hour, one man can kill hundreds of chickens.

You take a steer, if you don't hang him up and you just hit him in the brain he falls dead. He doesn't move. If you cut the throat, you cut the jugular vein. Everything is wide open, but you still have a little time before the steer dies. The same with a bull or a cow—it doesn't move, because you can't cut the throat unless the animal is tied; so it's hanging on one leg, in the air—it can't flop around like a chicken. And it doesn't make any noise.

Cows and steers and bulls are quiet, when you kill them. They don't know from nothing. But with a pig, it's different— the pig squeals when you kill it. And you can't fool around, because the pig is so strong. The way we used to slaughter a pig, we would grab him by his front legs on the ground and reach the heart with a special knife, like an ice pick, from under the leg. Then you stab it in the heart. The skin is thick. You don't want to damage the skin, because you make leather out of it. So you use a special knife.

My cousin Joe used to fool around sometimes, not killing the pig right away, but with little jabs. And when he did that, the pig would scream like a bastard. The pigs squealed too much when he killed them, and I told him he shouldn't do it like that.

So I had seen a lot of slaughtering. Years of blood. That was natural, in my business. You get used to it. But it's different when someone comes at you out of nowhere, and you hit him and maybe he dies.

I got back to the house. After a while Raymond came in with his wife and two kids and my mother-in-law. Raymond told people he was my cousin. He wasn't, but we were friends, and he was in the meat business and he was proud of us. I took him aside and told him what to tell Jean—about the guy still being alive. Then Raymond took Jean in my car, like I asked him, along with my mother-in-law, back to the hotel.

I took Raymond's car, with New Jersey plates, and drove to Newark to his house, until I go to meet Louie Saturday night at Raymond's shop. That was the worst part. I was alone and thinking about it.

Jean went back because it would look more natural. Also she had volunteered to work in a play that Saturday at the hotel. They needed somebody to act like a little girl, and she was just built for the part—she weighed one hundred twelve pounds. Then she thought nobody knew about the situation I was in, because nobody'd said anything to her. So she went on with the play because she'd promised them a week before she was going to do it. Baby bottle, diapers, beautiful girl, very cute, very nice. So she's acting Saturday night, and there's a telephone call for Mrs. Block. Urgent. Right during the play.

She goes to the phone. It's my brother-in-law again. Now the dummy tells her, flat out, "Tell Max to run. The guy's dead." He doesn't even ask where I am.

Jean fainted on the spot. And that canceled the play. They had to call the doctor, to revive her. Meanwhile, the people in the hotel understood. They knew before the papers. Before I knew.

Louie came to see me Saturday night at Raymound's place, but he couldn't decide on a lawyer. I wanted him to get Samuel Leibowitz, because at the time Leibowitz was the best criminal lawyer in the country. But he was in Alabama on the Scottsboro case, defending the nine black boys charged with rape. After years of confinement, the boys would be found innocent and released, and the case would establish the right of blacks to serve on juries. So Leibowitz wasn't available.

I told Louie to call Leo Healy. But Healy was off on a bender, so he wasn't available either. The next-best man would be Walter Hart—he was well-connected in Brooklyn. (Louie had phoned our friend John Sherman, a guy who headed the Democratic Club in Brooklyn by King's Highway, and Sherman suggested we call Hart.)

On Sunday, Louie reached Walter Hart. Hart said we should come to his office on Monday morning. Meanwhile the three of us, John Sherman, Louie and I, we go to New York, and on the radio we hear they're looking for me. I didn't want to get picked up by the cops, because in those days they gave you the third degree in back of the stationhouse. They'd break your head. So we went to the baths in Coney Island.

Monday morning, eleven o'clock, we go into Walter Hart's office, Louie and me. Hart asked what happened. I told him.

Walter Hart was not a great lawyer, but he had a good reputation as a fixer. He was a good politician with connections. I agreed to turn myself in. Now Hart said to me, "Okay, Max. Can you keep your mouth shut?"

"I suppose," I said.

He says, "If they ask you your name and address you can tell them that. If they ask you your business you can tell them that, too. But that's it. If they start asking you about the fight, do not say anything."

"Don't worry," I said. "I won't talk."

He called up a detective, and made arrangements with the police for me to come in the next day, Tuesday. My biggest concern was Jean going crazy, worrying about me.

At the station, Hart asked for the detective sergeant. Hart said to the sergeant, "My client doesn't speak English." He added, "Don't lay your hands on him. He has influence." And it was true—my connections were good.

They kept me there all day long, questioning me. They threatened me, called me names, they did everything. They gave me cigars. They gave me cheesepuffs, anything. Theatrics. They threatened to break my head. They worked on me in shifts, for hours and hours. The whole day went like that. They tried all the angles, but they couldn't get me to open my mouth. I wouldn't talk.

That was Tuesday. My wife was broken up pretty good. She'd seen the newspaper Monday about a guy who was in on a third-degree murder charge and the cops had broken his bones. They nearly killed the son of a bitch—she figured they'd do the same to me.

But I came out all right. Nobody laid a finger on me.

Meanwhile, Hart got Supreme Court Judge Mitchell May to sign the papers to let me out on five thousand dollars bail, and Gagen, the district attorney in Brooklyn, agreed to let me out on that. So Tuesday evening, about five o'clock, Louie, John Sherman, and the lawyer come down with the five thousand to get me out.

Now the desk sergeant says, "This is a murder charge. He hasn't been fingerprinted yet."

Hart looked at the desk seregant. "You know more than Judge Mitchell May? You know more than District Attorney Gagen?" Gagen, he signed the release. So who the hell was the desk sergeant to disagree.

Still, they took me downtown to Center Street. I went with the detective in his car. Louie followed in mine. It took about an hour until they finished fingerprinting, and they took pictures of me. I'd been fingerprinted before, when I was arrested for assaults on behalf of the Food Workers, so it didn't bother me that much, and I went through the motions.

Finally, I got out. I called Jean, in Mount Freedom.

"Where are you calling from?" she said, relieved.

"I'm calling from New York. I just got out of the police station. I'm coming down."

"I don't believe it," she said.

That was Tuesday night. I got there, to Mount Freedom. A few days later, we had to go back to New York—I was to be arraigned at the Snyder Avenue Court House in Brooklyn. Because I had the connections, I thought the whole thing would be dismissed right there. It was a clear case of self-defense. That's what I thought.

In the court house I went into the men's room. I came out, and the whole damn family of the guy who got killed was facing me. Now they all let out a yell—*"Murderer!"*

It went right through me. Then they're all running toward me. There's nobody else there—no cops to stop them.

They started pulling, punching on me, screaming—the mother, the sister, the whole bunch. I just tried to hold them off. Finally, the police stepped in, separated us.

In the courtroom, they started yelling again: *"Murderer!"*

There was nothing I could do. And they had a relative, an assistant district attorney in New York, who put up a strong argument because he was afraid the case would be dismissed.

Apparently the judge got scared, because of the commotion. He sent the case to the Grand Jury. Now I'd have to wait to see how that would come out, but still I figured I had a good case. After all, the guy came at me with the hook. I had the scars to show for it, and I didn't even know the guy. We thought the Grand Jury would see it the way it happened. Meanwhile, it was a murder charge.

I figured I had to go about my business as best I could. I didn't have much choice. So I went along. But it isn't easy to lead a regular life, with something like that hanging over you. I wasn't looking to be a "tough guy." My emotions were normal. Maybe you function okay, but you don't forget, because people were still getting the electric chair for murder.

If you do forget, it comes back. Sometimes it'd be hard to concentrate, treat other things seriously. You think maybe it'll work out all right, but still you wish it was over. And you're glad when the time passes; you're that much closer to getting straightened out.

So a number of months elapsed. Finally, the Grand Jury indicted me for second-degree murder.

I did a double take, surprised at the heavy charge. They said I hit the guy over the head with a bar, and that that killed him. But that was nonsense. Hitting with a club, there would have been an external bump, or a swelling, an opening —something.

They performed the autopsy, and they discovered the guy's skull was cracked from an indirect blow. Then there was my friend. He saw me hit the guy, and how I hit him. I never denied hitting him. But they claimed that after I knocked the guy out, I used a club. Then they said I left through the refrigerator, the box. But I couldn't have come back through the box—I would have had to come through the lobby, where everybody sees you. There was only one way to leave.

My friend, the clerk, testified I didn't come out that way. But they found a couple of supposed witnesses. I figured these monkeys must have been paid off. Why should they testify like this? They didn't see anything. How did they know what was going on behind this wall?

Now I had the trial to face. And the bail was raised from five thousand dollars to twenty-five thousand.

Meanwhile, Louie raised a lot of money, fighting in benefit matches he set up. Somehow we managed to cover the bail, and I got home that night, and I told Jean I was indicted for second-degree murder.

We went to bed, and at that age you want to do a little sex. I started looking.

"What are you looking for?" she said.

"I'm looking for a rubber."

"You don't need any rubber."

I said, "Now, wait a minute. I could be away twenty years for second-degree murder! I don't want to leave you here with no babies."

She says, "That's why. I don't want to be left alone. And besides, if I'm pregnant at the trial, it could help."

And of course, she got pregnant. By the trial, she was in her seventh month. My lawyer told the jury, "Ladies and gentlemen, consider in this case that the defendant is not one defendant. It is three, as you can well see."

The first trial ended in a hung jury. I have to go through the whole thing all over again.

I wasn't happy with the way Hart handled the case. I thought he questioned the witnesses too much. The prosecution witnesses. I'd say, "That's good. That's enough. Leave him alone." But he would lead them into areas that had no connection with the case. So now I would have to face a second trial.

6

Louie and I bought another butcher shop, in Richmond Hill, Queens, which was under contract with the Food Workers' Industrial Union. But I had spent too much time with the Food Workers, and I figured they weren't looking to help the boss but to kill the boss. So Louie and I decided to fight them. We signed a contract with A.F. of L. Local 234, and immediately the Food Workers set up a picket line.

So now we were the right-wingers. The Food Workers fought against us, and it went on and on. And all the things I did for them, the hitting, the killing, the cutting, they used against me in the circulars.

Meanwhile, the butcher shop in Richmond Hill was very close to Ozone Park, the hangout of Jimmy McLoughlin, the boxer that broke Louie's nose in the locker room and the guy I gave such a bad beating to in the ring. So one day a policeman comes in, Frank, the cop on the beat, and he has this guy with him.

"Here. This is the guy," he said.

I looked, and I recognize it's Jimmy McLoughlin. He didn't fight any more. He couldn't, after that fight. He got partially paralyzed. Anyway, he looked at me. I offered my hand and he shook it. He said, "Kid, I deserved it."

I called Louie over. "Say hello. Do you know who this is? It's Jimmy—Jimmy McLoughlin." And they shake hands.

After Jimmy was gone, Louie shook his head.

"Too bad," he said.

The guy had lost a lot of weight. He looked half the size of what he used to be. He was broke. He couldn't find work, because he was still partly paralyzed, and he wasn't eating.

I got Jimmy's address. Every week after that we delivered meat, groceries and vegetables. He lived with his mother, and we sent enough food for both of them. Every week as long as we were there, without charging him a nickel.

Meanwhile, Louie was still boxing and going to the gym. So he was younger. Whatever I did, he did. And he was winning. While I was out on bail, he won the benefit fights at the Broadway Arena in Ridgewood. We sold a lot of tickets, and that helped raise money for the case.

By now, the Food Workers had been picketing the shop in Richmond Hill for months. We had some bad fights over it, and we did a job on them. We fought them tough and hard. Then they tried coming around at night—some tough guys with knives. But we had better knives than they did, and we had more guts than anybody. We came out chasing them with knives, and they ran like thieves. Especially one guy who used to be a friend of ours.

When we were in the Food Workers, this guy left his wife and Louie and I took him in to our small apartment and gave him a place to stay. We gave him money, and helped him get himself together again. We really tried to help him. Now he shows up picketing us. I was coming back to the shop one time and I happened to see them, so I slipped into a telephone booth and I called the shop and told them to get some knives ready.

I had a feeling this guy—he knew what we thought of him, picketing us like that after all we did for him—and the others with him, would run as soon as we came out with the knives. So then we came out and they all ran like thieves. We chased them a couple of blocks.

By now the Food Workers had maybe a thousand or twelve hundred members, but they couldn't shake us. The people in the neighborhood supported us, and we did a big business, because we were good butchers and they liked us, and they knew about the murder charge, too.

My case dragged on for months. I was under pressure. Finally, the trial was held. For the second trial I had Hart, the same attorney.

I kept telling him, "You're questioning the witnesses too much."

He said, "Max, let me alone. Let me be the doctor."

I says, "I hope you don't kill me."

This time I was convicted of manslaughter. So I went to Sing Sing. But I went pending an appeal.

Taylor, the judge, was a tough son of a bitch, and he wanted me to take a plea for assault. But I wouldn't. He wanted to teach me a lesson. I thought he was a drunken son of a bitch. A bad son of a bitch. Some guys he sentenced got the death penalty for second-degree murder. He gave people thirty years that should have gotten two. He was that kind of character, but I was confident I'd be out right away on the appeal.

In the joint, the first thirty days or so you go through procedures and you live in a cell block, in a cell maybe three and a half feet wide by eight–nine feet long. It's an old building and you think the wall is going to cave in on you any minute. It's a very narrow room, and there's no toilet, just a pail. And a narrow cot. That's where you go at first. Then after about a month you're shipped out to another facility.

The food wasn't bad. But the place wasn't anything to look forward to. Not for years. Not even for days. As I was being processed in, I told everyone I met "I'll get out in a day or two." They all went through the motions of agreeing with me, but they all knew that nobody ever gets out of Sing Sing in a day or two. And I could tell they were humoring me, because they figured I'm a kid and they didn't want to disappoint me.

Meanwhile, you go through the procedures. They check you. Different doctors. A psychiatrist asked me what happened, and about my background. A rabbi asked if I needed any help and if I belonged to a synagogue. And he said he'd come to see me. I told him, "I think I'll be out of here in a day or two." He didn't reply. I guess he felt like the others.

Then the word came down—the judge, Taylor, finally issued a certificate of reasonable doubt. Now I faced another trial—but at least I'd be out of Sing Sing. As I was being processed for my release, everyone admitted how they were surprised. They didn't really expect to see me getting out.

Jean came down with her brother and uncle to meet me outside Sing Sing at Ossining, New York. After I'm out, I decide to get another lawyer. This time I get Leo Healy, who I tried to get earlier. Healy was a big, tall man, a natural lawyer, a former judge from Brooklyn. I made a deal with him.

Healy told me he knew the case, and that the minutes in the case, the transcript that he'll need to handle the appeal, would cost seven hundred fifty dollars. All he wanted me to give him was a thousand. I thought he was a doll. A gentleman. Walter kept pressuring me for more money, which I wouldn't give him.

So the case was reversed, a new trial ordered. In the new trial, we got the original judge, Judge Martin. He knew the case. And after listening to the arguments, we don't have to go to trial again and put up a defense. Martin dismisses the case.

I'm out. It's over. But I had all this hanging over me for two or three years. And of course, now I've got a reputation—I've been up on a murder charge. And that would have its impact on the course of my life. We like to think we control our own lives, but lots of times we move with the currents that push us. So the past plays a strong role in the future.

7

At the time the case was dismissed, we owned the butcher shop on Liberty Avenue and 117th Street, in Richmond Hill, where we lived. The A. & P. later bought that market. I had another one on 124th Street in Richmond Hill, and another one at 1603 Saint John's Place in Brooklyn. I was still buying the meat in the wholesale houses. There was that whole group of them on Sutter Avenue in Brooklyn.

The drivers here were taken out on strike by Martin Lacy of Local 816 of the Teamsters. Lacy was also head of the Teamsters Council in New York. He's dead now, but he was a widely-known charcater. He was supposed to be a tough guy, but he pulled the drivers out on strike a number of times, and each time, he left them stranded.

Now Lacy pulled a strike again, and the Murder, Incorporated mob in Brooklyn got paid off over there. Suppose somebody's on strike. The bosses, the employers, go to the tough guys for help. These guys, they don't do it for nothing. They have a contract. All deals are in cash, and of course there are no records.

So after three days, the tough guys told Lacy to take a walk, which he did. Lacy left the drivers hung up that way so they couldn't get a job. They were scared to death to join the union, because the union wasn't backing them up. The conditions were bad, but apparently this local wasn't that important to the international.

Meanwhile, some of the workers used to tell us, "Max, why don't you organize it? We trust you."

I thought about it, because I did believe in the union. I was sold on the idea. But not like the left-wing or Communist union that was out to kill the boss. And not like Lacy's setup, where the worker kept getting left up the creek. So Louie and I talked about it, and we decided to go ahead.

We got about a dozen applications at first, from some of the truck drivers for the wholesale meat houses in Brooklyn. Then we sent away to the Amalgamated Meat Cutters, instead of to the Teamsters. There could be some problems with the Teamsters, I figured, but I wasn't afraid of Lacy.

Denny Lane and Pat Gorman came to New York to see us. Pat was president, Denny was secretary-treasurer, but he was really the boss.

Pat Gorman was in his thirties. Very handsome. A distinguished-looking man. Tall, heavy eyebrows, lots of hair. The Amalgamated—Amalgamated Meat Cutters and Butcher Workmen of North America—was very small compared to the Teamsters. The Amalagamated had been around for years, but hadn't been very successful.

In the early twenties, they lost a strike that made national news. That was the one against the big four packinghouses, Cudahy, Armour, Swift, and Wilson. The Amalgamated suffered big losses. And after that, Gorman came in as president. Gorman wasn't involved in that strike, but its problems remained. The striker was still treated as a criminal by the company, the cops, even the public. And the companies still did what they wanted—reduced pay, fired workers, made up their own rules. So by this time, 1935, the union was still weak. They had maybe three or four hundred members in New York and only a few thousand in the international from Coast-to-Coast.

Some people thought Gorman would be a front for Kelly, who backed him. Kelly was in the syndicate, associated with the Capone people in Chicago, where a union could be just a gimmick so a company could avoid legitimate conditions. In later years, Mike Kelly would pass on a lot of power to his son, Emmett, at the Amalgamated headquarters. And when the big building was built in Chicago, in the early fifties, Gorman told me, Emmett Kelly shook down many of the builders. He got a lot of money from it, tens of thousands, and he was a power behind the organization.

Meanwhile, Gorman was no pussycat. He would hold on to his job maybe fifty years. And more than once he would side with me against Emmett Kelly. Kelly wanted to take over the international, and later he would fight me. But Gorman was an organizer, so he backed me.

Years later, in his book *The Picket and the Pen*, Gorman would credit me with organizing more of the Amalgamated membership than anybody else—tens of thousands—internationally—and by the time I retired we had more than half a million members. The membership of the district council I headed for the Amalgamated went from two thousand to eighty-eight thousand alone. And I had the largest local union, not only in the Amalgamated, but in the whole country. After I left, the membership would drop again. So the membership increase was possible because Gorman shared my view and supported me when I wanted to organize.

When the conditions are lousy, or when you got no conditions at all, like with the tens of thousands of workers in sweatshops you still got all over the country, you don't have to be a genius to know things aren't going to get better by sitting still. So I knew that wasn't the way advances were made, or would continue to be made, in the history of the union. But sitting around, the failure to organize, that was the pattern that too often would establish itself. Along with the mob influence, this would keep millions of workers from getting better conditions. And I knew that despite various factors—fear, payoffs, company or mob control of the unions—ultimately the continuing success or failure of the unions in America would depend on organizing.

Like me, Gorman not only believed in organizing, he was also anti-Communist. So I knew we could talk to the boss the way he'd understand. And like me, Gorman believed in getting along, once you sign. Because if you tried to kill the boss, like the Communists did, the way I had seen it done in the Food Workers, then nothing would get organized. Or if it did, before long there wouldn't be any jobs for the workers.

When I met Gorman and Denny Lane in 1935, a lot of changes were still a long way down the line. As to the way Gorman would keep peace in the industry, he later would say, "We haven't had a strike against Oscar Mayer in thirty-five years; Swift in twenty." And it was true. He was a peaceful man. But he was also tough, because he believed in organizing, the way I did.

So there was a lot of blood to flow, between this meeting with Pat and Denny until the time I would retire.

Denny had one eye. He dragged his foot, because one leg was a little longer than the other, and he looked like a pirate. He was a tough man.

Denny and Gorman had already discussed Louie and me getting the charter. They talked it over with some of the others in the Amalgamated or influential in the Amalgamated, and we had pretty good contacts there, including George Scalise.

Scalise recommended me because I was a butcher, and tough. They wanted someone who knew the business. And Louie and I knew the business. So they decided, and Denny Lane said, "The Block brothers, you're the only two we'll take a chance on. We'll issue the charter." They knew we were tough, and we had guts, and we'd fight. When you were facing the Block brothers, you were facing an army. And they figured we were the only ones that could stand up against the Teamsters.

So we went ahead. Louie was there working. He was the president of the union, on the payroll officially. I wasn't. But I knew people in the business. So if anything would happen, they'd come to me. That's the way we set it up, and then we began to organize the Wholesale Butcher Drivers, Local 640, under the leadership of Louie.

I was married. We had a baby, and I had to run the butcher shop. We needed that to support ourselves, because there was no money in the union yet for salaries. Also I didn't want my name too prominent—I had just gotten free from the murder charge. But I was deeply involved and worked closely with Louie in getting things started.

We began at the wholesale houses with some of the drivers who'd been abandoned by Lacy. Working conditions were bad. Lousy pay. No vacations, no sick pay, no accident pay, nothing. The drivers were afraid, but we told them we'd stick by them even if no one else would.

Finally, after we organized forty drivers, we pulled a strike.

We struck about six wholesalers in one area. I had already learned there was no percentage in striking just for the sake of striking. We were determined to win, but no matter how much you want to change the conditions, good intentions, even the strongest support of the cause, that wasn't enough. You need winning strategy. You need an approach where you give yourself the edge.

We thought about it. It figured that we couldn't organize one without the others, because one wouldn't be able to compete and survive, and so he wouldn't be able to accept that. So we pulled a strike on all of them at one shot.

It didn't take long for the return move. Julius Goodhoff, one of the bosses, came to see me. He spoke for all the wholesalers. He said, "Max, five thousand dollars—you know how long it takes to accumulate it?"

I said, "Julius, I can't do it. I'm not gonna do it. I gave my word to the workers, and we're gonna organize a legitimate union, and that's it."

He must have thought I was holding out, because he offered me more money. When that wouldn't work, Julius went to some of the boys.

They brought in the old-timers, Spunky Weiss and his crowd, from the Murder, Incorporated, organization.

The Murder, Incorporated, mob in Brooklyn was either to threaten us, to scare us away, or to knock us off—whatever was needed. The organization was already notorious in Brooklyn. But they wouldn't be around—there wouldn't be any money in it—if businessmen didn't hire them.

Meanwhile, Julius Goodhoff didn't know that I knew Spunky Weiss.

So Spunky called me. We set up a meeting at Joe's, an Italian restaurant on Queens Boulevard in Queens. It was near where my mother lived. I didn't want Louie involved. I figured he was too hot-headed. So I planned to go alone, and we agreed to meet on Sunday.

I was supposed to meet Spunky and a fellow by the name of Neely, along with Strauss, the leader of Murder, Incorporated. I knew Spunky Weiss and some of these guys as far back as 1928, from before I joined the Food Workers, and we were pretty good friends. Spunky and Neely knew me very well through a place I used to hang out at. I also had contact with some others in the group, when they were younger, before they got involved in all the killings.

I had a cousin, Benny Block, and during the prohibition period Benny was involved in the bootlegging business with another character, Ben Caruse, who used to be a safecracker. Caruse knew all these characters. So Ben Caruse was a bootlegger, and my cousin was with him. They were buddies.

They had a saloon, McCarthy's, on the corner of Second Avenue and Forty-fifth Street in Manhattan, and I used to hang out there sometimes, because my cousin worked the joint. That was how I met Spunky and some of these other characters. Later, through Ben Caruse, I was introduced to Meyer Lansky in that place. Lansky would become the brains for the Mafia and handle the biggest racing book in New York. So I would see Lansky, some of the guys from Murder, Incorporated, and some other tough guys around there.

I wasn't going to worry about the meeting. I knew I could talk to Spunky and Neely because they respected me, especially now I had just come out from a murder rap. Once I almost got killed in a fight with a couple of these guys, when they were young punks getting started, and of course, it was always possible one of the punks might come along Sunday with Spunky, Neely and Strauss.

The guys I had the fight with were Red Mendy, his pal Jackie, and some friend of theirs. Mendy was a bad one. He'd been in jail for many things. Mendy and Jackie, both of them —they started as kids, beating up different individuals, gang fights; that's how they developed.

The incident with me took place sometime before I joined the Food Workers. At night I used to go to the gym. A guy, Samson Stone, who later became a business agent for the Lathers' union, met me in a pool room in Brooklyn by Grafton Street and Pitkin Avenue. Louie was a little young, and didn't hang out much with Sam, but we were all friends, and we planned to play a little pool and then go to the gym together. I didn't hang out in pool rooms, but I had an appointment to meet Sam and also my friend Jack Burstein. So you look for someone, you find someone. We're on the ground floor. There's about a dozen tables, and we're all playing pool. There's maybe fifty, sixty people around.

We were there maybe twenty minutes, and I didn't see anyone come in.

Out of nowhere, there's a scream from Louie—"Max! Be careful!"

I didn't think much of the fellows in the pool room, and I didn't spend time there. So I didn't know who, what, when. The next thing, I get hit in the head with a cue stick, by this guy Red Mendy. I got it across the face with another cue, by the other one, Jackie. He broke the cue on me, and I went down.

I started to get up. And I hear Louie: "Max—he's got a knife."

I felt sudden slices with a knife, in my head and back. The guy doing the cutting was Mendy. Maybe he didn't want to kill me, but they couldn't keep me down. Despite blows from the cue, I was still ready to fight them.

Louie had got hit by a cue in the head too, and was dropped into the rack. But he got up and grabbed a stick. Meanwhile these guys ran out of cue sticks, so Louie hit one of them in the head—Jackie, who was down—and he was fighting the other, and I remained with Mendy, who was cutting me.

I managed to grab Mendy by the throat, and with my other hand I grabbed a cue ball. I started bashing the ball into his head—kept doing that until he dropped the knife and he was out.

I still had Mendy by the throat. Now I picked up the knife and I was going to kill him. I was going to cut his throat, like you do a calf. But Louie yelled, "Max, don't do it!" So he stopped me, and I dropped Mendy.

Louie had hit the other two with the cue, and they were out, but I wanted to kill Red Mendy. If Louie hadn't stopped me, maybe I'd have killed the other two with him—I'd have to. But I didn't know what it was. As far as I knew, we got involved for nothing.

Sam Stone was gone. It turned out he had a gun in his pocket—he must have been carrying it for protection—but he raced out. And Jack Burstein, he had backed out swinging a cue. When the fight started, Stone and Burstein left. Everybody ran out. So now there was just Louie and me. We looked out for each other. And so the other guys were out, lying on the floor.

Louie had got hit in the head with the cue, but he wasn't hurt bad. But when we walked out, I was full of blood. My back was cut in three places. My head was sore, from where I got cracked with the stick.

We went to Doctor Stone, a few blocks away. Doctor Stone was a Russian doctor, the brother to the other guy, Samson Stone, from the Lathers' Union, who it turned out was responsible for the whole thing. The doctor's wife would tell me for years how she never could forget that face of mine, how I was bleeding. Doctor Stone put stitches in my head and stitches in my face and in my back. He worked on me for hours.

After he fixed me up, I didn't go home. I didn't want my mother to see me, because of the sleepness nights she'd have. They put leeches on me to draw the blood, on both cheeks, on the cheekbones, because my face was swollen. And my mother kept asking Louie, "Where's Max?" and he kept telling her I'm all right. But my mother kept saying that she dreamed I was lying in a pool of blood.

It took a few weeks to get the swelling down. Then I went to inquire what happened.

Why?

I didn't do anything to anybody. Red Mendy was part of the Murder, Incorporated group, along with this Jackie, and their friend. But they were only flunkies, just doing the work for the top people. So when I inquired, why the fight came about, I was told they were looking for Samson Stone. And he was with me. But they were given instructions they'd have to take me first, if I was with them, because I'm very tough. In the meantime Stone ran away, with a gun in his pocket. Son of a bitch! If you have a gun, and it's your friends, and your life, you use it.

Meanwhile, Mendy had a real bad job done on him, with the cue ball. But Jackie, a neighbor of Jean's, I laid for him. One night it was snowing out. And he came home late.

I had a pipe with me, a lead pipe. I was waiting in the

hedges, bushes in front of his house, on Barret Street. He came home, about twelve, one o'clock, and I hit him over the collar bone—flattened him out. And he's been a cripple ever since.

I also took a couple of fellows from the gym, and we went with knives and guns looking for Mendy and the other guy over on East Ninety-eighth Street in Brooklyn. They're lucky we didn't find them.

So that was how I met these guys. But these characters didn't have any brains, and Mendy didn't know I wanted to slice his throat with his own knife. Jackie probably didn't know it was me that hit him with the pipe, because he must have made so many enemies. There were so many that these guys beat up.

That's how it happened. And they had it coming. Meanwhile I knew Spunky and Neely very well. I'd see them at the joint where my cousin Benny worked, and I knew where they hung out in Brooklyn. But I never told Spunky about the fight with Mendy. And maybe Spunky didn't know about it. Because Mendy and Jackie, these jerks were nothing yet. They were just becoming tough killers.

The whole Murder, Incorporated, mob was mostly Jewish fellows. And the Mafia used them. There were about fourteen or fifteen guys. They would hang out in Brooklyn by Saratoga Avenue and Livonia, by the pool room upstairs, and downstairs was the candy store. Officially, the organization only lasted eight years, and they killed a lot of people in those eight years—some said hundreds. These were people the mob wanted snuffed out or were killings contracted by different businessmen, or whoever had the money to spend.

Spunky and Neely used to get the contracts, and they handled the negotiations. For example, I go to Spunky. I want to get this guy knocked off. Spunky tells me how much it costs, and he makes the arrangements. I don't want to know who's going to do it, and they don't want me to know. And maybe Spunky never knew either. He needed a job done, he told someone to handle it. And that's it. Who did it didn't know why they were doing it. How they did it was nobody's business.

When they were younger, Spunky and Neely, they did some of the killings themselves. But by this time they had graduated—now they were just handling the business end.

There was Pretty and Joey Amboy, about twenty-five and twenty-six, and another guy, Abe Reles, a killer that used to hang out with Strauss. Pretty Amboy, one of the killers, used to travel a lot. He had contracts in California. He was always away. Here. There. Maybe not there. He'd already left to knock off a guy somewhere else.

The two brothers were different types. Pretty was really all over the place—strictly a killer. He had big ideas, traveled with high-class broads, high-class people, and was spending big money. He mingled with café society people.

Joey Amboy had his lieutenant around him, but he was a smaller fish. He was a tough kid, but didn't take any killing contracts. He always hung around Amboy Street and Blake Avenue in Brooklyn. Abe Reles was a bad one, and Mendy, he was just another hoodlum, not really known, but he was a killer too. At first we didn't know about Murder, Incorporated, but as time went on it came out how this guy was held for murder or questioned for murder. There was never any motive. The guys who did the killing work didn't know the victims.

So when these guys called me, I knew they respected me. We got along. They were gentlemen. I was pleasant. I wasn't a bully, like Mendy and Jackie. So we could talk, and I figured we could work it out.

On Sunday, I go over to Joe's. There's Spunky and Neely, and Strauss, the one who later would get electrocuted as the head of the organization.

Spunky and Neely introduced me to Strauss. He was friendly, very polite. We shook hands. I never met him before. He was very handsome, about six-foot-one, muscular. He was from Pittsburgh orginally, and he used to be a football player in college. Now he was also a professional killer. He killed many, and I knew he got top money. The price all depended on where, when, and who you hired and on who was getting killed. It's the same today. You can still get somebody killed for a few thousand.

Strauss was only about twenty-eight, the closest to my age, but he was the main killer. Neely was a level-headed fellow, about five-foot-ten, an average-looking guy in his mid-forties.

By looking at him, you'd never guess his occupation. By now, Spunky, shorter, a husky fellow who grew up in New York, was maybe close to fifty years of age.

The four of us ordered lunch. We bullshitted back and forth. Neely was Italian, but the killers were mostly Jewish. It didn't hurt that I was Jewish, and of course I had the reputation. I'm a young guy about twenty-five, and already beat a murder charge. They respected me for that.

Finally we got down to the issue. Spunky says there would be a lot of money for payoffs, and we could split it, if my brother and I would walk away from the strike. He was speaking for the three of them.

Maybe it would be about five thousand dollars apiece. Big bucks for 1935.

After listening, I said to them—and it was tough to say it— "It's not a question of big money." And right away, of course, they could see I was going in a different direction. I'd thought it out carefully, but I was watching their reactions.

They let me talk. I wanted to sound firm. I said, "I intend to organize a legitimate organization. However, as far as you fellows are concerned, I think I owe you something." Because I knew they didn't have to warn me—they could have taken the money and knocked me off, or tried to.

"In the future," I went on, "lots of things will come. And you'll be better off with me when I have a leg up. You'll be able to make more money and get more favors than you'd be able to make on this one deal.

"But if I leave, then I'll be finished," I said. "I'll have to walk away from the labor movement, and you'll have to deal with a bunch of Commies."

They listened. There'd be trouble, if they didn't like my decision, but Spunky and Neely knew me. They knew my word was good. And I knew that despite their reputation, these are sensible people—they think things out. They're not looking to be violent or to kill people for fun or to hurt some old lady in a purse snatching or for nothing like some dumb kids on drugs. They're businessmen. They're out to make a buck. So I figured, if they're smart, they'll know it's good business to see it my way.

All this time I spoke, they were quiet. Now I waited, and they looked at each other.

Finally, Spunky turns to me, then back to the others.

"Max is right," he said. Then I see Neely and Strauss are going along. So I knew it was okay. We finished eating. I was more relaxed, and Spunky came out with the remark, "Max, you're a level-headed kid. I think you will make good." And when we left, Spunky said, "Good luck. Don't forget, we're friends."

We all shook hands, and that was it. It was agreed that they'd walk away, which they did, and that we'd organize, which we did.

So the wholesalers couldn't break the strike. They'd gone to the toughest, and lost. They saw they couldn't shake us, that nobody would go against us. And so within a few days, we obtained a good agreement with these fellows, Julius Goodhoff and the other wholesalers, fair conditions and everything else we wanted. The idea was to give everybody a fair deal. After all, we weren't looking to kill the boss or to instigate people to become Communists. Our job was to achieve better working conditions legitimately.

Then the same type of people, the same organization you had in Brooklyn, you had in other places, groups like this, and we started taking them in. Our office wasn't nice. On East Seventeenth Street, one floor up, with the squeaking steps. But we signed each of the wholesalers in their own office.

That was the Brooklyn group. Within three weeks, we signed up all the wholesale butchers that was part of this group from Brooklyn, Manhattan, and the Bronx. About three hundred drivers and helpers. Maybe it wouldn't come easy, but we were starting to organize.

8 The first slaughterhouse we decided to organize was Schloss, in Newark, New Jersey. The plant was a good size, slaughtering maybe eight, nine hundred animals a week. They did a big business with the kosher markets because they slaughtered the best: young steers, two years old.

A steer is a young bull that has its balls cut out when it's a baby—that's how it grows up to be a steer. The meat is more tender than what comes from a bull, because it's more relaxed. The muscles are not built up, because the steer is always interested in eating and sleeping. But with a bull, the meat is tougher, full of muscles. The bull has got other things on his mind. He's not relaxed—he's always looking for a young cow.

Cows are slaughtered for the kosher market too, but not so many. A cow gives birth every year. She's pregnant ten months, and you milk her about eight. Then by the time she gives birth she's primed for a lot of milk. So the cow goes through this cycle four or five times, six times—then when the cows are used up the farmer sells them to the slaughterhouse for hamburger and brings in new young heifers.

With the bulls, the young ones are used for stud—then when

they're old and heavy, they're slaughtered. They're usually sold for bologna, frankfurters, salami, because there's very little fat and the meat is dry. It can absorb a lot of fat and water. The top of the neck is tremendously heavy, and bulls grow up to weigh a ton or more. The castrated steers are slaughtered when they're about a thousand, maybe twelve hundred pounds at the most.

Like Schloss, the slaughterhouses in New York and New Jersey mostly handled steers. But at Schloss and the other kosher slaughterhouses they handled the steers in a special way—with kosher and non-kosher. There's a tremendous difference the way the animal is handled.

Originally the Jews developed the Kashruth, an interpretation of the Torah, as a guide for the Jewish people in their lifestyle. Only that which was kosher, or clean, was permissible. This involved important moral concerns for the Jews, but you had practical reasons, too, for keeping kosher. Those days they didn't have refrigerators. They didn't have ice in the desert when they left Egypt, and meat spoiled.

Certain rules are proscribed. An animal, to be kosher, must have a split hoof—not like a horse. It must be an animal that doesn't eat other animals, because if an animal eats other animals then you never knew how the other animal died. It could have been found dead and then eaten. So if you can't tell the cause of death, you don't know—it could be by some disease. Even if it was alive you still couldn't be sure it was healthy, since the weaker animals tended to be preyed on first.

So you have to have an animal that can chew its cud. Cattle have a big "pouch"; swallowed food is brought back from their first stomach and chewed slowly a second time. Animals that chew their cud are classified as safe to eat.

With a pig, you had the serious problem of trichinosis. Tiny worms, seen only by microscope, are passed on to humans through under-cooked pork. The parasites no longer multiply in this stage but they burrow through the intestinal wall, and each one that reaches a muscle lodges there.

In Germany, a hundred years ago, autopsies showed that ninety percent of the human population was infected. In the United States, by the 1950s the figure dropped to about sixteen percent, and would drop even more after it was learned that deep-freeze temperature (not ordinary refrigeration) kills the parasites. But trichinosis is still a serious problem in many places.

So to be kosher the animal has to be healthy, and it has to be slaughtered properly. You have a specially trained person —a shochet, usually a rabbi who has been trained for years in how to kill the animal and how to make sure the animal is clean.

The shochet has to have a special knife. A very sharp knife, and smooth, so the animal doesn't suffer. The shochet blesses the animal, and the animal is strung up on its hind leg. Then the shochet goes up with the knife—he cuts the throat, quickly. Up or back, but fast, complete. In one shot most of the time —two at the most. And with the animal hanging, the throat is cut in such a way that the blood drains right away, because if there's no blood in the veins, the meat doesn't spoil so fast. And the animal is slaughtered so that the blood doesn't chill in the veins.

For the non-kosher market, I've seen a cow or a bull or a steer slaughtered all kinds of ways. You take an ax, a sledge-hammer, anything—you hit the animal in the head, in the brain.

I did it many a time. I did it when I was fourteen. I re-member the first time—I swung at a bull to crack him in the head, hit him with the sledgehammer. But the hammer bounced. It knocked me over to the next wall, and the bull didn't die—he really suffered.

When you're a kid, you don't realize. Now I wouldn't do it. I wouldn't have the guts. But it's a normal situation.

Today, with non-kosher, more animals are slaughtered with a gun. Because they haven't got time to fool around. They just shoot the cattle right in the middle of the brain with a special gun. When it's done for kosher, the blood doesn't chill. But when the others are killed—shot in the head or clubbed or axed—the blood chills in their veins. This happens even when you drain the blood right after.

At Schloss, which was typical, the cattle would come in by trainload in the back, and they'd be pushed through. They got them in individual pens, one behind the other and all in the same area as they're ready to be slaughtered, but they don't know from nothing. If it's for kosher, you hang the steer up by the hind leg, and the shochet goes up with the knife.

You let the blood run out. It doesn't take long. Then you have to take off the skin. Half way down, the rabbi opens the belly. He puts his hand in and he goes through everything all around, to make sure it's smooth and not grown to the ribs at any part. The belly and the chest are separated by the diaphragm. If there's any infection in the guts, or if you find anything grown to the rib, you feel it right away. If there is something, the shochet says right away that he has to take it out. He does this, without ripping it. So you cut a piece of the rib bone out with the belly, and you inspect it to see if there's heat that runs through and through after you remove the bone.

The lung is also covered by the skin. So now the shochet cuts through the diaphragm, and you get to the lung. You go through the lung the same way, and you feel all the way around. If everything is clean, it's kosher. If you can feel something, it isn't. Then you take out the lung, and you put it on a blower. When we didn't have a blower we used to put it in our mouth and then blow it up. After that you put water on the spot, wherever you felt something. If it bubbles, it's not kosher. It goes to the Christians.

With Schloss, doing a big business selling the four quarters to the kosher market, the meat had to be fresh, so they were supposed to kill every day. The hindquarters, not kosher, would be shoved on tracks into the coolers, where it could stay for weeks.

Meanwhile, the federal inspector in charge of the inspection at the slaughterhouse, goes through and cuts into some of the glands of the animal's head, to see that it's clean, that the animal doesn't have measles. If the inspector finds measles, the animal has to be put into the freezer for a few days. Then it's run on tracks out to the trucks at the platform and the company is allowed to sell it. But if it has measles, the rabbi puts a cross on it.

With religious Jews, if you drink milk or eat milk products, you're not supposed to have meat without waiting. If you eat meat, you're not allowed to have milk products for six hours, because it takes that long to digest the meat. Nowadays it's easier. The reality is different from when the rules were made. The milk is different; it's pasteurized. But in Biblical times they drank the milk fresh from the cow. It was warm.

And if you drank it right on top of the meat, it was very bad. So they set up the laws for health reasons to protect themselves. It's very detailed, the way you slaughter the cattle so it doesn't suffer, the preparation of food, the separate dishes for meat and dairy products, and so on.

With meat and poultry, before you cook it it's supposed to soak at least half an hour. You put salt on it and let it sit an hour. Then you wash it off good and you can cook it—it's kosher. The salt has drained the blood out of the meat. But with the chicken, you also have to burn on the fire—singe the feathers off—and the gentiles don't usually do that. Chickens have a tendency to get lice. Even after you boil a chicken, there are fine hairs left.

For a chicken to be kosher, the shochet gets hold of the wings and feels underneath to make sure it's warm. If it's cold, he throws the chicken away. He'll kill her for non-kosher, but not for kosher. The others can eat it.

The same with fish. The fish has to have thick scales—not like catfish, for example, that are scavengers.

I never kept entirely kosher, but I know what's right and wrong. Shellfish, usually scavengers, are not kosher. And they can be dangerous. I like clams and oysters, but one time I got very sick after eating them. Later I went back, it was a fancy restaurant, and I walked up to look at the showcase where they keep the shellfish—lobsters, crabs, whatever, piled one on top of the other six, seven high.

The clams were almost open, and I knew they opened when they die. They're supposed to be on ice, and the clams have to be kept refrigerated at thirty-four degrees or less for them to live. But I realized the only ones protected were the ones on the bottom layer. The other six piled on top of each other looked nice in the display, with the lights on them in the tank, but I knew they were dangerous.

I touched the showcase, toward the top of the tank. It was good and warm. So it looked fancy, but it was dumb. Later I learned some people got ptomaine poisoning, and I see the manager of the restaurant is twenty-five years old and knows nothing about food. Meanwhile, you got fancy, well-lighted showcases like this all over the country, but a lot of people are getting poisoned because so many people handling the food don't know anything about it. Or don't care.

Even in the supermarkets today, many butchers know very little about meat and poultry. A lot go into a butcher shop and they're given a particular job and they work on it and nothing else. Maybe one guy works on breaking up poultry. Another works on the chopped meat for hamburger or specialties in the market, or he works on the automatic electric saw cutting loins, chops, chucks for roast and steaks, and that's all he can do. So in an average supermarket, maybe there's one person who knows the business and understands it.

I once went into a large supermarket. I saw this big fish lying on top, instead of being packed under the ice. So I called the manager and told him the fish would spoil if he didn't cover it. But the manager didn't care. If he covered the fish, he told me, no one would see how big it was. It's like that in lots of places.

So you talk about sickness. People worry about cancer. Maybe they get it from diseased cows or steers or bulls, sold in state without federal supervision. Or maybe it's taken across the state line anyway. I know. Like I said, I used to kill those cattle since I was a young kid, but lots of times the whole carcass was diseased. Maybe it's sold to the bologna people, or chopped up for hamburger. All the big companies buy a lot of that stuff, and it's like moonshine. Then you have foods coming in from other countries, and you have a spot check that means nothing. You spot check a tiny piece in maybe one out of ten cases. Everything ought to be under federal inspection and protection as much as possible. But we have these strict controls in some cases, and in others no control at all.

Meanwhile, even the federal inspections are questionable. Depending on the size of the slaughterhouse, you might have one or two inspectors, that's all. Sometimes the inspectors are moved around, or you have one guy in charge of a number of slaughterhouses. There are payoffs—it's a question of collecting the price. So they go according to the book, but some get paid off, because there's plenty of money involved. Even without the payoffs, you can see a drastic difference between the regular federal inspection and the way it's handled for the kosher market.

*   *   *

The fact that Schloss did such a big business with the kosher markets made it easier to sign them up.

Schloss had died, and didn't have any relatives, so he left the slaughterhouse to three people who worked for him. Joe Kenney was one. Bill Kleinman another, and then Mark Herbst, a big heavy guy, about four hundred pounds.

Kenney was the guy I always dealt with. He knew me very well. So now I came to organize the slaughterhouse, about one hundred twenty workers.

Kenney said to me, "Max, why come to us first? You got so many other slaughterhouses you could organize."

I told him. First, I had some of his people signed up. Second, there was the way he dealt with me when I had the murder charge hanging over me.

"You remember, I was a good customer of yours? But the moment I got my case on Johnson Avenue, you told me you couldn't give any more credit."

I added, "Why shouldn't I come to you first? You were telling me you're my buddy. You're my best friend. I'm your best friend. So how come you cut off my credit? You're the only one that cut me out."

"But Max," Kenney said. "I love you like my Joey."

"I know how much you love me," I told him. "I saw what happened when I was in trouble." I had called Mike Nagel, right there from his office, and was told to come get all the meat I wanted. My credit was good. But not with Kenney.

So that was it. First we got the drivers out. Then they had a couple of scabs in New Jersey, but they came out on the other side of the tunnel, coming into New York, and we made them turn back.

Then the partner, the fat one, told me he was going to go see F.B.I. Director J. Edgar Hoover who was supposed to be a friend of his.

"Go fuck yourself!" I said.

We stopped the trucks on a Monday, a busy day when they normally slaughtered about two hundred steers. Meanwhile, because it had to be fresh, they were supposed to move the kosher meat out every day. But now they couldn't move the meat and they had no room for the cattle coming in.

They couldn't operate. We had them tied up. In one day they signed. Otherwise, they couldn't have stayed in business.

Louie and I went to Insel and Insel, another slaughterhouse in New Jersey, to organize for Local 640. The bosses were two brothers, and about four o'clock one afternoon they were both there, along with a few customers and a guy that handled the trucks. The brothers paid this guy for handling their meat that was slaughtered, and so he headed a half dozen or so trucks that picked up the stuff there.

Louie was doing the talking. I listened but the Insel brothers didn't. Then this guy that handles the trucks moved up to Louie and told him to get out. Louie told him to mind his own business. The guy shoved Louie, and that started it —with the two going at each other.

Louie is short, but husky. He could handle them any size. The other guy was a lot taller, but I knew Louie would beat the shit out of him, so I didn't interfere.

They started fighting at the front of the slaughterhouse as you come up the steps. This was the platform where the trucks loaded, and they got the rails running across, and the meat is coming out on the hooks and goes into the trucks. So they were fighting by the tracks. Then the guy tried to hold on to Louie, and they started wrestling. Pretty soon they ended up down the stairs. Then Louie started giving it to him, bad. Bang! Bang!—he kept pounding the guy over the ears, from both sides. I knew how that hurt—the power Louie had. So Louie was all over him, and wiping the floor with him.

Suddenly the guy got free. They were wrestling again, and all of a sudden Louie ripped his elbow against the license plate of our car. I grabbed the guy by the hair to pull him away. Then Louie sailed into him pretty good. So I gave him a shot, too.

Louie could fight, because he trained with me at the gym. And the bosses, they knew my ability and my reputation. But I was a little bit afraid, because I had just beat the murder rap and had to use restraint. Anyway, we left the guy sprawled on the ground and we drove off. Louie's arm wasn't cut too badly.

Next week we tied up Insel and Insel. They couldn't move. We followed their trucks when they came out of New Jersey. We followed them when they came through the Lincoln Tunnel, like with Schloss, and we saw where they went. Then we walked into the butcher shops and told the owners not to take the meat from Insel and Insel, because the company was on strike.

So the shops didn't buy. They were afraid. We were respected, and the butchers figured why should they have trouble. It was just as easy for them to get their meat someplace else.

Most of the drivers hadn't signed up with us, but we did have some that wanted to join, because conditions were so bad. So we got some information from the inside, about certain big customers who were supposed to get deliveries the next day in New York. Then we contacted these shops. We also stopped the drivers from going in.

These were tremendous trucks. And the drivers were big men, husky. We were half their size, but they respected us. None of the truck drivers argued—they knew not to fool around with us. We kept following the trucks when they came out the tunnel, and after two days the company surrendered. We signed an agreement. And once the bosses signed, any workers that had objected went along—especially since they got a little raise and improved conditions.

9

We followed the pattern. I continued running the family butcher shops because we were spending so much money organizing. Meanwhile, Local 640 didn't stand still. Louie organized all the time in the wholesale field. Finally, months after we started, we went to Johnson Avenue, Brooklyn, where I had killed the guy at Aaron Brothers and where there was that whole row of slaughterhouses.

First we went to Lehman Packing, where they slaughtered bulls. The load was very big. A heavy quarter. And each driver of Lehman's handled the beef, so he was anywhere from six-feet-two to six-eight. Big guys. Louie had spent time talking to them individually, and now he made arrangements with them to pull a strike on Lehman.

He told them we'd be out there at three o'clock in the morning to establish a picket line, because this was when they were supposed to pull the trucks out. But before we went to sleep, about eleven o'clock, Louie said, "Max, we better go over there. I haven't got confidence in those big bastards."

We took a ride over. We pulled up about midnight and didn't see anybody. Then we went into the garage, and all these guys were there, getting ready to pull out early. They had the trucks in the garage. Fifteen or sixteen. If we'd waited, they'd be gone. So instead of starting the strike at three, they made a deal with the boss to pull out just after twelve—he gave them a five-dollar raise—and they'd be on the road when we got there and that'd be it.

So the giants were loading, almost ready to pull out. And Louie is about half the size of these guys, because Louie is maybe five-six. I'm five-eight. And these were such big characters. But Louie walked up to them, and I come up alongside of him, and they knew I had reputation as a killer.

"You cocksuckers," Louie said. "I'm gambling my life and the union's money to help you and you're gonna double-cross your own fucking selves! You dumb bastards. Get out and put on the signs."

We started to picket right there, just after midnight. I wanted to get them started—because once they're started, and the boss gets mad, then that sets it off. So they started picketing, and we watched them and they were afraid to move, those big bastards.

By eight, nine o'clock in the morning we sat down with Morris Lehman. Morris was a German Jew, a nice gentleman. He knew us. We could have got a lot of money. He said, "Max, you can have a bundle."

"We don't want any money," I said. "We only want to organize a legitimate union. That's the truth."

We signed him up, and then we organized the others on Johnson Avenue. Aaron Brothers. California Calf and Lamb. Mike Nagel.

At Aaron Brothers there was no problem. They were friendly. They knew I was a straight kid. They liked me, and they knew I could fight. They were smart, and they realized that once Lehman signed they'd have to sign too. After that, we didn't have any trouble at California Calf and Lamb, either.

At Nagel's, Mike asked, why we came to him last, because it had been months now since we started organizing with Local 640. We had covered the wholesalers, then the other independent slaughterhouses.

"Why didn't you do it before, Max?" he asked.

"I'll tell you why," I said. "It's very simple. You remember when I got in trouble with the murder rap across the street? Well, I was a steady customer of Leon Schloss and Company.

After the trouble I went to Kenney in New Jersey, and I told him, 'I need some meat.' And he said, 'Max, you know, you're indicted for murder. We can't give you credit.' I said, 'My credit is good all the time,' but he wouldn't give it to me. So I went and called you on the phone, remember. I asked if you would sell me meat. You said, 'Of course, Max.' I says, 'You know my problem?' But you said, 'It doesn't matter. You need help. So come and get all the meat you want.' So I never forgot it. That's why I came to organize you last."

Local 640 had been organizing about a year, under the leadership of my brother Louie. Now there was this vice-president, Jack Walsh, in New York, New Jersey, Connecticut, representing the East. So one day Walsh came to see me and he asked me to get in and organize the locals in New York City.

"Max, I want you to organize the retail meat cutters," he said. "They're not organized. There are three or four little locals, and nobody's doing anything."

It was true. There were a number of groups under Communist leadership, and they were constantly on strike, constantly breaking the workers' backs by breaking the backs of the bosses, the employers. So they accomplished nothing. Then you had Local 234, the Hebrew Butcherworkers Union. The Kosher Butchers had some three hundred members. Local 342 in the Ridgewood area of Brooklyn had about sixty members. And there were some other locals like that, standing still.

I agreed. We put the shop on 117th Street in Richmond Hill up for sale, to provide some income while I started organizing the retail meat cutters.

Local 233 was a small group, about a hundred members all over New York. They had a secretary-treasurer and a business agent and a few helpers. Their office was an old building with a squeaky floor on East Seventeenth Street. They didn't have the Communist problem but they were constantly fighting and accomplishing nothing. They were selling out for a dime —not doing anything but picking up a few dollars here and there. So Walsh advised me to join Local 233 and become their leader, and he brought me in and introduced me.

When I got in, things changed. They couldn't continue the way it was, because I went out to organize the big retail butcher shops in Brooklyn and Long Island. This was the fall of 1936. Within a year, the membership would go from about a hundred to five hundred.

I started organizing by distributing thousands of leaflets in Brooklyn and Queens. These called for a meeting. It took close to two weeks. Two or three people I stopped in certain areas helped distribute the circulars, and then I called a meeting on Fifth Avenue, Brooklyn.

About twenty people showed up. A few were employers. A couple others were phonies. But I realized that this thing had been tried many times. Some people got hurt. Some got scared.

By now I had listened to speeches at the Food Workers' meetings, watched how the speakers handled the people. I told the workers what was happening with the industries. People were working like slaves. I knew it, because I had done it too. I had worked in the meat packing business since I was thirteen. But what I didn't realize until I first joined that left-wing union, I said, was the difference between the union and non-union shops. So I was telling the workers all the things the company should be giving them, particularly tools and laundry. We used to pay for those ourselves out of our small wages.

I knew the business. I knew what I was talking about. The workers sensed they could trust me. I told them we had distributed ten thousand circulars, and this was the small number that showed up. A handful. But I said I was not disappointed, and I was not discouraged. I said that next meeting we'll double the attendance, because I expected each man present to bring another member. And the meeting after that would be doubled, and then doubled again. And eventually, I promised them, there would be thousands.

The first time we set up the picket lines at the butcher shops in Brooklyn they were not really strikes, because we didn't have the membership. The workers didn't want to join the union, and they gave the usual reason why—they'd get black-balled.

So officially there was no strike, because the workers didn't really walk out. Though sometimes we kept them out. Our picket signs read, "Unfair to Organized Labor," or "Unfair to

Local 233." But if we got lucky and happened to take out a guy from the shop on to the picket line, we called it a strike. There was one guy like that, I remember, and he stood out by himself—he picketed with the others we brought in until the strike was settled. A big strike, and he really gambled his life.

So the workers, they're the hardest to organize. Each individual one feels, "Why should I pay dues to this racketeer?" Or, "Why should I pay this racketeer an initiation fee?" Or shit like that. Either that, or they're afraid.

When I started, there was no organization of butcher workers in Brooklyn. But I brought in men, and we set up the picket lines at the different shops, beginning in the South Brooklyn area.

Meanwhile the employers had an association and they reacted. During two weeks of picketing the shops, we had fights on the lines. The workers were scared, and they didn't want to strike. So then we gave the businessmen a lot of headaches. Broken windows. Things like that. It wasn't baby games. Finally, the Association of Employers asked me to attend a meeting in Brooklyn.

They had offices on the second floor of a bank building. There were maybe fifteen to twenty employers on hand, all big shop owners in Brooklyn. I didn't have to act tough, because they knew I was tough. So I met with the owners. There was a Mr. Rosen. He was the richest butcher in Brooklyn. A gentleman, an English Jew. And it was his son's shop I had been picketing so hard. There was Phil Maxwell, who had a few shops. Then Emery Gross. I think he's still alive today, over ninety. He had a chain of butcher stores in Brooklyn and Long Island. So these were the rich butchers with a lot of stores.

First they felt me out. They thought they might buy me off. Or scare me off. They were mostly Jewish, but it didn't matter to them that I was Jewish. They knew I understood the business I was brought up in. So I didn't talk Jewish labor to them. And I didn't talk to them like a Communist—about the boss and the workers. I talked to them from a strictly business standpoint.

"Now you're going to be organized sooner or later," I told them. "So you have the Communist group in the Bronx. They'll be coming around to bother you. But with me you can talk, you can discuss. I'm not going to hurt you or your business. I'm going to organize the whole industry, not just your group. Deal with me on a legitimate basis, and I'll organize the industry."

Mr. Rosen said to me, "Young man, why did you establish picket lines on my son's place, not mine?"

"Mr. Rosen," I said. "I knew if I would hurt your children, it would hurt you more than if I hurt you."

"You're a smart boy," he said. "You got a contract."

I signed the agreement with them, for the whole bunch. Sixty hours a week for thirty dollars. And a dollar a week for tools and a dollar a week for laundry. So the shopowners had the association, and we had the union. And we got a three year contract. I promised the same terms for all of them. And I went out and organized under that condition.

The employers had all signed in the office. Now we had to get the workers.

It would take weeks. We had to go to every shop, bring in the applications. Some workers still resisted. That's human nature. Some were phonies—they made believe they didn't want it, so they could tell the boss they were on his side. Once the boss asked them to join, a lot joined immediately, but others held out. So when we started with the first agreement, the employers had to push them in or pull them in by the ankles, or the employers had to help us get them in.

Sometimes we put pressure on the employers to help. After one shop signed it was more in his interest for the other shops, and the other workers, to sign. So when we got them all in, this group was a good group, and they worked under the same conditions, the same contract. It was a start, and then gradually we could keep improving the conditions. That was the idea.

In between picketing in Brooklyn, there was a lot of other activity. I started organizing in Long Island and Flushing. The original Local 233 had never moved in that area.

A few workers came in, but most wouldn't. So we started picketing. First with the small shops, then other shops in the same area so the conditions would be equalized. Then we went to the larger shops.

We moved further into Long Island, into areas like Main

Street, Flushing. Big shops, busy butcher shops. We set up picket lines, and after we started the picket lines they often offered payoffs. When we refused these, the shop owners would sometimes run for help to the tough guys.

It was big businessmen, Dick Stroh, one of the owners of King Richard's, a big shop on Main Street, and the owners of a few other big shops, who tried to get tough guys.

We were lucky to get away without getting hurt. But nobody was able to move us out. A lot of the wise guys didn't want to go against us because we had friends too. I had a reputation that I'm not easy even with the tough guys. But my reputation among the big tough guys was good. So when the businessmen checked me out with these people, they were advised to leave me alone.

In those days, to make me walk away there was a group that would pay ten thousand dollars, and that was a lot of money. And I would get half and the mob would get half. Or if they could get me to walk away for free, if I was scared or something, they'd keep whatever they'd get. Or else they'd talk to me about splitting it. Like the guys from Murder, Incorporated.

There were lots of cases where union organizers were bought off by big companies. I'm sure of it, because they offered the money to me. They must have made the same offers to most organizers. But I gave them my usual answer.

I'd say, "Okay. I walk away. I'll take your money and I'll walk away. But I guarantee you, a month or three months from now the Communists will come around and they'll organize you. With them you'll be in trouble all the time."

Finally they decided they had to deal with me. In Flushing, Dick Stroh and some of the others talked it over among themselves. They said I'm a good boy, my word was good. And they told me, "Okay, we'll make a deal with you." And that's how they operate. They don't deal with someone they can't trust. But they trusted me, and the threat of the Communist union was effective.

10

We didn't look to make enemies. Normally we didn't deal with places already organized. But still the organizing that went on didn't happen without opposition from various directions.

Sometime in 1937 we were having a meeting of Local 640 on East Seventeenth Street, where we had the office in New York. We rented a hall for twenty dollars whenever we needed it, and we had fifty or sixty members there, and Louie was talking.

It was Saturday night, and we had all the drivers in the hall upstairs. While this was going on, one guy approached the front and he stepped up to Louie.

"I come from Joey Amboy," he said, "and I want to declare myself in the union." And he became threatening.

"Go fuck yourself!" Louie said.

But the guy had a gun in his pocket. Before he could take it out, I rush up and grab him in the back of the neck by the collar, and I drag him a little ways to the steps. I already had him. He couldn't do nothing. He didn't have a chance.

I spun him around and hit him a shot in the head, and he went down the steps head-first. He was lucky he didn't break his neck, and he just barely managed to get up and out of there before I gave him some more. Every time I run into some old-timers that were at that meeting, they still talk about it.

Now I figured that if I didn't go see Joey, this guy may come back. So I go find Joey Amboy on the corner of Blake and Amboy in Brooklyn. I tell him the story:

"Did you send this bum? He mentioned your name and said you sent him."

And Joey says, "No. I didn't send nobody." But then, while we're talking, the guy approaches.

"There's the son of a bitch!" Joey said. "Why didn't you kill him?"

"I hit him," I said. "I knocked him down the steps."

We were standing in front of a coffee shop on the corner. It was fairly dark. Joey had a broomstick nearby, and the moment the guy walked up Joey grabbed the broom and started whacking away. He beat the shit out of him with the broom.

Joey didn't ask any questions. He just kept whacking the guy. The guy may have been one of Joey's lieutenants, but Joey said he didn't know anything about his coming down. And he didn't like the guy using his name. So Joey took care of this fellow. I never knew his name, and I never saw or heard from him again.

It was about ten o'clock at night, and I went away. I said, "Goodbye, Joey."

"So long, Jackie," he called after me, because he knew me by my boxing name. I'd see Joey after that. I'd see him a few times, because the gym wasn't far from where he hung out by the coffee shop on the corner there.

Local 640 was growing. Now we started to work on the wholesalers in the Fort Greene Market.

In Fort Greene, you had about a hundred markets on each side going down a long block and around a corner, and around the next corner a little bit. These were the wholesale meat houses. You walk in front of a scale where the meat comes out. There's a little office, and then you got an office upstairs. On the back street, where you walk out, there's a big cooler, maybe fifty feet long or so. Here you got all the rails, and you got meat hanging.

So you have the packers that unload, and meat men that cut

the stuff up, and clerks. Those days trucks didn't have refrigeration and they didn't pack or freeze anything. They had hooks in the trucks, or sometimes you just dropped the meat on the floor.

At Fort Greene we started to work on the wholesalers one at a time, but they organized immediately among themselves, trying to fight us. They paid off the cops, and the cops hassled us. This went on for weeks. So when we had a strike against a wholesaler, Louie and I made sure the retailers didn't buy from him.

We never stood still. There was always someone to organize. In New Jersey, after we took in the independents we decided to pull a strike on Cudahy, one of the big four packinghouses.

At Cudahy, conditions were really bad. The workers got fifty cents an hour. They had no vacations, none of that stuff. No breaks. A break in the head was more like it. The workers were like slaves, and they slaved for pennies. It was dangerous work too but there was no accident pay. Workmen's compensation wasn't in yet.

At the Cudahy plant in New Jersey they slaughtered mostly good steers and young calves to make veal. They had about eight hundred workers at the plant when we called a strike for the Local 640 drivers and wholesale workers. So this was for the drivers, luggers, cutters—everyone. We called for a boycott of all Cudahy products. We tied the company up at their branch distributing plants in the wholesale markets all over the city.

The strike lasted sixteen weeks. Apparently the company tried dealing through the mob in New Jersey, but nobody moved against us. Then we were told they wanted to buy us off, but we didn't respond. So the strike continued. Every Friday, near the slaughterhouse, we distributed meat to the workers—whoever wanted it. We got the meat as donations from the wholesale houses. If we were short, we bought some. At ten cents a pound, we could buy all the meat we wanted.

There was some violence, but not much, because the company didn't try to bring in scabs. The slaughterhouse was paralyzed. It didn't operate.

The Communist groups still had some of the Cudahy branch

houses organized, but this got them nothing except recognition. They had caused a lot of stoppages every couple of months, until finally, late in the year, we took it all over. The head of the Teamsters then was Tobin; and he was anti-everybody, and especially us, because we were organizing everything. But we worked out a deal with Lacy, to let him keep his jurisdiction.

Finally we reached an agreement with Cudahy, and Cudahy became the first big packinghouse union-shop contract signed in the country with one of the big four—Cudahy, Armour, Swift, and Wilson. So now everyone in the Cudahy plant had to be a member of Local 640.

We cut the hours down, increased pay, added a coffee break and got the workers an allowance for their tools and laundry.

We had waited long enough. The United Packinghouse Workers of America (U.P.W.A.), under Communist leadership, didn't have one contract with the New York Butchers' Slaughterhouse, owned by Armour. So now we moved in New York. We decided to take it over.

In those days there was no National Labor Relations Board to smooth things over, so there was really no law. And the West Side of New York, Ninth to Eleventh Avenues was a territory considered the roughest part of the New York City —Hell's Kitchen.

We signed up some members and struck. At first it was standard for the company to try to buy its way out. They made overtures, but we said we only wanted to make a deal to get conditions, because things were so bad.

When the company couldn't buy its way out, they turned to muscle. Armour attempted to bring in scabs in buses. They tried every angle. They hired tough guys as drivers on the buses, and they hired others to go along.

They were tough but we were tougher. Among scabs in the bus were some people we paid off. But we didn't care. That's what the money was for—to organize.

So when Armour had forty or fifty men, we'd come up with a hundred. And guys in the packinghouses are strong men. And we were the Block brothers, and we were young and ready to fight. When we could, we grabbed the buses as they were coming in. There was a lot of trouble, a lot of fights, and it was a bad scene. The strikers threw rocks, and then they turned over the buses. When they were overturned, some of our members got hurt. But not many. The other side got hurt more.

In a couple of days we knocked over about twenty buses. Armour couldn't move. They couldn't sell. We tied up Armour that way for nineteen weeks.

Meanwhile, there were a lot of arrests, and as fast as our people were arrested, we'd bail them out. When we'd sign a contract, all the charges would be withdrawn on both sides. That was standard.

Finally the owners wanted to meet the Block brothers, because they couldn't find anyway around us. They had tried tough guys, and of course, there were a few around, looking to make a buck. They didn't care which way they went. Suppose this guy is offered twenty thousand dollars to put us away. He'd tell us to take a walk, and if we didn't walk, he'd kill us.

But we were lucky and respected, and these guys wouldn't touch us. Finally a fellow by the name of Green, a vice-president in charge of labor and industrial relations at Armour and Company said, "I came to meet you kids, because I was told so much about you. We went to every mob. Every tough guy. But nobody would touch you."

All during the strike against Armour, Cudahy loved it, because Cudahy was getting the extra business—the way Armour liked it when we struck Cudahy. The same way the small independents in New Jersey loved it when we struck the big plants.

Finally Armour signed—we got the same deal with them that we made with Cudahy. And we worked out the deal with Martin Lacy. Before the strike, Lacy had the drivers in the slaughterhouse in his union. But the Teamsters had no control, and the people didn't pay dues. When we settled the strike with Green of Armour and Company, all the drivers had to be in good standing with the Teamsters. Now they had to pay up back dues, but they didn't mind because they got benefits and increases.

11   Local 640 kept working on the wholesalers in Fort Greene, and we got a lot of threats. The cops gave us trouble because they were being paid off by the bosses. They used to harass us, frisk us, try to lock us up for nothing. Eventually we got ourselves straightened out. We paid off the cops just the way the bosses did.

Fort Greene was all wholesalers. You had mostly Italians hanging out there. Mostly the tough guys. That's where I met Carlo Gambino, who later would become the godfather of the whole Mafia, and we became friends. So when the bosses went to the tough guys, the Italian fellows, they already knew us. We were buddies. That was out of Gambino's family, and some of them were also in business over there, and so we didn't give them a hard time and they wouldn't fight us because they respected us. But Fort Greene took about a year, to get everything organized, and the wholesalers formed an association by themselves, and we dealt with them as an association.

Meanwhile, while we concentrated on Fort Greene, we worked on the other wholesale markets a little at a time. We used the same approach on Fourteenth Street. That was very big. Five, ten times the size of Fort Greene. Over there they

94

also had the cops on their side, but by now I'd begun to know the cops. You meet someone. They introduce you, you get to know the lieutenant, the captain, whoever. If a holiday comes up you bring them something. Or you just give them a little money. Fifty or a hundred dollars was a big deal in those days.

Meanwhile, we were respected by the Teamsters. We were respected by the unions, and by now we had a lot of guys, maybe a thousand in Local 640. So the company knew, if they didn't cooperate we'd take a position against them and put on picket lines. Or we'd set it up so the retailers wouldn't buy from them. Or the drivers wouldn't cross the picket lines.

Eventually we signed up all the wholesalers on Fourteenth Street. After a few months, all the wholesalers sat down with us. We signed a contract for everybody in the market.

In the same way, we went after the wholesalers in Jamaica; 125th Street, Harlem; and the Bronx.

It was the same scenario all the time. First they offered to pay us off. Finally, they all signed.

In 1938, Local 233, which I headed for the retail butchers, merged with Local 342 and Local 400. Local 342 was the group of Butchers in Ridgewood, Brooklyn. Local 400 of the Amalgamated was the left-wing group in New York and the Bronx that had a number of members from the old Food Workers' Industrial Union.

The left-wing group had tried in Brooklyn, but they couldn't make any progress. They had a few shops in Manhattan, but that was it. Within a year or so Local 233 which I had taken over increased from a small number to five hundred or six hundred members in Brooklyn and part of Long Island.

We had the main office of Local 623, the newly merged group, on Sixty-second Street and Broadway. So now I saw the old guys again. Before, I had fights with this bunch. Now we were all forced to merge by the international, the Amalgamated. Jack Walsh talked us into it, but I knew we'd have serious fights with the Communists when we went back.

I told Walsh, "It won't be any good, but I'll take a shot at it." And sure enough, it was no good. For weeks, it was constant political fighting. Just fights. No organizing. Meanwhile, the other A.F. of L. groups did nothing. They didn't make any progress either.

It went on like this for months, and all the time Louie kept organizing Local 640. So I helped him, with the wholesale end.

In Brooklyn you had hundreds of people involved. The Fort Greene Markets, and also on North Sixth Street uptown, Harlem, and you had Brook Avenue in the Bronx, and Jamaica market. Even in areas we had covered there was always some new place opening up. So Local 640 was organizing drivers and everyone around the wholesale field.

But little or no progress was being made in Local 623. So now we had a meeting on Saturday and Sunday, and different guys got up and made speeches. One guy came back from somewhere, but he said there was no issue. Another guy said you should create an issue. Anything to fight the boss. Meanwhile, nothing was being organized. In over a year, we had gotten nowhere because the Communists and us were so busy fighting.

The leadership of the left-wing faction was still Conrad Kaye, Shine, Leshnick, and Joe Cohan, and after all this time I saw no future with these bums. Instead of organizing, we were only quarreling among ourselves.

Now each one of these guys gets up and makes a speech about how reactionary I am. So when they're all finished, I take the floor. I'm supposed to be answering them, but I'm not really talking to the officials, but to the people watching us.

"Conrad Kaye gets up and talks about heart," I said. "He tries to prove I'm a reactionary. And he talks about his record in Spain. But let's look at the record here," I said.

"Max Block organized more in one year than all of you did. What happened last Thursday. Brother Shine comes out of his office with a nice pair of slacks, and a tennis racket, and he walks to the elevator. And he goes over and presses the button and waits for the elevator to go one floor down; then he's away for the weekend. On Thursday afternoon, Conrad Kaye didn't do anything. Conrad Kaye got lost somewhere, the way he does on any holiday weekend. Same with Leshnick," I said.

"But the unemployed didn't have a pound of bread to take home, and they were sitting in that unemployment room," I went on. "Now let's look at a reactionary, Max Block. Max

Block made all kinds of phone calls and got work for all these fellows for at least one or two days."

After that meeting I was elected president for four years. I was elected by the biggest vote. But still I saw no hope of working together, so I didn't even show up for the elections, because that's when I started planning to split the organization.

There was a general meeting at the Mecca Temple in Manhattan, and I organized my people to sit behind, where they could make a lot of noise. And I told them they didn't need pipes rolled up in their shirts, things like that, because they could use the chairs. So a lot of the members were from the old Food Workers' group, and I knew this was going to be a showdown between the two factions.

I prepared my men, and I gave the instructions. I knew the Communists and their buddies were always looking for the front seats. So we'd sit behind them. That's how we'd know who to deal with. And the instructions were, when I adjusted my tie, we'd let them have it. Finally, I adjusted my tie, and they could see because I was on the platform up front, with the other leaders. So it started.

Chairs were ripped from their brackets and smashed over the heads of the guys in front. The whole thing didn't last long.

Conrad Kaye, sitting next to me, said, "Max, why don't you stop it?" But I said, "Stop what? What are you talking about? I don't know from nothing."

There were a lot of folding chairs. And a lot of ambulances. Maybe fifty or sixty people got hurt. In the end we had to pay for the chairs, but chairs were fairly cheap in those days.

Right after this, on the Fourth of July, everyone was going on holiday to the countryside. So that weekend, with everyone out, I went in with a few of my men, and we moved the office. We took most everything—all the files, the membership from before the merger that we had on the other side of the bridge in Brooklyn, and Long Island and Staten Island. I took Local 342, kept that charter and merged in Local 233, and I left Manhattan and the Bronx to Local 400. After that, they still didn't organize. And we were organizing all the time. So later we would organize the retail in Manhattan and the Bronx, too. It was inevitable, because we were organizing and Local 400 wasn't.

I moved Local 342 into a vacant office on Fulton Street by the Flatbush Extension, and we began to organize. We'd go out on Fulton. Most of the population there was black, so I appointed a black organizer, named Butts. Since it originated in the Ridgewood area of Brooklyn, Local 342 dated back to 1905. But they hadn't organized anything—they had maybe sixty members. After the split from Local 400, I brought five hundred or six hundred members to 342, and within a year added three or four hundred more.

In Ridgewood, which was all German, you had some Nazis, but I became president of the local anyway. On Myrtle Avenue, you had a lot of butcher shops. We set up a picket line at one of these shops, and the German manager, a big guy, used to come outside and scream, "Jew bastards!"

However, there were no Jews on the picket line. Because he was so openly anti-Semitic the people I sent to walk the picket line were German. The business agent I sent down, Otto Rucker, was also German. I also made sure not to send any blacks, because the owner was so bigoted he would never hire Jews or blacks.

Then the manager hired scabs and I couldn't take that from that son of a bitch. I thought, I got to take care of him. So I watched his activities every day. I did that until I knew where he moved, what time, and when he left the store. I saw that every Saturday night he took home a bundle of meat, and he was a clumsy powerhouse, a walker.

Saturday night the shops were open late on Myrtle Avenue, a busy street alongside the streetcar tracks, and I knew this shop would be open until midnight. So I took a ride in the car with my Jean.

She didn't know from nothing. We went down and I parked the car on one of the side streets a half block down from the shop, but I didn't say anything. Meanwhile I had it all timed carefully, and we started going for a walk on Myrtle Avenue. I was acting casual, browsing, looking into the shop windows. Now I saw the big manager, with his package of meat under his arm, and he was coming toward us. It was about midnight, but it's a busy street, and there were still a lot of people out.

Jean was walking on the inside closer to the shop windows, holding my arm. The guy was coming closer. Now I said, "Honey, get your arm out a minute." So she takes her arm out.

Just as the guy approached, I hit him a shot. Right on the chin, a good one. The guy weighed about two hundred-twenty to two hundred-fifty pounds, but he went up into the air. He landed in the street, by the gutter.

Meanwhile, I'm not going to stick around. We walked. We continued walking, and now the people began to scream—but they didn't realize who hit him or what happened. And the guy was laying there. I had busted his head.

About three or four days later the boss gets hold of Otto Rucker, the German business agent I sent over. The boss wanted to sign a contract. He didn't want to fight. His manager didn't come to work for thirty days—he got hurt, but they weren't sure what happened to him.

Meanwhile, while we were fighting that shop, we signed up the rest of the butcher shops on Myrtle Avenue.

After the incident, when the guy went flying into the street, Jean and I just kept walking to the next corner, made the turn, got into the car, and then I'm going. And as we pulled away, Jean said, "Honey—please, promise me you'll never do it again." She's crying.

I says, "It happened."

"Why didn't you tell me?" she said. "Maybe I shouldn't have come with you."

"I needed you to walk with me, to make it look legitimate," I said. She was a good kid. I didn't discuss union business with her. She didn't ask. She knew I was always busy. I was always doing things. I was never standing still.

12

Local 342 continued building up in Brooklyn and Long Island. We worked first on the independent shops. The only chain we had that amounted to anything was Bohack and Company, which we signed earlier, in 1937, for the butcher departments.

We didn't have any problem with Bohack, because they knew my reputation—they knew they couldn't fight me. But after Bohack, we had some major strikes. Some rough ones. And there was a lot of violence and problems.

In Astoria, Long Island, I walked into a butcher shop. It was called the Open Market. It's about one hundred feet long, narrow, and I'm walking in to talk to the employer about a union contract for the shop with Local 342.

I walked up to the cash booth, and he was counting money. I handed him my business card. He was an Italian fellow. He got wild, and he grabbed a meat cleaver and he ran after me. I ran, very fast, and he threw the son of a bitch—whop!

I heard the air rushing past. It just missed me—hit the wall. It would have killed me.

Across the street was the King Richard's shop that we had already organized, part of a chain of meat markets. There was the shop manager, Harry, and I told him what had just happened. It was the first time I'd seen this other guy at the Open Market. He had no reason to know me, though he must have seen me because we had organized King Richard's and Tessa Brothers down the street.

"Oh," Harry says. "That's a crazy son of a bitch. You're lucky he didn't kill you. He's a maniac. It's a good thing you ran."

While we're talking, the telephone rings and this crazy character is calling Harry, and he tells Harry he's very sorry for what happened. He says he lost his head.

He knew he would never survive that incident, because I would kill him—because he knew I was tough. But he was ready to kill me. If he had, he could have said he thought it was a stickup. Anyway I was going to get him before the day was out. And the moment I'd get him outside, he'd be finished.

But now he called and we made an appointment. We met in an ice-cream parlor around the corner, on Broadway. He apologized, and we shook hands and we signed a contract for him and his two sons to join the union. We didn't have no trouble after that, because once we shook, that was it.

In Jamaica we had a very rough strike with an independent shop, and this would go on almost two years. The place was Frank Baloney's market. They had a big shop on the corner, and they produced their own provisions there. Frank Baloney was the owner, and he was tough. A Polack, a stubborn mule. He had two sons working there, and his wife, and about fifteen workers.

Frank must have been about fifty, and I was much younger, not thirty yet. But he knew me. Meanwhile, because Louie was representing Local 640, Baloney had a tough time purchasing meat, because the wholesale houses were organized by my brother, and the drivers didn't pass my lines.

Frank Baloney had no sense. So we fought him all the way. But on account of him, this strike was so tough we organized the whole area easy.

The industry had it in for Frank anyhow, because he always undermined everybody. Maybe he'd mark the chicken at two pounds for a quarter, and it actually cost him fifteen cents a pound. So the others couldn't compete, but he'd make up for it by robbing the customers on the scale. He had pieces of lead hanging by every scale, and every chicken or turkey, he used to stick a piece of lead through, into the belly, and the lead was attached to a string. So if it's a big turkey or a big chicken, or they had a sucker customer and it looked like they could get away with it, they'd pull the string harder. The lead pushes the weight up a pound, pound and a half, whatever they want.

They're still doing it in some butcher shops today. So the manager does it, because he steals himself and he has to cover the loss.

Frank Baloney was the biggest thief on Jamaica Avenue. So the industry didn't like him. And then, if his shop was open late, and the others closed early, it was no good for them. So either they had to pay for the extra hours, or they'd lose business. Meanwhile, without the union, Baloney could pay his workers little or nothing for the extra work, one reason, of course, Baloney wanted to keep the union out.

So it would cost, to improve conditions. But you could see that Baloney was also opposed to the union on principle; like a lot of shop owners. And they'd complain about the cost, the extra money, the better conditions. They didn't understand that when you treat the worker fairly you usually get more out of him. He works harder, and produces more. That's why the Japanese are murdering us today.

Baloney was a slave driver. His men worked long hours on a cement floor. The workers never went to lunch. They would bring buns and coffee and a big salami, and that's it. The pay was lousy and they worked from six in the morning to eight or nine at night.

So if you like to boss people around, and then suddenly you have to start taking orders from the union, you feel you're not the boss anymore. You go through hell to start up your own business, to have something, to be somebody, to get out from under; the next thing you're facing the union, and maybe it seems like you're taking orders again. So it became a matter of principle for Baloney to oppose the union, and maybe he was afraid that if he wasn't boss he'd get a taste of what he was dishing out.

It's hard to reason with guys like Baloney, maybe it's impossible, because he had to know it was tougher fighting us than joining us. We made sure he learned that much.

But Baloney kept at it, and the strike went on, and then it became a principle for him, to win if only for the sake of winning. It doesn't mean anything to be boss of nothing, and that's where he'd end up. So it meant some tough decisions, but I was committed too, because once I started I knew we'd have to organize the whole industry. There wasn't any choice about that. I knew we'd have to go all the way, because you don't just jump in the river to swim half way across.

So we fought him.

The police station was right around the corner, on 168th Street. The police bothered us some. But I also paid them off. Sergeants, captains. The stationhouse was maybe two hundred yards to the back door of his building. And Baloney's building would get blown up right there in the back.

At least it was the right building. In Philadelphia, the local of the Amalgamated had a strike against the Cross Brothers slaughterhouse. So the company brought in scabs, and they had lots of fights and bloodshed.

Jack Berl was the business agent there. A big guy. He weighed about three hundred seventy-five pounds. So they have all these colonial-styled homes in Philadelphia, with the pillars in front. And Berl decided to pull down the pillars of this house owned by the manager of the plant, because the manager was bringing in strike breakers, tough guys, and so on. So about three o'clock in the morning the guy went in a little Ford car, and he connected the two pillars with a chain to the Ford. Then he drove forward and pulled down the pillars and the whole house caved in.

The next day in the newspaper it says that police couldn't give any explanation as to why someone pulled down the house. The owner worked in a bank, a nice guy, and didn't have any problems with anybody. So Berl realized he'd pulled down the wrong house. Everything was white and all the houses had identical pillars.

But Frank Baloney's was the right place, and he got it good. We fought the strikebreakers. People got hurt on both sides. Finally, after one year of striking, the building burned down. When we were picketing, the cops had been staking us out from around the corner. After the building burned, we laid down the picket signs. That gave us a breather. But we didn't waste our time. It was publicity, because no sane person would want to go through that hell. So we organized all Jamaica and Flushing, all these areas where there were butcher shops. They saw how the guy got slaughtered. We fought him all the time, and we organized all of Long Island after this. Nobody wanted to go through that trouble.

Baloney was a stubborn mule. He remodeled and brought in scabs. So we started again with the picket lines. I wouldn't give it up, and we kept going with the strike until his building burned down a second time.

We drove him crazy, and every day we had more pickets. One day he came outside, and he picked out a union picket sign. He put it on his back and he was marching up and down picketing his own shop, singing. He kept telling the people, "Frank Baloney's on strike! Frank Baloney's on strike!" And he wasn't joking. He went nuts. It was like temporary insanity.

I can't say much about the fires. Maybe he started them himself. He was running dry. But finally he must have gotten tired of it all, because it just kept going on and on and he saw we wouldn't quit. He may have figured he would go out of business, and maybe his sons talked to him.

He signed a contract with us. Then he told his sons, "Fellows, in the future, whatever you do in the business, when I retire don't do business without Max Block."

He was okay. He got to like me because I was so tough. And I understood him. Like I said, every employer wants to dictate his own policies. So I didn't blame him.

13

After the independents, like Baloney, we started with the small chains. We already had Bohack. They had a reputation for being anti-Semitic, originally, because they were controlled by a German family. But they had signed with the Clerks international, for the grocery clerks, and I convinced them to sign an agreement with me, for the butchers. They had shops in every town in Long Island, and some others. Then they added shops in Brooklyn, Queens, and Nassau and Suffolk Counties. And as they added new places and workers, we'd sign these up too.

After Bohack, the first small chain was Merkel, then Trunz. Between the two chains, they had maybe five hundred retail butchers. If Merkel opened up, Trunz opened in the same area. They had the same kind of stores, pork stores, in Brooklyn and Long Island. The only thing, Trunz had two or three in Manhattan.

But I started with Merkel in Queens. The old man, a tall guy, he's a tough man, and he sticks his big finger into my chest. But the son, Merkel, Jr., got scared. So the son sat down and talked with me.

I told him how I wanted to organize the industry, that I wouldn't leave him out there hanging alone and that as soon as we organized him we planned to do the same with Trunz. He agreed to an election.

I went through the procedures. We had an election and I lost in a close ballot. But I came to tell the son that after all, almost half the people wanted the union.

"I don't need all of them," I said. "I'll call a strike, and I'll tie you up." So he signed the contract, and I didn't have to fight him. After that, I went to see Trunz.

Charlie Trunz, Jr., was a man around town. He used to hang out on the golf course and he knew some of the wise guys in New York. So he came with two guys to talk to me.

They introduced themselves. They told me who they were. Trunz must have paid them off. But after listening, they wouldn't take me on. They knew I was legitimate, but tough. Reputation travels. And I knew that once I signed one chain I'd get the other automatically, because I always felt that the employer was the best organizer for me. He sees he can get along with me, because once he's signed up, we didn't have unnecessary strikes, stoppages, or phony issues. And so he was better off with me than against me. The Communist groups always fought the boss, whether they needed to or not. But with me, you could get along, if you wanted to.

The direction was clear. First we organized a small operation, then a little larger one, then a small chain, another little chain, then a bigger chain. But all along we kept adding different operations, new shops, family stores, and so on.

The industries now have chain operations, and they're spread out all over. Maybe the families were tighter knit in the old days. There were larger families, and maybe now one son wants to be a lawyer, a businessman, an engineer. There are not so many family operations left where there's one butcher shop or two butcher shops and the family controls and operates it.

You take an outfit like Kossman's, in Queens. Kossman, a little German guy, had three sons and two sons-in-law, and they had five butcher shops and they were all together. Each one was a manager in a prime beef shop.

Kossman's main store was on Jamaica Avenue but we met in the market on North Sixth Street. This is where he used to buy his meat.

"Mr. Kossman," I said. "My name is Max Block."

"I know you," he said.

"I would like to talk to you about a contract for your shops."

"Would you give me a week?"

"Sure. Today is Tuesday," I said. "I'll meet you here next Tuesday."

"Fine," he said.

I saw him again the following Tuesday in the market. It was about five o'clock in the morning. "Good morning, Mr. Kossman," I said.

He spun around angry, and shouted "I don't want to know you—goodbye!"

"But you said you would discuss things with me."

"I'll never sign with you," he screamed.

"Well, Mr. Kossman," I said, staying cool. "Never is a very long time."

So that was it. Now he goes out to buy, and he can't buy a pound of meat in the market. I established a picket line in the Jamaica Avenue store. We had a couple of members there. The main market where he bought was still North Sixth Street, and we followed him all over, and he couldn't get meat.

The wholesalers simply wouldn't sell to him. They wouldn't fight us. There are a lot of wholesalers, but he was followed around. So he couldn't do anything. If he called up to have something delivered to the store, it'd be a union driver, and the driver wouldn't cross the line.

How long could he fight like that? We'd drive him out of business.

So never is a very long time but within four or five days we had him. He asks Lester Travis, one of my business agents, if he can get me to come to his store.

I go to the main store on Jamaica Avenue, and I walk in. Now he puts his hands up in the air, as if to say, "I surrender!"

I said, "Mr. Kossman. Do you ever go to the fights?"

"Oh, yes," he says. "I love fights."

The fights are like life. There's always some risk in life but you don't bet only because of the odds. You bet because you think you're going to win.

I tell him about the Louis–Schmeling re-match.

In Sunnyside, Queens, Long Island, an ice cream parlor

was across the street from my mother's place. Two Germans owned the parlor, and I remember when the Joe Louis–Max Schmeling fight was re-matched. I began to discuss the re-match with these two German brothers, and they wanted to bet money. They were cocky. They offered ten to one odds, and I thought that was a big mistake. I chipped in with a few others and we bet them a hundred dollars on Louis.

They never thought Louis could win. All the Germans, even those that weren't Nazi sympathizers at the time, were rooting for Schmeling.

I liked Louis, but I didn't bet the first fight because I knew Schmeling would knock him out. Louis had a left hook, but he would come in low. He would drop his hand too low, coming from the bottom up, and Schmeling had a good right cross, a good right hand. So I figured Schmeling would beat Louis's left hook and knock him out. And that's what he did.

The first fight I saw in the movies. The second match I went to see at Yankee Stadium. I was in the third or fourth row from ringside. There were fifty thousand people there.

This time I felt Louis would knock Schmeling out, because I figured they had to show Louis the movies of the first fight, and so he'd correct that part about leaving himself open to the right cross.

I was right. This time Louis covered himself. He didn't throw a lot of punches, but he kept at him. And Louis had a solid right. Before you knew it, he knocked Schmeling out in the first round.

It was a real victory for Louis, especially during those times, with the Nazis starting up, and all that talk about the Master Race. Some people were disappointed that the fight ended so quickly. I wasn't. I was rooting for Louis and I collected lots of money on that fight.

I tell Kossman this because I want him to know how sure I was that we were going to win with him. And I tell him that at the end of the fight the fighters shake hands again, and everything is fine. That's how I feel about it.

"Oh," he says. "You're a good guy. I like that attitude." Then he says he wants me to meet all his sons and his sons-in-law. So he calls in his boys, and I meet them all and he tells them, "Go to the lawyer and sign a contract with Mr. Block."

We go to his lawyer's office, and his lawyer is told to sign a contract with me, and I have the contract out. But I say, "Wait a minute." I take out a pen. "This part we can scratch out." And I initial it. "This part we can scratch." I initial it. Because it's the first year's. In the beginning you have to break it in. We reduced the hours from fifty-four or fifty-six hours a week to fifty and got them salary increases and money for tools and laundry. But you can't take everything right away because they may not be able to stay in business.

Now the lawyer turns around to the older son and he says, "Joe, why'd you fight this guy? This guy's a good guy."

And Joe says, "Well, we didn't know how good he was."

Now Joe says to me, "We put up a good fight, didn't we, Max."

I said, "Yeah, Joe. Terrific!" But he didn't have a chance.

We signed, and took in everybody into the union, about thirty-five workers in all the shops. And after that, the Kossmans invited me and my wife to attend their weddings, and all their parties.

I had become a close friend of Dick Stroh, who owned the King Richard's Market, and I made arrangements to meet him on vacation in Flordia. I remember it was the first week in December 1941, because we were attacked December Seventh at Pearl Harbor.

Stroh was in Florida ahead of me, because first I had to go to the Amalgamated headquarters in Chicago for a few days. All I took was summer clothes, and in Chicago it was freezing, about fourteen degrees below zero.

I told my friend Jackie Perno, "I want to go and get a suit and a coat."

"Come with me," Jackie said.

He took me into an old broken-down candy store. Then we walked right through the candy store, and in the back was a warehouse, a tremendous warehouse, with a high ceiling, all kinds of boxes piled on top of each other, all types of clothes, jewelry, shoes, appliances, whatever. But I was only interested in a coat and a suit. So I bought a coat, charcoal gray, beautiful, and a woolen suit, and I had good clothes for the two or three days I was there.

I had plane reservations for Florida. It snowed like hell, took five hours, and the plane arrived early, about five o'clock in the morning. I took a taxi to the Shelborne Hotel in Miami Beach, where I had the reservations with Dick Stroh.

Apparently Dick got up early for breakfast. He came in and said, "Max, you better wake up. We were attacked by the Japanese in Pearl Harbor."

I called my wife that night, while I was still in Florida, because I had reservations to visit my cousins in Cuba that I hadn't seen in years. So I get Jean on the phone.

"When you coming home?" she asks.

"When my vacation is over in two weeks," I said.

"Honey, we're at war."

I tell her, "By the time the Japanese would reach our coast, I'll be able to get through my vacation." I thought maybe I'd have to go to war anyhow, but after that I went to visit my cousins in Cuba and then went home. Then a number of months elapsed and I went back to Chicago for a meeting with Pat Gorman.

Now I want to go back to that store, where I went before, because they had such good stuff, and reasonable.

I said to Jackie Perno, "I want to go over to that same store, to buy some more clothes. Maybe I'll find something for my wife, too."

Then he tells me, "They're out of business."

I said, "How come? What happened? The police caught up with 'em?"

"No," he said. "The overhead was too high."

"What do you mean, the overhead was so high? They steal the stuff."

"Well," he explained, "they travel in different cities, St. Louis, Milwaukee, Detroit, and there's different department stores that they rob. But they have to cover the travel expenses, and they have to take care of the security people of the department stores. And then in case of any arrests on the road, the bail bonds are high, and the lawyers' fees are high to defend the people, and the local police have to be on the payroll all the time. So all these things add up and it doesn't pay for them to operate anymore.

"Besides," he went on, "they had other problems. After all, when the wholesalers buy clothes they have credit arrangements. But here, to get the stuff, they have to pay cash on the line. And then if they don't pay, they get busted." That was

110

another problem, because without the cops you can't operate. So maybe you got the goods cheap, but you had to sell them cheap, too, and you still had all the other overhead. That's what he told me, and they went out of business. So it goes to show you, being a thief isn't always as profitable as it looks.

We became more active in the community. Abe Stark was president of the borough of Brooklyn. Later he ran for mayor of New York and lost but before that, in the early forties, he was the one that started the Boys' Club in Brooklyn, on Linden Boulevard. It was the first in the country.

Louie and I were close friends with Abe, and he came to us when he wanted to start up the Boys' Club, and we helped in the financing. On account of that, being active for the Boys' Club, I had photos taken of me with Governor Thomas Dewey, and also with Mayor O'Dwyer.

About the same time, Martin Guerra and a few other Italian fellows started raising money for a Boys' Club in Italy, and I was active in that. I knew Guerra before, when he was head of the meat department for the Bohack chain. I met him again when Carlo Gambino brought him to my house one time at three o'clock in the morning. Gambino's boys were going to military school nearby and Gambino and Guerra were coming back with their wives.

This was during the early years of the war, and all of a sudden it was difficult to get meat. There was an involvement of some kind with this chain of groceries in Brooklyn, and it was a big chain, and they had maybe fifty or one hundred stores. So Guerra sold Carlo on the idea of installing meat departments. Not a butcher shop like you'd usually see then, but a meat section inside the grocery store or the market.

All Carlo's nephews were in the meat business. The young ones still are. The old ones died off.

And so Gambino and Guerra worked together, raising money in the Fort Greene Market for the Italian Boys' Club, and I contributed money to Gambino for that.

14

Opportunity comes up and you take it. One day I came around to McCarthy's saloon to spend a few dollars, and my cousin Benny, who was still working the joint, told me the owner, Benny Caruse, didn't have the cash to renew the liquor license. So I made a deal with Caruse. Two-thirds for Louie and me, and a third for Caruse, and we promised to make a steak house out of the place. Then we paid to renew the license, and we remodeled the place a little bit. We made it into McCarthy's Steak House.

The war had started, and it was difficult to get meat, but we got the best meat, and I had my business meetings there, so we had a tremendous steak house right away. We made a lot of money.

Caruse was our partner, and now we had more contact with the characters around there, some tough guys and some people from the mob, like Meyer Lansky. Lansky was Jewish, but he was the brains for the whole Mafia. And then the Mafia used to hire some of these guys from Murder, Incorporated, and maybe they made some deals at McCarthy's. We didn't know and we didn't ask. We were just running a restaurant and bar, and handling some of the business for the union.

Carlo Gambino, the godfather, didn't come into McCarthy's,

but I got to know him, through the years. I didn't know everything going on, but from our first meeting in 1939 he had made it his business to be my friend. I didn't know until later in life that he would be the top man in the Mafia. We had some dealings, and we were friends.

Later I would come to his home in Long Island, on the Sound. A big home. He also had a house in Brooklyn, on Ocean Parkway. I'd go to his home on a Sunday, in Long Island, and you'd see the boats. He'd point them out.

"Those are the F.B.I. guys," he'd say, meaning they had him covered. And he'd invite me to sit down with him. One time he motioned for the two of us to sit down, and I said, "No, it's by the open window."

"You're a smart boy," he said to me.

Gambino had a couple of sons, both in the dress business. One of his kids would become a partner in my family. So I knew Carlo.

I first met him during a strike we had against a buddy of his, Tony Conti, and Conti was tied up in the Fort Greene Market in Brooklyn. It was a big operation, so Gambino came to see me.

He introduced himself. He came up and he said, "Max?" and I said, "Yes, sir."

I didn't know who he was, but he said, "My name is Carlo." So I said, "Sit down."

He told me he was a partner to this fellow Conti, and he'd appreciate it if I could help him.

I didn't have the workers. I promised Gambino I wouldn't bother Conti's operation until his people joined the union, which they never did. And so, Gambino and I became friends.

Gambino had a deep Italian accent and could hardly speak English. He came here when he was about twenty-one. He never learned to speak well, but he was a nice person to talk with. Very soft spoken. Later when I went, I didn't go just to say hello. Guys would take me to see him. One of his nephews used to drive me up.

I remember once there was some battle in the Teamsters Council in New York, and people would ask Carlo who he thinks should be president of the council, who we should back. Certain locals would do exactly what he wanted. And so he used to send out the word.

Gambino also had an office of industrial relations, and he had a guy by the name of George Schiller fronting it. In case a company had problems with the unions, these people handled it. They'd straighten it out. They were very effective.

During the Second World War I had no problem with the meat shortage. Instead of drafting me, the government put me in classification 3A because they wanted me to produce meat for the army.

There was this big plant in New Jersey and the owner, Ben Grunstein, came to see if we could help because he could get a large contract with the government, but only if he could convince them he could produce enough meat. He used to get a lot of contracts from the army. A general didn't think he could produce so much, so I went to see the generals, and I guaranteed it.

The problem wasn't just getting meat, but boning and processing it. It was difficult. There was a shortage of butchers, and few new applicants, because the young ones were in the army. The contract called for a lot of meat. The stuff had to be packed and shipped overseas. Whole fillets, shells, ribs, but all boned out—boneless. The meat had to be fabricated and cut up according to certain specifications. But to have boneless meat is a job. You need professional boners doing it.

I had the workers, and I made sure I sent Grunstein enough boners and butchers to produce all through the war, and I was very involved in that. Sometimes, when Grunstein would run short of help, we had to work day and night. And we had some of my business agents working day and night, because they knew the business and they were butchers, and so we produced.

15

During the forties both Louie and I were organizing all the time, and Locals 640 and 342 continued cooperating with each other. So after the wholesalers, 640 took in the slaughterers and then the packinghouses. Now we went after the renderers. The whole rendering industry, where you render the fat and grease and the skin and bones.

When we had to, we'd fix it so the drivers didn't pick up the fat from the markets. Then when we had a strike against the renderers, the employers wouldn't sell them the fat. Things like that. Because the employer figures, the hell with him— instead of selling here, he'll sell somewhere else.

But it wasn't all peaches. The biggest rendering plant was Van Iderstein in Queens. We had the workers. We organized. Then we called a strike. There were maybe five hundred workers in that plant. At first there was not much activity but we had problems with a couple scabs. One fell into the hot fat tanks and died. A couple of things happened like this while we were organizing. It wasn't planned that way, but the organizing didn't get accomplished without some risks.

In Kearney, New Jersey, we had a long strike against the owner of a rendering plant, Theobald. He was an anti-Semite, a real Nazi and a slavedriver. Most of his workers lived on the premises sharing little huts with rats.

We could talk to Theobald's sons, but not to the old man,

115

who was in charge. He was stubborn. A mule. He was another Frank Baloney. So we followed the trucks, and then nobody would give Theobald any fat. He tried all kinds of gimmicks. Other people would try to pick up the fat, and he'd give them credit for it. But eventually we'd find out, and we adjusted things all the time.

Finally it was obvious Theobald was going to go out of business. That wasn't our intention, but he wouldn't give up, so we wouldn't give up. The strike went on for ten, twelve weeks. He lost twelve hundred customers.

Then Theobald's sons came to see us. Theobald had five sons and a daughter. Now, with the kids we got along swell. No problem. They realized the father was wrong. He'd destroy the business. So the sons agreed to sign, and they asked us to help them build the business back, because nobody was going to cross our picket line. They knew the connections between 342 and 640. They knew we were brothers and the same organization.

So we signed with the sons, and then we put out the word and we started working at it, and we helped them build their business up. It took weeks, but we got them back most of their customers.

From time to time we had problems with Martin Lacy of the Teamsters. Lacy talked rough. Sounded rough. Looked rough. But I figured he was full of shit. A character. A shlub, as they say in Yiddish. And I never wanted to have much to do with him.

After that first strike in Brooklyn, he didn't interfere. The workers wouldn't even go near him then, and he may have figured we wouldn't last long anyhow. Because he was told by the mob to take a walk, which he did, and he thought we'd do the same thing.

We didn't normally interfere with places organized by other unions, because there were too many still unorganized. We had to give Lacy his jurisdiction, like with Armour, even though he had nothing and wasn't even collecting dues until we handed it over to him.

Anyway, I didn't care for him, and I left him alone. But he'd get jealous and try to show that he was in control of things.

116

One time he stopped a couple of our trucks at the waterfront, where the drivers were organized by Local 640. That was a big mistake.

I called in all the business agents of Locals 342 and 640. I gave the agents instructions that beginning the next morning, midnight, they were to stop every Teamster truck from loading, or unloading. This involved all the wholesale meat markets all over New York City.

Now Lacy calls me up, crying. "What'd you do?" he says. "You stopped two thousand of my trucks."

I said, "You stopped two of my trucks on the waterfront yesterday. Didn't you?"

"Well," he said, "you stopped two thousand."

"My two trucks are just as important as your two thousand trucks," I told him. "Next time we'll stop three thousand. What do you think—you're playing around with children here?"

So we set up a meeting, to talk about it.

I had knocked him out in the first place, a long time back. I never forgot the time Louie and I went up to his office in the late 1930s. He interfered somehow in our operation, and when Louie called up on the phone he opened up a big mouth. So Louie said to him, "Tell it to me, to my face."

And he said, "Come up to my office."

So Louie said, "I'll be right up there with my brother Max."

We got up there, and he had some of his buddies around. Characters, with big fat bellies sticking out. But Lacy took water. He got scared and backed out.

Now Lacy wants to meet with us again.

Louie and I went up to his office, and he had a half dozen guys there, with the big bellies. And we were in good condition. Good boys. Plenty of guts.

We walked right up to him. "What is it, Marty?"

"Max, I got to respect you. You're a big man. You've got a lot of power. You made a lot of progress. Call off your crowd. We won't bother your trucks anymore."

So I said, "Okay. Fine." And that was it. They never stopped our trucks again. We took care of him once in a while, like with the packinghouses, and he cooperated with us, and we got along.

16

I had to organize a lot of independents for Local 342. New ones, old ones—all kinds. Whatever was around. You had thousands of shops in Brooklyn, Long Island, Staten Island. Long Island was growing. So there were always new shops to organize.

Meanwhile, we were also adding the chains. And some operations that we'd signed earlier grew and added new stores. One important chain was County Fair, and the president of that company was Max Kolner. This was a German outfit, and their headquarters was in Queens. Kolner already had a complete meat operation. He also had a wholesale plant, and then later he got into supermarkets. So they had the wholesale house, which Louie had already organized, and the factory. But the butchers in the markets belonged to an independent union, which included the County Fair retail markets and also the King Cullum Markets.

The independent union was nothing. A phony union financed by Kolner and King Cullum to keep out the more legitimate union. But we established picket lines all over, tied them up, and within two days we broke their whole setup. So they signed and after that we had no problem, and I took in the fellow that represented that group, Charlie, and made him a business agent in my organization.

❋   ❋   ❋

Jimmy Clark, the guy who used to own the gym in Brooklyn, was in trouble. Louie called and said, "Jimmy's up here. He needs a job." Jimmy had some problems. His kids couldn't breathe, and he went to Arizona. Then he came back and he was broke. So I said to Louie, "Put him on as a business agent in Local 640." And Louie did, and everything was fine.

Meanwhile, we had McCarthy's Steak House. We did a tremendous business. We didn't look to get rich out of it. My brother, my brother-in-law, another brother-in-law, everybody could make a living. We put Jimmy Clark in as president of the corporation and head bartender. He was a good type for that. A good storyteller. We trusted him and he fronted for us in the steak house, because we were busy with the labor movement.

One Saturday afternoon, some friends came into the bar and we began to talk about fights.

"I'll tell you a story about a fight," Jimmy said, and he told about a substitute that he brought me down to fight, Snowflakes. Then he said to me, "You think you knocked out that big coon? You knocked *me* out."

I said, "What are you talking about?"

So he tells me, "I was supposed to bring a guy that would lay down."

I said, "Why didn't you tell me that?"

"I knew you wouldn't do it," he says.

And I'm thinking, Oh, you thought Snowflakes would kill me anyhow, because I wasn't in shape. So I looked at him and I said, "You're fired, you son of a bitch!" And I fired him, right on the spot.

Then Louie calls. He says, "Jimmy called me. What happened?"

So I told Louie the story. "That son of a bitch," I said. "I always thought he was our buddy, and he took me down there to get killed." And I remembered, too, how Jimmy had asked me to take it easy instead of knocking the guy out right away, because Jimmy knew I couldn't last the ten rounds then.

So I told Louie, and he said, "The son of a bitch!"

After a while Louie and I became concerned about the crowd at the steak house. We didn't like the setup. We wanted

119

to get away from some of these tough guys, and we didn't want to be associated wtih that. Also Benny Caruse was a bootlegger in prohibition days and he was arguing and fighting quite a bit with Louie. And I was afraid there was going to be a killing.

We began to look around. Finally, we sold our interest to Caruse and a friend of his, Dave Polter, who was involved with the stock market somehow and was a front man for the tough guys.

Meanwhile, a guy named Ed Fudim, from the old left-wing group was now with Local 342. He was a so-called hot Communist, but he couldn't hang on to a job. One day he started a fight with me, but I knocked him out fast. He didn't have a chance.

Then his brother Phil came to talk to me about Eddie. How Eddie was having trouble. Couldn't hold onto a job. And this Phil is a good kid. He said I should do something for Eddie and his wife, who was seven months pregnant, and he asked me to help because Eddie couldn't make a living. So I say, "Okay," and I go ahead and put Eddie in business.

This was still during the war, and I told Eddie he would be partners with me and my brother in the wholesale business. So I gave him the connections to buy meat. It was still tough to get meat those days. I helped him get set up and pretty soon he was making a lot of money. We made a buck too. And it was one third for Eddie and one third each for Louie and me.

I knew in advance what the business was. So I said to Eddie, "I trust you." And he said, "You know more than I know, how much I owe you every week." And it was true. Beacuse if I buy meat for thirty cents a pound and they're selling it for forty cents, I know he's making ten cents a pound. Now if he cheats somewhere, if he gets a little more someplace and puts it in his pocket, then I figured, Fuck him! I wasn't going to worry about it. Because he never made that kind of money in his life—five or six hundred dollars a week, legitimate. Before he couldn't hold a job for fifty dollars.

We had a wholesale business, and he was selling to other butchers. The shop was maybe forty feet by twenty feet, with a couple of cars of meat. This was in the Fourteenth Street market, straight beef, and we had a few people working there, cutting meat in half. Sometimes you wouldn't have to cut it at all.

Then Eddie started accumulating a lot of money, and after he got a little fat he began to do wrong things. So we dropped it.

"Eddie. Forget it!" I said. "Go out on your own." And he wound up in business by himself.

But Eddie couldn't get any meat once I dropped him. So he wanted to talk to some tough guys to help him. A guy by the name of Scarsie from New York was one fellow. The other was Benny Caruse, my original partner at McCarthy's.

So Caruse called me. Maybe he made some kind of deal with Eddie, figuring that if Eddie could get straightened out he'd be a good source of cheap meat. I didn't know, and I didn't care. But I didn't like to leave things open. So I agreed to meet these guys at the Pierre, an expensive hotel in New York over on Fifth Avenue facing Central Park.

I didn't trust these guys, and I decided that maybe I should bring some backup. I didn't want Louie to be involved, especially since he didn't get along with Caruse anyway. I also didn't want to seem too threatening, because you don't show up with an army on something like this.

I got hold of my friend Solly Krieger. Solly was a good fighter. He was middleweight champion of the world. He and I were buddies. He was always having trouble keeping his weight down. In between fights, sometimes he'd put on a lot of pounds. But he was still tough as hell, and for someone who didn't know, when he was a little heavier like that he might look even tougher.

Solly had not only won the middleweight championship, but had also beaten Billy Conn, and he had to beat him decisively because the fight was in Pittsburgh, Kahn's hometown. And Billy Conn almost beat Joe Louis for the heavyweight championship. So Solly knew how to take care of himself, and you wouldn't want to mess with him. And these guys knew who he was.

Solly knew what we were going into, because I told him. He wasn't the kind of guy to look for trouble, but he wanted to help, because we were friends.

We went up to the hotel room. Caruse and Scarsie and Eddie were there. Eddie stayed in the background. He wanted the tough guys to talk for him. So we bullshit a little bit. Then they tell me they want me to release Eddie to let him buy meat.

But I'm figuring, because his brother came crying to me, the son of a bitch wound up a rich man, through me. And I didn't like him. He used to be a left-winger. Now because he had a little money he was a right-winger and wanted to be a big businessman. Then he makes deals with my former partner, Ben Caruse.

Scarsie I didn't bother with, because I figured I could talk better to Caruse. There wasn't much to talk about anyway.

Solly was quiet. He let me do the talking for the two of us. I wasn't looking to be friendly, but I didn't want to create any unnecessary friction with Caruse, if I didn't have to. We were ex-partners, and I didn't think he was too anxious to go up against me. Still I wanted them to know my position, so when Scarsie started to get into the act I turned to him.

"I'm not worried about you or anybody else, and that's it."

"You're fooling around with your life," Scarsie said to me.

Solly tensed up, enough for me to notice. I knew he wouldn't make a move unless it was necessary. But he'd be ready if it was. He had great timing, and he was there to back me up, and that was why I brought him.

Now I looked at Scarsie and Caruse, ignoring Eddie. "I don't like rats!" I said.

It wasn't exactly friendly, but at least I didn't call Caruse a rat, and he knew who I was talking about.

"He's our partner," Caruse says.

"I don't give a damn whose partner he is," I said. "He's no good. He's a rat. That's why I dropped him. You got him. Sleep with him. As far as I'm concerned, I'll do what I want, and that's it."

Apparently they could tell I meant business. And they must have known that if they started anything Solly and I would wipe the floor with the three of them, so they didn't want trouble on the spot.

Solly and I left. I wasn't worried about these guys.

The outcome was that Eddie had them as partners. The tough guys couldn't do a thing with me. For a long time Eddie had a problem getting meat. But then as the war ended you could buy meat anyplace.

17

With the money from our interest in McCarthy's, Louie and I set up another steak house. We found a closed-down place, which we remodeled, and in December 1945, we opened up on East Fiftieth Street in Manhattan, between Third and Lexington.

We couldn't think of a name, and I asked our lawyer, Fred Scholem, to check on different names in Europe, in England and France and so on. There was an Angus Restaurant in Scotland, and I realized the black Angus cattle was the best in the world—so I chose that, and we called the place the Black Angus.

After that, we always watched when the black Angus cattle were being slaughtered, and we used the black Angus ninety-nine percent. Other restaurants that later took the Angus name didn't use the cattle. Probably a lot didn't know what the Angus was. People would ask our waiters, so we put a picture on the menu along with a little write-up on the back, with some of the history.

We had large rooms, and seating for about three hundred seventy-five people, the legal number. We remodeled everything. There was a beautiful small bar in the front with a foot railing, and about ten stools. In the two front rooms there were about two dozen booths, with curved black-and-white calfskin upholstery. In the other two rooms, we had tables, expensive wood paneling, all kinds of paintings. It was a beautiful place, and we expected a big crowd.

From the Waldorf-Astoria you would walk down a half block, then cross over Lexington Avenue to the Black Angus. So we had another place to hang out and to meet, and the family could make some money out of it.

Right away the place was successful—an important eating-out place where you could get the best steak in New York. We also served large orders of double steaks.

A lot of different groups began to come in. It became a popular hangout for fighters, entertainers, politicians, journalists, writers, a lot of colorful people.

Billy Buckley, Jr., used to eat dinner there all the time. He would invite me over, and I'd sit and converse with him. He was knowledgable, but also a good listener. We discussed a lot of things, about labor and so on, though I didn't tell him about all the stuff that I knew was going on.

Another guy, Walter True, used to come in with his wife. He was the president of a bank, and he'd invite me over to his table, and we'd have a drink together.

"Max," he asked once, "Do you ever miss the school education you never got?" Apparently he knew my background.

I says, "Walter, sometimes I miss it. But then again, if I were to go to school I wouldn't get the education I received on the street."

I knew that school education was easier. The education you got on the street was a hard one. And sometimes I felt I was climbing up a straight wall and slipping down and getting hurt all the time. And finally when I'd reach the top of the wall, there'd be some son of a bitch with a club in his hand, hitting me on the head and trying to knock me down.

We were accumulating a lot more power as the organizing continued, and of course there was always some wise guy that saw an opportunity. But that wasn't anything new.

I remember Eddie and Mike Bentz. They were members of the union, and they attempted to strong-arm me to take over Local 342, after I made the break with Local 400.

124

We had the offices on Fulton Street near the Flatbush Extension in Brooklyn. I was in a board meeting one evening, and Eddie, one of the brothers, came over. He wanted to muscle himself in.

Billy Casale, my secretary, tried to stop him, but Billy was not a fighter. He was a pencil man. And Eddie grabbed Billy and roughed him up a little. So somebody came into the board meeting and told me about it. I hurried over. Meanwhile they had called the cops.

Now Eddie says to me, "I want to be a business agent, and I want my brother Mike to be a business agent."

"You know, Eddie," I said. "It doesn't work like that." I looked at him. "Right now, there's no room."

"What'ya mean, there's no room? Make room!" he said.

I said, "Eddie, take a walk."

He made a move toward me. I wasn't going to stand there. I hit him on the chin, and he went down the steps, head-first. He was out cold. I left him there, stretched out, and I went back to the board meeting.

When I came out, this cop was there. "Gee, Mr. Block," he said. "You hit harder with your fist than I do with my club." By now he had called the station for a wagon, to take the guy away.

Meanwhile we finished the board meeting and I went back to my office, and the next thing somebody said Eddie wanted to see me. He came to and straightened himself out, and he said he was sorry.

I opened the door and let him in. He had his head down. I said, "Okay, go!" So he leaves.

Now the wagon comes. The cop can't find Eddie, so he thinks I hid him someplace.

"Mr. Block, I have to have a prisoner. I called the wagon."

I said, "Take me." Fine. So I get in the wagon. But by the time the wagon is ready to pull away, they grabbed Eddie. The workers found him in some saloon nearby and brought him into the wagon, and they let me out. They took Eddie to the stationhouse, and then they let him out on bail, because I bailed him out.

Now he's waiting outside for the cop, and when the cop came out, Eddie slugged the cop and knocked him out. He was tough. Meanwhile I had the bondsman get Eddie out for five hundred dollars. So he knocked out the cop, but then the other cops grabbed him, and they charged him again and he was no longer out on bail. This was after he had his head down and made like he was sorry, or whatever.

Eddie was in jail until he got out after thirty days or so, and then later we had a meeting of Local 342.

Now Eddie shows up with his brother, and the two of them are tough, bad people. You never knew if they would use a knife.

There's about four or five hundred members in the big room upstairs, which we rented when we needed it. Jack Walsh, the vice-president of the Amalgamated, was at this meeting, and he had just turned the floor over to me. So then I saw that these two guys were approaching me at the head of the room, like they wanted to take the mike away from me or cause some kind of trouble.

Edide and Mike were big, husky fellows, about twenty-eight, thirty years old. Blond hair. I knew most of the members. These two guys couldn't take me, no matter what, because the members would run up. But still I had to show my ability, my guts, because the members respected me. So, I wasn't going to let these guys fuck around. I'm supposed to be in charge of the meeting.

Eddie and Mike approached me by the front of the floor, about six feet apart. Jack Walsh was an old man by now, but he told them, "Don't fool around. Get away and sit down." Because he knew I would take them. But they wouldn't listen. They wanted to get wise.

Eddie came up, and right away I cracked him one, and he went flying. The brother, Mike, backed away. He was already finished. He saw he had no chance against me, because the same would happen to him.

I never told Louie about the first incident, when Eddie came to the office. It wasn't as if they were from the mob or something—I figured I could handle it myself, and I didn't bother to mention it.

But now Louie must have been told I was in trouble or expecting trouble or something. He came over and waited downstairs. He got them as they came outside.

126

Louie and his friends beat the shit out of the two of them. They got a terrible beating.

I said, "How'd you know?"

He just said, "I was told you were having trouble, so I came over with a couple of fellows."

18

18 A lot of entertainers came into the Black Angus, and everyone had a plan or a dream or a pipe dream. But you had to have some kind of idea what you were doing with your life, and you had to try, or you could end up just sitting around the bar going nowhere.

Then you never could tell about the future. I knew Victor Mature, the actor. He seemed like a nice fellow. His father was a butcher, and Victor used to come into the Black Angus, and I'd have a drink with him.

One day he came in, and I said, "What's new?"

And he told me. "I'm going out to Hollywood," he said. And he left, and I haven't seen him since. He did all right.

Dean Martin, before he tied up with Jerry Lewis, used to hang around me after I'd come out of the barbershop at the Waldorf-Astoria. Or sometimes he'd wait for me at the Belmont Plaza. I'd buy him a couple of drinks and then we'd go over to the Black Angus. We'd spend a little time together, and he'd have a steak. I thought Dean was talented, but I knew what he was up against getting started.

I thought Tony Bennett was a tremendous singer, and I knew his manager. But one day his manager told me he couldn't get any work for Tony, and yet Tony was a terrific singer. So

I told the manager, "You got to get in through the boys. So he'll get the work." And sure enough, Tony got himself connected with the mob somewhere, and he worked and got everything going since then.

But before, he was starving to death, the same as Dean Martin when he was hanging around and down and out and couldn't get any work.

This Jerry Lewis used to work in the Glass Hat.

"This kid's gonna be good. Funny," I said to Dean. "You ought to make a deal with him somehow."

"What do I need with him?" Dean said. "I'm a crooner."

That's the way he answered, but somehow, a little time elapsed and he tied up with Jerry. So they both started working together.

Then Dean got himself in with the mob, with Frank Sinatra and that setup, and they made him big. But Jerry got nervous because of the mob, and that was why he later split the team —he didn't want to bow to the tough guys, for them to stay on the payroll. Jerry was lucky they didn't shoot him. The last I knew, Martin was still controlled by them.

I didn't know exactly, but the idea was simple—the mob gets a piece of the action. They get a percentage. So maybe they're partners some way with the manager. But that's how they'd operate. They had the front. They had the connections with all the known nightclubs and everything.

For example, I used to sit and discuss things with Frank Costello. He was behind the Copacabana. He told me he owned twenty percent of the place, and I was surprised—it was so little. Because Costello was one of the top men in the underworld.

"Why only twenty percent?" I asked him. And he told me. He never takes more than twenty percent on any legitimate deal, because he doesn't trust people, and he doesn't want them to rob him. On twenty percent, he explained, he figured he'd get his twenty percent. But on fifty percent, he figured he'd never get it. He'd get robbed.

The boys had always been involved in the entertainment thing. It was a natural. I already knew stories about Westchester County. How they set up Sinatra, the whole thing. They tried to sell me stock too, in some fancy place in Westchester, the Premier Theatre, but I wouldn't buy it. This guy was friends with a relation of mine, but he was also friends with these guys playing a lot of golf, and he knew what was going on. And they got Frankie Sinatra to go there, to help them open this place in Westchester, and then they took away the money, and all the people who invested in the place went bust. There was a whole write up. Pictures of Frank Sinatra with these monkeys, when they were tough guys in Westchester. But Dean was not really a tough guy. He was just an entertainer, and as he said, "I'm just a crooner."

Adding a little splash to the Black Angus, some of the top fighters would often come by for a double steak or a few drinks. Gene Tunney. Jack Dempsey. Rocky Marciano. Also, the leading union figures would come by. George Meany. Phil Murray. Jimmy Hoffa, a little later when I got to know him. Then you had other people coming by on union business because now we made most of our appointments at the Black Angus. We had to meet somewhere. This was more convenient and more comfortable than going into the office.

Joe Kennedy, father of John, Bobby, and Teddy, would come to the Black Angus for a drink or dinner. Publicly, he wasn't that widely-known yet.

"Hi, Block!" he'd say. My dentist and he were in the same building and Joe used to talk to me about things. But we met originally in the Waldorf-Astoria in the barbershop, where he and I used to go every day. Frank Costello was also a regular.

A little earlier, before we started the Black Angus, the Murder, Incorporated, organization had gained notoriety after some arrests and convictions in the early forties. This was under District Attorney Bill O'Dwyer, who later would become mayor of New York.

Strauss was charged as the leader and convicted. Eventually, he got the electric chair. Abe Reles, a little guy, another in the gang that used to frequent McCarthy's, was killed when the police threw him out a window of the Half Moon Hotel in Coney Island. They said he was trying to escape. But I figured the police threw him out the window, or maybe he was dead before they threw him out.

Red Mendy was charged and in and out of jail on different

130

things, along with some of the other guys, but not as part of the Murder, Incorporated, organization. They had some convictions, but the organization continued, different guys, and for all I know it's still going on.

Later, Bill O'Dwyer, the D.A., would come to me for support when he was running for mayor of New York. I supported him, and he was elected, and after that we became friends. He would stop by the Black Angus to say hello or have a drink from time to time. Bill Donahue, his secretary and his buddy, used to hang out at the Black Angus all the time. We were very close.

The place used to be a tea house owned by the San Carlos Hotel, before we bought and remodeled it. Of course, anyone can go into a public restaurant, and some of the characters who used to hang around McCarthy's would now come to the Black Angus. Our tough guy clients included Carlo Gambino, Johnny Dio, Little Augi Paisano, George Scalise, Joe Parise, Frank Costello, Anthony "Tony Pro" Provenzano, Meyer Lansky, Joey Gallo and his brother, and some of the lesser-known mob characters.

You could write a book about most any one of those guys. These fellows were connected to Lucky Luciano, Vito Genovese, Al Capone, and now with Carlo Gambino. And they were the leaders of the Mafia families that controlled a large part of what was going on in America.

Meyer Lansky once said the Mafia was bigger than U.S. Steel. Some district attorney claimed it was bigger than U.S. Steel, General Motors, the telephone company, and a few other corporate giants all put together.

It's a lot of money, and nobody pays any taxes on it. And some mob business was undoubtedly conducted in the Black Angus, and not always in the back rooms where some of these wise guys were involved in payoffs for the biggest book in New York.

Perhaps an important transaction—or for all I know a contract to get someone killed—would take place in one of those booths in the front or the middle dining room, maybe next to some tourist or someone out on the town having a nice steak and a few drinks. They wouldn't know what's going on. How would they know who's sitting next to them? And who's listening, and who cares.

Louie didn't know about stuff like that. I probably wouldn't know myself, and I wouldn't ask.

A lot of the tough guys were involved with the Mafia families that sometimes fought each other, until Carlo Gambino became head of all the families. But even then all the conflicts didn't die away.

These guys are still killing each other. The last I knew, there were many killings of people in the mob going on in Brooklyn and New York. That's what I was told, and in recent months some of the people got knocked off. A lot of them. I was told when I was in New York. Apparently some others were looking to move in, and some of Gambino's people got killed. So all the jurisdictions are still controlled by the mob, the Mafia, out of New York, New Jersey. Anyplace. And you still have mob guys that want to increase their territory.

But the Black Angus did not belong to any mob. It was neutral territory. Sure these guys were friends of mine. Once in a while they'd come in, have a steak, have a drink, "How you doing?"

"Fine."

I didn't always know what was going on, and neither did Louie. But maybe because I was Jewish, that put me more outside the inner circle of any one Italian group, and so they all trusted me.

Some saw us as tough guys too, but I was busy organizing the union. I wasn't looking to take over any mob. And I never squealed about anything I might have heard, and they all knew my reputation and that my word was good. Then Carlo and I became friends, and later on in life he probably saved my life half a dozen times.

It's easy to get yourself killed in that crowd. Because they always wanted to kill each other. There was a Teamster guy. He latched on to me, and I did him favors, Milton Silverman. He was always organizing. He looked to organize anything, and he didn't always ask questions first. So that caused some problems.

Johnny Dio wanted to kill him. So one guy from the mob came to see me.

"Look," he says. "Look what he did. You always protect him. We want to kill him."

132

I looked at him. I said, "Listen, Joe. You need guys like this."

"What do you mean?"

"If there were not some people like this guy, you're in trouble," I told him. "He's creating issues. If you kill the guy who's creating issues, then there's no need for you. Who needs you?"

So he says, "Nobody ever told me this."

"You dumb son of a bitch," I said. "If you give me the details, I'll straighten it out tomorrow." Which I did. But he was so excited. He wanted to kill. But I just told him these people would come to see you because this guy would give them a headache. And you need a guy who gives them a headache. So that was it, and they dropped the issue.

Larry Brescia—Chappy—was a friend of mine. He was a partner and bodyguard to Lucky Luciano, until Luciano was deported. And Chappy always told everybody he was my partner, and you'd always hear about it in the Black Angus. He must have made a buck unbeknownst to us for these guys always look to make a buck.

But Chappy behaved like a gentleman at the Black Angus. Otherwise, I wouldn't let him hang out there. He was a high-class guy. He'll get mad as hell anyway when he reads this, and I'll say, "I intended to say worse, but I cut it down."

When "Charlie Lucky" (Luciano) was convicted and sent away to Italy, Chappy was held on ten thousand dollars bail, and they kept him on it for years. Today you couldn't get away with that. Those years you could, but they had nothing on him. Still Tom Dewey was appointed by Governor Lehman as a special prosecutor, and he kept the bail on, and this went on for a long while.

Dewey was a friend of mine, because I had supported him, and I went to Dewey and asked him to release Chappy from the bail, and he did; and ever since then I was obligated to Dewey and I backed him in all his elections, when he ran for President or whatever he was running for, and we remained good friends. Later, Dewey would help me get Hoffa out of jail, and some other things. And so after the bail was dropped, Chappy was sort of obligated to me, and we became good friends. He always invited me to his parties and weddings, when his children got married. He had his home in Atlantic Beach. He had a few houses, but his home was also there.

Joe Gallo and his brother, they were in Brooklyn around the Broadway section, and they had certain things in their control. They came to see me a couple of times, for favors.

Johnny Dio was another well-known mob guy that I'd see sometimes. Dio was in jail for a while, and then when he came out he got himself involved in kosher provisions. He had formed a company, and then he filed the Chapter 11 bankruptcy. He gave me the report. I told him not to do it. I said he'd go back to jail for the way he was doing it, because it's federal law once it's in Chapter 11, and the feds were watching him.

"Everybody else is doing it," he said. "My lawyer told me it's okay."

But I told him, "Everybody else will get away, but you'll go to jail for it."

So what he did, he took the assets away from the old company and put them into a new company, and he got arrested and convicted on it and sent to jail. And he died in jail. But before he went to jail, Dio also set up a distributing company, and last I knew the company was still operated by his son and his nephew Tommy. There were some problems, and Tommy's father, Jimmy Boyle, got killed a few years ago.

Anyway, Dewey spoke to somebody about getting Johnny Dio out, but then he came back to me. "Max," he said, "the guy makes too many waves. We can't get him out."

We got along fine with the police. Without the police department, nobody can operate. I can tell you. The police station was on Fifty-first Street and we were on Fiftieth Street, and I knew all the cops, all the inspectors, and most of them were paid off by different guys all the way down the line. So many of the inspectors and captains used to hang out in the Black Angus. They'd be there for lunches and dinner parties. The money collections from the biggest bookmakers in the city used to be made in the back dining room.

Meanwhile the traffic department never gave any driver a summons when they mentioned that they were friends of the Blocks in the Black Angus.

Without the police, the mobs couldn't carry on. So you had

some of these guys in the back dining room, with different payoffs and deals. But we were good friends at the Black Angus with the police, and we tried to help them when we could.

One day the shoefly for the inspector showed me that both him and the inspector received their papers to get off the force and retire. (A shoefly is a driver and a go-fer.) So I went and I called up Mayor O'Dwyer, and I asked him what is the story about.

"Listen, Max," he said. "You know the commissioner is a tough man," because it was the commissioner that wanted the shoefly and the inspector to quit.

"So who in the hell elected him?" I said to O'Dwyer, because it was O'Dwyer that appointed the commissioner.

He said, "You're right, Max." And then the next thing the shoefly comes in, and instead of getting retired, both he and the inspector got themselves promoted.

One time, two o'clock in the morning, I was being driven home on Hutchinson Boulevard in Westchester, heading into the New England Throughway. I was asleep in the back seat. The driver, a little Italian fellow, Patsy, was going fast in the limousine, a seven-seater Cadillac. So a cop was chasing us, but Patsy didn't realize he was racing with the cop—he thought it was another guy, fooling with him.

Finally, the cop pulled us over.

"What do you want from me?" Patsy said to the cop. "I got Max Block sleeping in the back of the car."

"You're full of shit," the cop said. Then he opened the door and he saw me. "Oh, Max! I'm sorry."

All the cops knew us. On almost any city street, it was the same thing.

One day I was driving with Jean, and I look in the mirror. There was this motorcycle cop. A big fat guy, and I knew him, and I see he's timing me. So I stepped on it. I pulled away. Finally he pulls up and stops me.

"Oh, Max Block. Hello!"

"I did it on purpose," I told him. "I wanted you to stop me, so I could say hello."

If people would get stopped, they'd say they were friends of the Blocks. They'd use it like a password. And occasionally they'd leave a few dollars in an envelope, and I'd give it to

135

the motorcycle cops. Usually when the captains and inspectors would go in, the others wouldn't. But all the cops were friends of ours.

Maybe sometimes you had tough guys there at the same time as the captains or inspectors, but the police didn't look for these guys. You don't look for somebody unless you got orders. And they wouldn't arrest them in the Black Angus anyway. They wouldn't want to embarrass us.

A few times characters came in. Not mob guys but different characters that didn't want to pay a bill or that picked a fight, and we gave them a tremendous beating and threw them out. Then they'd go around the corner to the station-house because we'd break their heads, break their legs—the headwaiter, Dave Gould, used to be a good heavyweight fighter. So someone would go to make a complaint around the corner but the desk sergeant, anyone they'd talk to, would tell them they made a mistake.

"They don't fight in the Black Angus. It's a high class place."

19

We had our home in Woodside, Queens, and for a period during the war I'd bicycle to the office every day, maybe twenty miles each way. Then in 1945 we moved to New Rochelle. It was a beautiful place, a huge stone house. A Japanese ambassador lived in it, then the war started and he left or was taken somewhere. I bought the place from the bank.

We had a boy and a girl, Alvin and Iris, and after the war we adopted a seven-year-old, Danielle, from France.

My brother-in-law, in the army, wrote us about the homeless kids. Jean used to send packages and also ten dollar bills in the letters, and then one day this lady wrote to us from France. Somebody on the block had the letter translated, and the lady said the girl would have a better home with us.

So my wife, Ginny, says, "Max, maybe we'll adopt her?"

I said, "Okay," and that was that.

A friend of mine had some business in France. I gave him the information, but we had some problems with the records and getting her over, so I went to Washington, to the White House, and I saw Vice-President Barkley, from Kentucky, the Vice-President under Truman. Then immediately they took care of everything. My friend left a few days later, and he brought my girl from France, and we loved her ever since,

137

along with the other kids. She went to a fancy college in New York on Park Avenue, like my other daughter Iris, and now she's married and lives in Houston, Texas, and has two children.

A lot of the guys from the Jewish mob on the West Side of Chicago would come by to see me when they were in New York, and then, whenever I was in Chicago, usually to stop by the headquarters of the Amalgamated, I'd visit them. We were close friends for years.

I met some of these guys when I joined the Amalgamated. So when I'd come to Chicago, they'd entertain. We had a lot of fun. There was Big Sneeze, a big man in size, and his brother, Little Sneeze. Jackie Perno, an Italian guy, was married to a Jewish girl, but he spoke Jewish better than the Jewish boys do. Jackie was in control of the fish market in Chicago. He had a charter with the Amalgamated, and he also did some work for the Teamsters.

Doc Brown, a doctor from Chicago, used to hang out with us. Joe Glimko, who represented the taxicab drivers in Chicago, was also part of the crowd. And my friend Irv Green, the son of Al Green. Al was president of the Mercury Record Company; then later Irv became president. All the boys had a piece of the action. Then this guy got killed and that guy got killed and that guy died.

Maxie Hoffman had a piece of Mercury Records. He was also part of the crowd, and when I was in town we'd see Maxie. He owned the Shangri-La, a famous Oriental restaurant with the best food in the Loop.

This was the so-called Jewish mob, in Chicago, and there was another guy that would hang out with us, Wanny Shatsky, when he'd be in from Minneapolis. But Wanny got into a problem. Wanny and another guy, Hank Savers, had a night club in Minneapolis, and then a couple Teamsters started coming in and giving them a hard time, acting abusive and nasty. They were just bad characters. Miserable people.

They kept annoying Wanny, and he warned them that if they came back, he'd kill them. Then they came back.

The last time maybe these guys had a few drinks, and they

dropped a glass on purpose. Maybe they felt like tough guys, but they weren't so tough, because Wanny was a killer. A handsome guy, a six-footer.

So these guys came in, two brothers. They were always acting like bullies, and they'd been warned. This time Wanny told them to get out. They refused. Then they made a move, so he shot them both. One died immediately, the other soon after.

The Jewish tough guys, the Jewish mob in Chicago, figured Wanny wouldn't get a fair deal. Then the trial was going on, and he escaped. It was amazing—he saw an opening. He ran from the courthouse, and nobody caught him.

Wanny went over the border to Mexico, and we helped him. In Mexico they had a black fellow that used to be a friend of the organization in Chicago, and this guy had a pool parlor. So Wanny went out, and this guy took good care of him.

Meanwhile, the authorities went through with the trial and convicted Wanny, and he got maybe one hundred and fifty-four years. We got money together for appeals. Louie and I contributed most, because we liked him. So Wanny was away in Mexico. This black guy, a solid citizen, put Wanny up in a nice apartment. But Wanny had a girlfriend, a blonde, in Chicago, and the F.B.I. guys kept trying to get her to frame him. Finally they showed her some phony pictures of Wanny and some other woman. They convinced her Wanny was screwing around, and they scared her, because they wanted her to cooperate to bring him out of Mexico.

After a while, Wanny's girlfriend got hot enough. She made arrangements to meet Wanny on the border. He came up, but while the two were walking on the bridge, the cops grabbed him.

When they grabbed Wanny and put him in jail, Truman was President, so I figured Truman could get him out, because Wanny wasn't even present at his own trial.

How did I reach Truman? Well, Nick Blassie, who represented the local in Saint Louis for the Amalgamated, was very close to Truman. Nick had lived in Saint Louis, where Truman was from, and that famous line "Give 'em hell, Harry!" that was my friend Nick Blassie that screamed that out.

So I asked Nick, who was a good friend of mine, and Nick worked out the deal with Harry Truman, and Truman pardoned him.

Nobody had to tell me that sometimes you could push things too far. Or that you could be too smart for your own good. But it was that way with a lot of wise guys.

Little Sneeze started pushing his luck, but Harry Truman couldn't help him. Little Sneeze had a habit—he used to stick up joints that belonged to the syndicate. He wasn't a stickup guy, but he did it. He was a wise son of a bitch. He only stuck up their places. There was the Italian mob and this was the Jewish mob, and he had a habit of sticking up the tough guys, the Italians. He didn't knock off any Jewish stuff, just the Italians, certain big crap games the syndicate used to run, things like that.

Little Sneeze carried on quite a while. At first they didn't know who it was. Then they discovered it was him, and they warned him. But he didn't pay attention. He was tough as hell. And while he was sticking them up, he originally figured they're not going to squeal to the cops—but he forgot that they could kill him.

One day the group was eating at Maxie Hoffman's place, the Shangri-La, and some of the tough Italian guys got Little Sneeze in the parking lot and they killed him. They shot him. After that, the Jewish mob didn't do anything. We all figured Little Sneeze had been asking for it—he was warned.

When you're dealing with the tough guys, or if you get warned, you have to take it seriously.

I was invited to a New Year's Eve party in a home on the East Side of Manhattan, uptown. Six couples came to a dinner, and there was one single man. He was supposed to be a comparé, but he must have messed up somehow, because they got him down in the basement and they killed him.

I realized what was going on because I was going toward the bathroom and I saw something downstairs—by the steps going down.

They cut this guy's throat with a big knife, and they were holding him. So I went on to the bathroom, but I made sure I took a good look. By that time he was dead, and I realized that this was the single man.

140

So they killed the guy. They cut his head off, and they cut every part of his body apart and then they put all the pieces into bags. After that, without saying a word, some of these guys went out somewhere to get rid of the bags.

After the car pulled away, the women naturally were left behind, cleaning up and washing, because the basement must have been full of blood.

The women got a little nervous, cleaning up. Jean realized something was happening. She saw the women run down to the basement. She wanted to know, what was going on? Where are they?

Jean may have seen one of the women come up with some bloody rags, to wash in the bathroom. Or she may have seen something when she was going by the opening there by the stairway.

She fainted. I brought her to. At first, I didn't know what happened, why she fainted, because nobody said anything. There was no conversation. Nobody talked. So I figured Jean must have seen something—maybe some blood.

Jean didn't know they cut this guy up the way they did. She thought they must have stabbed somebody or killed somebody. Although she didn't know for sure.

But whoever the single guy was, he wasn't going to see the New Year. His time ran out.

Of course, I had no way of knowing what was going to take place. I figured the guy must have squealed, or tried to move in on someone, or done something. And I didn't know if it was planned, or something that just came up. But after that, Jean begged me—never take her to anything like that again.

20

Some decades ago, Billy Rose owned a nightclub, the Diamond Horseshoe, just off Broadway. They had good food, and it was the biggest nightclub in the city.

I used to sit in a box with Billy at the Diamond Horseshoe. I knew him from the late twenties, when he hung around the Ziegfeld Follies. He offered to use his influence to get me a job with Ziegfeld but I never took him up on it.

Billy Rose started as a poor guy, a hustler, and he hustled Fanny Brice, who became his wife and the star of the Follies. Billy introduced us, and I met her just once, but I thought she was a nice lady.

Later, when World War II was on and during the shortage of meats, Billy had a man, Nick, in charge of the food operation, and Billy asked me to help Nick get straightened out that way because they were running short. So I made connections for them to get meat, ribs and loins and so on. Nick knew his way around food, and I'd come by and talk to Nick, or spend a little time with Billy, sitting in the box with him. He told me a lot of stories about the Follies.

*   *   *

Louie and I kept organizing, adding new places. In the late forties, I became president of the Butcher Council for New York and New Jersey, which was made up of the heads of the local Amalgamated unions in these areas.

When I took over the Butcher Council, it changed from night to day. There used to be fights all the time. Now these stopped. The whole thing was set up to get cooperation to help one another, and we'd discuss different problems and see what could be done.

Longie Zwillman from New Jersey might call, or he'd come by the Black Angus just after midnight sometimes and have coffee. He'd say, "This guy's okay," or "Watch out for this," or something like that, the same way I might go over stuff with Meany or Hoffa when we'd discuss things of mutual interest to the internationals.

The A.F. of L. internationals—the Amalgamated Meat Cutters, the Plumbers, the Teamsters, whatever—it was all autonomous. Each was supposed to run by itself. Each had its own direction, but it was all part of the A.F. of L.

In the Butcher Council, mostly I looked at how to increase the organizing, and how to increase the benefits. Of course, this wasn't always popular, even within the union, especially where you had people protecting the independent shops. You had the retail meat local of the Amalgamated in Chicago, for example, under Emmett Kelly, and for years they ran a private racket there and they were on the payroll of every employer— and they were the sole organization there, and it was paid off, protecting the independent shops.

So you had butchers working late at night, stuff like that, or getting paid the same as the wrappers. And that was ridiculous, because you can go in and wrap and inside of an hour you know what you're doing. But a butcher, he started as an apprentice—maybe it took him four or five years to learn his trade, and he went through all these hardships to get to that point. But that's the kind of situation you get with guys protecting the independent shops. Pat Gorman, who believed in organizing and not tolerating that kind of stuff, used to say to Emmett, "Talk to Max." But he wasn't interested. He had his own thing going, and meanwhile the Kellys had Gorman by the balls.

*   *   *

What I'd see a lot of the time, either someone was getting paid off by the boss or he was trying to kill the boss, to put him out of business.

One week, all the organizers for the international were called in for a meeting in Chicago. You had lawyers, professors of labor, and so on, and they asked questions all week long. But all you got was answers from books and theories. Then on Friday morning, the last day, Belsky, the senior vice-president of the international, said, "Max, take the forum."

I said, "I don't want to—I'm disgusted with the whole thing."

"Max," he said, "go and talk for five minutes."

So I get up and I start talking. "I've listened the whole week," I said, "to the questions, and to the answers by the professors and lawyers. And most of the questions had to do with something like, 'How do I handle the situation when I come into a town that's anti-union—the cops, lawyers, public, everyone?' Then you got opinions on how to handle it. But I want to ask one question—why should these employers be pro-union?—are you bringing them a little business? Money? Profit? All you're doing it taking things away from them. Taking money, control of business. And the one thing the employer hates, that's to lose control. He wants to be boss. So why should they be pro-union?"

Then I went on to make my point, "You don't kill the goose that lays the golden egg. If I sign up a shop, I get conditions I want for my people. But the guy next door, he isn't organized. So I don't leave this guy alone and ignore him. My god! You got to organize the fellow next door. That would help the organized shop stay in business and would help the worker get good conditions. And after you organize this guy you don't harass *him;* you annoy the next guy, until he's organized.

So you don't look to kill the employers. You harass the ones you don't have. Then the organized shop automatically becomes the organizer. People come and ask him, 'How are you getting along with the union?' He says, 'Beautiful. Fine. Wonderful.' You get them that way. And this is the way I'd do it.

"But if you continually harass your own organized shop, then you put them out of business. You wind up with nothing. And everyone is going to fight you. If you have to fight every inch of the way, you bleed to death."

21

There was always the possibility of trouble.

One day in 1949, my brother Louie was sitting in the Black Angus with the police captain from Fifty-first Street and Third Avenue. I had just gone home. The shoefly, and Frank, the inspector's runner, was also there. And the captain, about six-four, was sitting with Louie about three tables over from two characters that came in and asked for me.

It didn't look kosher. So Louie told them to take their hats off and behave like gentlemen.

This must have been when I arrived home, about ten, eleven o'clock at night. Next day, I'm back, but I stick around a little later. Again, these characters show up. One of them, a butcher, I knew from Local 342. And we saw he was hanging around outside by the front door, while the other one came inside.

Now Louie went to the back to get his gun—because he had seen Lou Taco, the guy outside, hanging out with some of the tough guys in Astoria. And he knew that the night before, the two were carrying pieces.

We walked up to the front together. As we reached the first guy, I grabbed his wrist. I swung his arm around behind him and raised it up hard, applying pressure; it just about broke his arm. Now I started walking him outside. Meanwhile, Louie covered the other guy. He went up to Taco with the gun, then pointed it straight at him. He told Taco to take his hand out of his pocket—carefully, without the piece, because Louie could see that Taco had the gun in his pocket. Now the guy saw that Louie would blow his brains out, so he did as Louie said, took his hand out.

Outside, I hit my man on the chin—he went flying across the street with his head into the door of a parked car. By the time he got up, I had moved right up to him.

"Let's go!" I said, and we started walking to the station-house around the corner.

"Let me drop my piece," he asked.

I let him drop it by some parked car, and Louie let his man drop his. Then we walked them both up to the station. We only pressed charges for assault, since we let them drop their pieces and they locked them both up. But who cares about them appreciating that. They'd kill me in a minute.

They were lucky they didn't get killed or shot. Because the night before, Louie and the shoefly and the captain saw that these guys, Taco and his buddy, were carrying. If not for Louie, the cops might have killed or shot them right there—they wanted to shoot them. The cops do that. Sure. Maybe in the leg or the ass, or whatever. The cop had his gun under the table. He figured these guys deserved it. They came for no good.

I was surprised. I thought Taco was a sensible guy. He was a good butcher. I didn't know he hung out with some of the tough guys in Astoria. Apparently Taco and his buddy did some checking. One guy that tipped me off about it later told me he warned them to be careful—the Block brothers were tough. But Taco just said, "Don't worry about it," or something like that. So these guys thought they'd grab some action for themselves. They must have felt cocky because they belonged to the group, the mob. But instead of making sure who they were dealing with, they didn't find out until after they were in jail. Then they found out about my friends.

Now I had a compare from the mob come to see me. Because the authorities wouldn't let these two out on bail. Then this compare has my buddy Chappy call me, because apparently the guys were connected a little.

"How come you didn't tell me?" Chappy says.

"What am I gonna tell you? These monkeys were in there with guns," I said. "You weren't around. In the meantime I was able to handle them. I'm gonna go look for you, I'd be dead."

But I asked Chappy, "Why didn't they come to you before? Why are they coming to you now? Because these monkeys could have gotten killed."

"You're right," Chappy says. "But what are you gonna do?"

"Okay," I said. "I'll see what we can do."

The judge was Charles Murphy, a personal friend of ours. When the two came up to him, he dismissed the case. We didn't press any charges, but they could have killed us.

Lou Taco was a member of our union for so long, I was surprised he could get involved like that. But he saw our operation, and he wanted in. Maybe the mob in Astoria talked him into it. They told him he'd be a business agent. They must have made a deal like that, so he'd have an in and they'd have an in, and they figured they could control us. But among the friends they talked to, they didn't see or hear anything about us. Yet we were very well-known in the Jewish mob and the Mafia and with the police, and all over. And we were respected, because we'd been through the hell and we stood up.

22

Joe Parise was about six-foot, a big man, two hundred forty pounds, a nice person to talk to. I knew him a long time, from the movement. He was the head of Local 27, for the paper and pulp, in the Teamsters. He was invited to a luncheon when I was the first Jewish labor leader to introduce Israeli bonds in the United States.

Of the big companies I dealt with, there was altogether ninety-two that were invited and ninety-two that showed up for the luncheon. Finally I was called up to say something.

I had "tears in my eyes," I told them, because "every employer said what a bad year he had. He couldn't buy ten bonds (these were a thousand dollars each), he could only buy five, because he had a bad business year. Or he couldn't buy five bonds; he could only buy two.

"First of all," I said, "this is not charity. This is an investment—guaranteed by the U.S. government. And so far the Israelis haven't defaulted. But I can't understand it," I went on. "Every year when we negotiate a new contract, you always come to me with a package you want to give me—a lot of cash. Now, this is a good cause. An investment. I don't know why it bothers you so much."

Now Joe Parise says, loud enough for everyone to hear, "Only Max Block could get away with that remark."

So that's it. Everybody bought more bonds than anticipated —I sold over a million dollars worth right there at the luncheon.

Jimmy Hoffa took a bond from me for fifty thousand dollars. Then he asked me, "Is this enough?" I kissed him on the forehead, and I said, "You're the first man I ever kissed."

And he asked why the kiss? So I told him, because the others said they didn't want to buy ten bonds, only five, or didn't want to buy five, only two. And here he comes along, and he isn't even Jewish, and he buys fifty thousand dollars' worth. And then he asks me if it's enough.

So I was the first one to come out with bonds for Israel in the labor movement. My membership was mostly Christian, but no Jewish labor leader had been willing to raise the issue yet.

I raised so much money that soon after, on March 14, 1955, the Israeli government gave me a birthday party in the Waldorf-Astoria, in the main ballroom, with about thirteen hundred people attending.

I did what I had to do, because the industry wasn't about to organize itself. So there's always ways to tie up an outfit, if you're really willing.

I never took an outfit to organize unless I studied it sometimes for weeks or months. I knew exactly their makeup. How much money they had. If they had credit. How they were purchasing their merchandise. How they were selling. I always checked. So when I moved, I had everything, all the information I wanted, right in front of me.

That's how we used to work. The organization didn't exist and come by itself. You don't sit and wait for the worker to come join up. Of course, you can say, "The hell with him—if he doesn't want to join the union, let him drop dead." But in order to protect the people, we had to get the industry in line—everybody.

It wasn't always easy. And I had to use all kinds of tricks. The Clerks union used to go with dirty hands, and handle everything in a store, and they'd let mice loose. That stuff I didn't use. We broke windows. We had fights, and little things. This was when we were striking, when we wanted to organize a shop. So we tied up a shop one way or another. We stopped them. They couldn't get meat, because we had also organized the wholesale markets. Or the renderers we'd organized didn't pick up the fat and bones and grease and skins in the stores for a week in the summertime. It was hot. It stunk. We did all those things.

This was if there was no strike line—if you tried to organize a shop and they got an injunction against you and you couldn't picket, because over the years, some of the laws made things more difficult. But there was always an angle on how to get around any law, there's no question about that.

The way I did it with the Grand Union, one of the largest supermarket chains in the country, I didn't have an application from even one butcher. I had tried before to get the meat people unionized in the Grand Union, but we couldn't get to the people. The Clerks had attempted a couple of strikes, stood out a few weekends, got mad and walked away. We constantly tried to get applications to the butchers, but we couldn't get inside to see them.

First I tried talking. Barney Lubeck, one of the vice-presidents of Grand Union, was a tall German guy with a red face and red hair. He and I got friendly. He used to come to eat at the Black Angus. So one day I called him up, invited him over.

While we're eating, I said, "Barney, all these years I didn't ask you about organizing. Now I'm ready."

So he says, "Would you give me a week? I'll talk to my boss."

I said, "You got a week. When you going to be back?"

"Next Friday."

He came Friday. We had a dry martini and dinner. He was about fifty years old, married about one year.

After we get through eating, I said, "So what did you hear from your boss about an agreement?"

150

"Max," Barney said, "I'm like an old maid. I'm afraid to open my legs."

I asked him, "How long you married?" I waited. I didn't come up fast. I wanted to give him a chance.

"One year," he said.

"How you getting along? How's Ida?"

"Wonderful," he says. "We're getting along fine."

"That's what's going to happen with your company and the union," I said. "You're going to get fucked and like it." He turned red as a beet. He didn't know what to say or what to do.

I selected forty-two of Grand Union's best shops out of a couple of hundred. Then I called in eighty-four workers, with applications and circulars, and I gave instructions. "Everybody must have a watch," I said, "because at 11:30 the store managers go to lunch—so everybody goes in at 11:35."

At 11:35, everybody went in, in all the stores. They started handing out applications and collecting signatures. Then I pulled a strike.

Meanwhile, there were three union men I had sent in to work ahead of time. But still I didn't have a single application, and on a strike, especially an illegitimate strike—and this was illegitimate—they can get an injunction against you within twenty-four hours.

But there's always a gimmick. So when I pulled the strike, it was the week before Christmas. Sunday midnight, I established picket lines around the company's warehouses—one in New Jersey, one in Albany. Meanwhile, it was one of the biggest shopping times of the year; they had all this stuff sitting in those warehouses.

I had to pay up some money, because the officials had this warehouse organized by the Clerks international. A guy by the name of Baldy, in the Teamsters, was involved here. He used to represent some funeral-drivers' union in Brooklyn. Baldy was involved with Maxey Becker, who had connections with the New Jersey mob. Maxey represented the Clerks in New Jersey, and had this warehouse organized, but I paid him off so their people wouldn't cross the picket line.

The Grand Union was a chain of supermarkets, but now we started with the warehouses. Sunday midnight we set up the lines. Everything had been prepared. The Teamsters wouldn't cross the line, and everybody else who wasn't in the unions, but who delivered fruit and vegetables from the South, they didn't cross the line either—they were afraid.

We had a lot of people walking out there. And we established a picket line on every shop they had in the New York area, and nobody crossed it. So we had a strike going, but meanwhile I still didn't have any members. I didn't have people. I didn't go through the procedures of elections. Nothing. Of course, I couldn't get an election because I didn't have even one legitimate application. We had to do it all one way—the hard way.

Meanwhile, I had told my attorney well in advance to establish for Monday a claim of unfair labor charges against the company for firing certain people—the three men I had sent in to work ahead of time. I paid them the difference, because they were good butchers. They asked Grand Union for jobs, and they got in. Then when I told the workers what day to come in with applications and start talking to the people about organizing, I knew these three would get fired for "joining." Which is what happened. They got fired Friday night. That was the company policy. So on Monday morning it was all set up to file the unfair labor charges.

My attorney, Arnold Cohen, a hunchback, a very sharp guy, asked me how could he file unfair labor charges when nobody has been fired yet.

"Never mind," I told him. "Take my word. Just go ahead and file the charges." And he did. So now, in order for the company to get an injunction against a union for having an illegal strike, the judge tells them that first they must have the unfair labor charges cleared up at the labor board.

That was why I set it up. Because unfair labor charges, you can drag on for three years. You have hearings and hearings and hearings, and when you lose the decision you take it to Washington and drag it on again. It's a very slow process. By the time it's settled, the company will be out of business.

After a couple days, the company realized what was happening—they can't move. So they got hold of me. Barney Lubeck called and wanted me to meet with Mr. Lansing Shield, the company president. I said, "Fine."

I was driven over there, to a hotel in Paterson, New Jersey. I met with Mr. Shield, a high-class gentleman. And we discussed the situation. He had a satchel with a hundred thousand dollars in it, and he wanted to give this to me to walk away.

I couldn't take it, I said. I'd have to bury it underground anyway. I wouldn't be able to use it. I say I'm only there to get an agreement.

Apparently Lansing had discussed it with some of the boys —he already had Maxey and Baldy on the payroll anyway— but they'd come back and told him they couldn't handle me. Maxey and Baldy had raised the subject with me the day before, and they must have figured they could offer me thirty or forty thousand cash from the hundred thousand, and I'd walk away. But they didn't realize I wouldn't do it. And I'd grind them down to a little pebble, because I wasn't afraid of Maxey and Baldy, and that's what I told them.

So after these guys let it go, Lansing figured he'd try me himself.

"What good is it?" I told him. "You know you're knocking yourself out. You'll be organized sooner or later anyway, and being bothered anyhow by bad characters. With me, you'll get a fair shake. Legitimate. And everything is fine.

"You know my reputation is good. As far as the unions are concerned, everybody we've been dealing with didn't get hurt."

Now he says, "What kind of deal am I going to get?"

"You pick your own," I said. "Here's all the contracts."

I didn't have an equalized contract, an extended contract. Those days, each company negotiated a contract, so each one figured he got a bargain here, the other a bargain there. I told Lansing he could pick any contract he wanted, any contract, any company—"It's up to you."

We shook hands and agreed we had a deal.

"You're tired. You haven't slept for three days," I said. "Why don't we handle it Friday?"

He said, "What about the strike?"

"I'll call it off. We got the thing settled, don't we?"

He said, "Yes."

I called my business agent and told him to remove the picket lines. Everything was settled.

The next day Mr. Shield calls me back. "Gee, Max. I'm not going to be able to meet with you Friday."

I said, "Why not?" So he tells me his wife made a surprise

party for him on Friday. I says, "I'll tell you what we'll do. We'll settle it after New Years."

"Gee, Max," he said. "I didn't know you were such a good fellow."

After New Years I made an appointment for Lansing Shield and me and Barney Lubeck, his man, to meet in the Bankers' Club on Fifty Church Street in Manhattan. So we met for lunch. We finished eating, and Lansing said to Barney, "I'm going to leave you two, and you'll settle it. Whatever Max puts, you sign it."

That's what he told his man. After that, he left.

Barney and I sat down and got the contracts out. I said I can help you out on this side and this side and this side. Of course, it's a new agreement, a new company I was dealing with, and I realized it'll take a year or two to work it in. So we both signed and initialed everything, and that was it.

Meanwhile, I still didn't have one application out of the Grand Union workers, so I called a meeting for the following Tuesday at the Union office. I had a room that would hold three or four hundred people. I could have got a larger room, because I knew it was going to be very tight, but I wanted it tight.

Barney called me in the afternoon. "Max," he said. "You've got a tough meeting."

I says, "Why?"

"Because they're all full of piss and vinegar and they're going to give you a rough time, the workers."

"Barney," I said, "if I can't handle my men, I don't belong here. Don't worry about it."

I gave instructions to my business agents. I told them it was very cold outside and to keep the windows closed, so no one should catch a cold. But what I wanted was to keep the place smoky, until smoke would be coming down finally below their heads. And it's hot, and I know there's little wooden chairs and these guys had big fat asses that couldn't fit into them. And they all smoked.

I kept them waiting until about nine o'clock. They were sweating pretty good, and getting nervous. Now I had a microphone, which I didn't need, but I wanted to knock their eardrums out. And I gave instructions to the secretary to read

154

the contract we had signed, but very slowly, verbatum. Every word, because I didn't want to miss anything. Actually what I wanted was to drag things out as long as possible.

Finally, I called the meeting to order. I had to get the Grand Union workers to sign up for the union and approve the contract, because they weren't in the union yet. None of them.

We salute the flag. Do the pledge of allegiance. Then I say, "We're going to get Brother Casale to read the contract." I call on Casale, and he gets up and starts reading, very slowly.

After he's reading for three quarters of an hour, a hand comes up.

I say, "What is it, young man?"

He was a little guy, a young one. He said, "We don't want to listen to the contract. We don't want to listen to that."

I said, "What's your name? Okay, sit down."

Again a small hand comes up.

"If we don't read the contract," I said, "you would doubt. You would think there is something wrong here. I'm obligated to read to you every word. However, the majority rules here. We run a democratic organization. We'll vote. If the majority rules for no reading of the contract, it's okay with me."

We took it to a vote: Unanimously, no reading of the contract.

"Okay. Fine," I said. "Now the floor's open to questions. I will answer."

The same little guy jumps up. He didn't know what to say. He wanted to kill people. Finally I get another guy up there, a Swede, Hanson. He said he worked for the company a number of years. Then he got a hernia and went for an operation and he came back and they wouldn't accept him.

I said, "Okay."

Now this little guy gets up again and he's all worked up, excited, and I let him kick the benches. And he says, "Why don't you answer?"

And I say, "I'll answer when I'm ready. Don't teach me the business." I said, "Look, John. Do you think you're the only smart guy here? Don't you think they have brains?" And they booed him down for hogging the floor. But there were twenty hands up, and I kept recognizing him. So now he doesn't get up no more. He was one of the worst trouble-makers, the main one.

"Now," I said. "I'm going to answer you. You ready? I'm going to answer every word I heard here. Everything that any-body complained about." So I say, "I know it sounds a little fishy to you. Why should Max Block come and organize the Grand Union, increase the wages, reduce the hours, and, most important, get job security? Why should he do it? You didn't join the union. You didn't pay the union. You didn't pay Max. Why? Why should he do that for you?

"So I'm going to explain to you how it works. When I started organizing this local union, you must realize I came from the shop. I worked since I was thirteen. I scraped the blocks clean. I sawed bones. I broke my back from lifting heavy meat when everything was by hand. We used to work day and night. There was no such thing as vacation, sick leave. Tools and laundry we used to buy ourselves, when the pay was small. The hour for lunch I never got. We used to eat on the run.

"Then when I joined the union, we got an hour for lunch. That was enough to join the union. We relaxed an hour during the day. So I went out to organize. I decided to organize the industry. It was a slave industry. As I remember, a few of us handed out ten thousand circulars in Brooklyn and Long Island. It took two weeks to hand them out. Twenty people showed up.

"I wasn't worried about it. I made up my mind right there and then, I'm young and strong and I'm willing to do it. Or-ganize the industry, get conditions that are due us.

"So you must realize that we are an *industry*. It takes years to learn the butcher business. The boss always wants to hire a young apprentice, a young good-looking guy with curly hair behind the counter. And he hires you and continues to think of you as an apprentice and finally gives you a buck raise or two. Meanwhile the boss works us day and night. Then here's John Hanson. He works fourteen years for the com-pany, and now he has a little bald head and a double hernia and he's finished.

"They wouldn't accept him to work. Is that right? Well, this is the situation that I'm trying to correct. I'm trying to get conditions established. Vacation periods. Sick leave, and everything. And we have it. It's on the drawing boards and we have it. We'll have everything.

"Now we have this other fellow, Tom Jenson. The same thing. He goes to the hospital for two weeks, he comes back, and they don't accept him to work no more. But I can tell you one thing, fellows and girls—if they don't accept these two people Monday morning, *nobody* will work. We'll strike."

Jesus! They gave me a hand. A tremendous ovation. They ripped the building down.

I said, "Meeting adjourned." Just like that. "The only thing, before every one of you leaves you've got to sign a new application. Just sign the application and you'll become members of the union. All you got to do is come on time."

They came to rip me apart. Now they were signing up. But that's how I organized the Grand Union. It was an illegal strike. Illegal everything. But I didn't do it for me.

I had to wear a lot of hats. I dealt with the workers, but also we had some interesting executives coming into the Black Angus.

Tom Boucher was vice-president of Johnson and Johnson, which made the bandages and pharmaceutical supplies. Tom's brother Jerry Boucher was a partner in a very well-known stock firm, where the brokers advise you and handle investments.

The two brothers used to come to the Black Angus, and one day they brought their mother, a little old lady about seventy-five, maybe eighty. I had a drink with them. We talked about different things, then they began to talk about politics.

"Look who we got for President—Truman!"

"Terrible," one of the boys remarked, and the mother agreed.

I didn't want to get involved with politics, but Mrs. Boucher says to her sons, "Why don't you ask Mr. Block's opinion? He's a smart man."

"How smart can I be?" I said. "I didn't go to college."

But she says, "That's why you're a smart man," and they want to know my opinion now.

So I said, "Mrs. Boucher, since I remember, every President that we had in office was no good. If he was a Democrat, the

Republicans knocked his brains out. And if he was a Republican, the Democrats knocked his brains out. As a result, we did very well. We made so much progress. More than any other country in the world, in spite of them. And our system must be very good, because we're doing very well. We're making a lot of progress."

Mrs. Boucher looked at me and said to her boys, "Better listen to Mr. Block. You can learn a lot from him."

So that was how I got to give advice to a stockbroker and an executive trying to patch up sore spots around the nation.

Sometimes you're better off taking advice than giving it. You never know when things are going to turn out the way they're supposed to, and then you can make a lot of money.

There was another fellow, David Shore, who used to work in the same office as Jerry Boucher. It used to be the Harris Upham Company, and then they merged somehow and now it's Smith Barney Harris Upham & Co.

David Shore used to be very friendly with me, and he came to the Black Angus often. We'd discuss different stocks, and that's why he came to see me. He was a hustler, and a go-getter.

So one time Shore came by. He told me that some people were going to open up a chain of hamburger places, and that a rumor was that the A&P was going to get involved, and he tipped me off to be connected with it.

They were going to call the chain "McDonalds," he said. He asked if I'd heard about it, and he said they were going to open up tremendous, a big chain, and that's why he came to see me.

I didn't invest any money that time, but I should have listened to him.

23 The family had an opportunity to acquire a country club in Connecticut. The man that built it originally in 1937, he brought over most of the stuff from Italy, a lot of impressive things—big statues, big pieces, marvelous things, out of this world. He spent over a million dollars. I know, because we knew the builder.

Louie had built a house in Harrison, New York, and the builder told us how he had built this estate and that it was for sale. It was fabulous. And we bought it cheap, about two hundred and thirty thousand dollars. The guy, a fellow by the name of Blake, was dead. He had been the president of a railroad company. So we got it from the estate cheap, but by then it was expensive to keep up. You couldn't get help for it easily. And it was large. It was wooded, so we had to chop down a lot of woods to build the golf course. There was a beautiful pool, so we used the same pool, and we developed the whole thing and made a terriffic club out of it.

Gene Tunney lived nearby, and used to visit with his sons. The young one, John, later would become a senator in California. They were cute little kids. They'd come with Gene, and they tried to play golf in our club. We were his neighbor.

I knew Gene pretty well. I'd meet him at the Biltmore Hotel

in New York when I went to the health club. We didn't go to the gym, but to the steam room. We did that a lot. We'd sit and talk, and he was very bright. He had arthritis real bad, and his fingers were crippled. When he'd shake your hand, his fingers couldn't get hold. The thumb would, but the rest of the four fingers it was like they were bunched together. He was pleasant. We didn't talk much about fights. We talked about the club, the area, in Connecticut. He had some property out there, and then he went ahead and organized his own group later on. They built a club for themselves—a golf club, right next door to us. We had eighteen holes on our course. It was beautiful—gorgeous.

Once in a while we'd talk about the fights or the other fighters. If one of us heard some news or had seen someone, we'd mention it. Gene was ten or eleven years older than me, in his early fifties by this time, because he was twenty-eight when he won the title from Dempsey in 1926, in Philadelphia. And Dempsey was about three years older than Tunney. Dempsey had lived upstairs over the Black Angus in the San Carlos Hotel for quite a while, and I'd see him a lot of the time. Usually just to say hello.

"How are you? How you feel?" I'd ask.

"I'm getting old, Jackie," he'd say, using my boxing name.

Rocky Marciano, twenty-nine or thirty, won the title a while back from Jersey Joe Walcott. He'd come by the Black Angus fairly often and have a double steak, and we'd sit and talk. Sometimes he'd bring his mother with him, for dinner. A little woman. A nice old lady. And he was a nice, mild-mannered fellow. He spoke softly. You'd have a hard time hearing him. But you could feel his punch, because he was a solid heavyweight, a great fighter. He wasn't tall enough, like some others; he didn't have their reach, but he could fight. He was my style. My build. But heavier, and a little bigger.

So Dempsey and Marciano were nice, ordinary guys but tough as hell. Tunney was not as tough as Dempsey, but he was smart and a classy boxer. So Dempsey couldn't overpower him, and Tunney got the title. But now, years later, Tunney wasn't worried about who was tougher or whatever. He was interested in setting up a golf course on his property next door. Things like that.

I remember some of the other great boxers I had known.

160

Max Baer and Jim Braddock, each one took the heavyweight title after Dempsey and Tunney. I used to see them a little bit when Sammy Goldman had me working out in Stillman's gym, over by Eighth Avenue in Manhattan. Barney Ross, who won the welterweight title in 1934, was another great fighter. He'd come by a lot, to the Black Angus, and we'd buy liquor from him. He worked somewhere as a salesman, so we gave him the business.

Dempsey didn't have much tied up. He had a few partners in the restaurant business, and he may have made a few dollars for a couple of things, but it wasn't much. The only rich one was Tunney. But that was because he married into a rich family. His wife was from Connecticut. From our country club you'd look across the mountain and see the place, his home—it was tremendous.

So no matter how tough you were, it didn't matter. Except for a small handful, the chances are you wouldn't make it big in the ring anyway. And if you did, sooner or later someone would come along who was tougher. You had to remember, you could always get hurt. Even if you didn't, probably you wouldn't end up with any big money. Or if you did, chances are it would disappear somehow, because of the lifestyle.

I knew Jake LaMotta. He used to come by the Black Angus and have a few drinks. Jake was pretty tough. Yet I didn't think he was a very good fighter, because he would take a lot of punishment, even when he won. But he had a lot of guts and he always mixed it up. He'd move in and fight, and the public liked to come see him fight because there was always a lot of blood. And a lot of it was his.

If you're trained, and in good shape, you can take a lot of punishment. In some ways, maybe that makes you a little stronger. But in the ring, you learn there are limits to everything. And you had to know how to cover yourself, not just punch away without some good idea what you were trying to do. It was the same with organizing the union or anything else—you had to think it out. You had to prepare, as best you could. You had to plan ahead.

That's what I liked about Gene Tunney. He liked to use his head. When he was younger, he may have been tough, but when he got in the ring he also knew what he was doing. He wasn't just looking to slug it out, the way you see so many matches today. He was always trying to learn . . . he had been a classy boxer, and he was that way as a person. A gentleman. So it wasn't enough just to be tough, because I'd seen plenty of tough guys that got nowhere. And most of them weren't as tough as they thought they were.

So there's always lessons. But then a lot of people don't learn. In Manhattan and the Bronx, Local 400 of the Amalgamated was still under the left-wing leadership of Al de Prospo and Joe Cohan. Cohan was manager of the local, and de Prospo was president.

Almost right away, after I organized all the shops in the Grand Union—including the ones in the Bronx and New York —word came down that local 400 was claiming the jurisdiction; they didn't feel I should be organizing in the Bronx or Manhattan.

But Pat Gorman backed me up from Amalgamated's headquarters in Chicago.

"Max makes the decision," he said.

Before long, a couple of tough guys showed up at the Black Angus. Louie was there. I was in Florida. So I didn't know these characters and neither did Louie, but he knew they were tough guys from the mob. He told them I'd be back in a couple of weeks. But I came back a little sooner.

The next thing I know, this guy Benny Macri and his brother had been hired to see what they can do about getting me to give Local 400 the jurisdiction for New York for the Grand Union. Benny Macri had been convicted and sent to jail for murder for killing a guy in the dress market, but he got out somehow when the conviction was reversed.

So when I got back from Florida, I came into the Black Angus one day and there was a "sit-down"—that's what they called it—and Carlo Gambino was there along with a few other guys, and Benny and his brother, and Joe Parise, from the Teamsters. I knew Joe Parise and his brother a long time in the movement, but now I realized he was close to Gambino.

We sat in the middle room, in a booth with an added table, because we had seven or eight people. There were some other people nearby, eating, but what did they know. There was no noise. We had dinner. We bullshitted quietly, and it wasn't during the dinner hour but about ten-thirty, eleven o'clock at night. Louie wasn't there. He wasn't involved in things like that.

So we were all sitting there, and the arguments came in. The Macri brothers said I can't do this and I can't do that. But then when they got through talking, Gambino took his hand and he banged it down hard on the table, two, three times for emphasis.

"Whatever Blockie says, goes!" he said. And so that was it.

The meeting was ended. The Macri brothers left, but they still weren't satisfied. Because the next day, they showed up at Joe Parise's office and they tell him they're "not satisfied with the decision the old man made." That's what Parise told me later.

So Joe smacked Benny in the face and chased him and his brother out. And he told them, "The big boss makes the decision—call him!" And maybe he said something else that I don't know about.

After that, Parise called and suggested I get out of town for a few days. So I took his advice and left town.

That was Thursday. Friday night they find Benny Macri dead in New Jersey. They found his brother's car nearby, somewhere by a big lake. They never found the body, but it was obvious. So both brothers were dead—they pushed their luck.

Now I hear about it—that I must have killed the Macri brothers because they wanted to kill me. But I didn't ask for anything. I didn't make any requests to get these guys knocked off. I would have told them not to monkey around. But after they went to see Parise, you could see they weren't going to drop the issue—Carlo's decision was not satisfactory to them. I said so to Joe. They said so too. And here was a case where Gambino and the others saved my life, because I wouldn't give up this jurisdiction and they didn't want these guys to kill or hurt me.

So that's a sample of how the mob gets in and how they got friendly with me. And it was years before I realized . . . I didn't know how great in the mob Gambino was until I read in the newspapers, boom, boom, boom right down the line. But he was a fine gentleman.

Carlo Gambino. What did that name mean to me? Nothing.

163

But he came and spoke to me about helping out his friend with this strike, with this and that. So we had coffee and breakfast together, and we worked out something favorable that everyone was satisfied, and he and I became friends.

Then they automatically put it on record that I'm their man. Stuff like that. And that's how I met him. And the whole family I knew in the business before. And that's how they get to know certain people that they think can be a friend.

And people say you shouldn't associate with this guy or that guy. And the law would put them in jail. But you got to do something. You got to work out some sort of arrangement. And it wasn't my business to ask all these questions. It was the government's business. I'm not a cop or the district attorney asking a lot of questions.

So you got to have some sort of understanding with these people. Or they're going to blow somebody's head off and step in anyway. I nearly got killed a couple of times, and Carlo saved my life, without my knowledge. Maybe there were other times like that. And then, whenever there'd be a killing planned that might concern me, someone would get the word to me that it might be a good idea to get out of town for a few days.

24

At the Delmarva peninsula in Maryland you had several thousand duck and poultry workers nobody could get to. Conditions were terrible! You had a high percentage of migrant workers, and even if you could get into the place it was almost impossible to organize them. Then you had the Ku Klux Klan, serious racial problems, rotten facilities, and tough, stubborn owners.

The local groups of the Amalgamated and the Teamsters had been trying for four or five years, but didn't get one person organized. The owners had fences around, and you couldn't get close. So you had all these big plants with maybe a couple thousand workers altogether, and the locals trying every angle and getting nowhere.

As president of the Butcher Council, and becoming more involved with the international, I would help out where I could.

Jimmy Hoffa said to me, "Max, we went for over a million dollars, and we accomplished nothing there."

So that's when I got into it. And I made a deal with Jimmy. I said, "Okay. I'll go in and I'll organize them. The only thing, we'll have to make a dividing line."

The way we worked it, from the platform out, where the trucks load, that would belong to the Teamsters, all those members; and from the platform in, that would belong to the Amalgamated. That's what we agreed on, and that's when I went to work on the poultry workers in Delmarva.

Before I went out, I was warned by Harry Pool, vice-president of the international, "Max, don't go! You'll have a meeting between the white people and the black people. The white people will come around and shoot you or they'll tar and feather you and chase you out." That's what happened to him —they chased him out, because there were Klan rules about the whites and blacks not mixing together. And the bosses, they didn't care, because if the workers were fighting each other they weren't fighting the bosses.

So they chased Harry out. But I wasn't worried. I guessed I'd get around it somehow, but first I had to figure a way to get in and to get the owners to deal with me. Then I'd worry about getting the workers set up. Meanwhile, I didn't have a single application. But I felt we could organize the place anyway. I thought about it and finally I came up with a plan.

I decided to stop the trucks coming in to deliver the poultry in New York. The trucks would deliver to the wholesale markets—Sixth Street, Fourteenth Street, Fort Greene, Harlem, Bronx, and so on, where all the poultry houses are. By now, we had all this organized under Local 640.

So I called in Louie. We got all the business agents together the day before in a meeting. We had both offices there now, by Thirteenth Street and Broadway, and we made arrangements for early Friday morning, just after midnight, to stop all these big trucks coming in from the Delmarva peninsula. We had the agents from Local 640 and Local 342, all former butchers and a little on the rough side, in case of any trouble.

It's July, a very hot time of year. And these days there are no refrigerated trucks. They used to use a lot of ice. Meanwhile, the 640 shop stewards were given instructions not to let the trucks unload.

Then the trucks came in. Huge. Forty or fifty of them; each load weighing maybe a couple of tons to five tons. So they had well over a million dollars' worth of poultry sitting in those trucks. And the ice was melting. And the trucks were all over the streets of New York—but the stewards wouldn't let them unload.

166

I knew I'd hear from the owners pretty fast. The poultry was going to get ruined.

Nine, ten o'clock in the morning, I get a call from Harry Landis, one of the big owners. Landis knew Jack Penn, a business agent for the poultry retail union in New York City. So he knew these people, and somehow they got together. They tried to make a deal through Jack to pay me off, and I wouldn't do it. But apparently Jack tipped them off that I loved pinochle.

Landis invited me out to his place in Ocean City, Maryland, a well-known spot overlooking Washington, D.C., from the other side of the river. He promised we'd negotiate an agreement. Also, there'd be a pinochle game for me, and this was the incentive.

"We'll sit down and negotiate a contract," he said. "And the others, too." Because he knew I had them by the balls.

"Okay. Fine," I tell him.

Now he says, "What about the trucks?"

"I'll let them unload," I said. "We got a deal, don't we?" Otherwise, they'd go broke. So I realized, and I let them go.

I called Jimmy Hoffa, told him we were going to work out a deal. He said, "Okay. Beautiful." He was happy. He trusted me.

The following week, Jean and I went out to Ocean City. We spent the weekend with Landis, and he got the other owners of these plants to come down, including Calhoun, the toughest. All big guys. Herb Calhoun, not tall but muscular, about one hundred eighty pounds. Homer Pepper, about six-feet, a couple hundred pounds. They're all well-dressed, rich people. Tough men. But before we left Sunday night, we signed an agreement.

We didn't have the workers at all. But we got control and improved conditions. Obtained contracts.

Because the majority were migrant workers they were traveling all the time, rotating. They had little huts to sleep in, but with no furniture except the most broken-down stuff. So we made arrangements, got them furniture from different companies, got them set up in little cottages, fixed up the church, and this was part of the package for the workers. It was a start.

Many of the workers were paired off as man and wife but weren't actually married. A lot of the men would get drunk, not put in their regular hours, and the women they lived with used to work overtime. But a number of the men would use the money to buy wine. Then they'd kill one another. Stabbings every weekend.

The workers were half black, half white. I went out and talked to them. No one tarred and feathered me, but I don't think half of them understood. Probably a lot didn't speak English. Then I asked Jack Burroughs, the local business agent for the Amalgamated, to have another meeting with the workers to explain the conditions we settled for, and to sign them into the union. He did that, and he signed them up. And the same thing with Hoffa. I told him I had settled and that he could instruct Reynolds, his business agent there, to sign the workers into the Teamsters the way we had agreed.

About three months later, Calhoun, Pepper, and Landis invited me back to Ocean City. Jean and I went. Then we go out to see the homes of the workers again . . . and all the furniture we bought and everything we set up, the workers used it for firewood.

We saw the church, where everything had been fixed up, and that was ripped down—even the banister was used for firewood.

25

Local 342 had become the largest local in the international. So we had Grand Union signed up, all the butchers, and Local 400 of the Amalgamated, for Manhattan and the Bronx, was still mad as hell over the jurisdiction. Though they had nothing before, anyway.

Local 400 wasn't involved in the sit-down, with Gambino and that group, but the Macri brothers, speaking for Local 400, knew that before they could muscle in on me they'd have to talk to the others. So when the others wouldn't accept the decision, the Macri brothers got themselves killed. I didn't know about it until they found Benny's body, but now I figured Local 400 wouldn't be sending any boys around for a while.

Meanwhile, Local 342 kept expanding. This was the early 1950s. The chains were growing, and many independent markets started falling by the wayside. Some smaller chains merged into larger operations. Daitch and Shopwell, which we signed, used to be separate meat and dairy shops. These came together into a larger operation, moving down from the Bronx across New York.

As the larger chains grew, they threatened the other chains and the smaller operations. And to equalize the industry, we had to organize everything.

I decided to organize the A.&P., the largest retail outlet in the world. We'd have to do it, sooner or later. And once I established the A.&P., I figured we'd have the whole thing locked up—we'd be able to establish conditions all over. Otherwise, it's unfair. The guy that's not organized, he can beat the price, because he doesn't have to pay his worker. And if you organized only one group and the prices are higher than others in the industry, then you're destroying your own people, your own business, your own jobs. Everything. Because you knock them out of business. They can't compete. That was my theory all the time.

The Clerks' union had some of the A.&P. workers signed up, the grocery clerks. But they had nothing. No recognition, and no conditions. So I wasn't going to worry about the jurisdiction. Apparently they couldn't organize it because they never did—they'd live a thousand years, it wouldn't make no difference, they couldn't come close. So we went ahead.

We put together a book about the A.&P., a three-color red-white-and-blue book that included reprints of all the antitrust cases against the A.&P. The book was devastating. It had a picture of the Attorney General, and documented all the legal actions taken against them. Then we began distributing thousands of copies in Brooklyn and New York.

Meanwhile, the A.&P. had a reputation for being very anti-Semitic. They wouldn't even talk to a Jew. I figured it might be difficult to get to them, but the book was very bad publicity —it really knocked their brains out. The next thing, within a few days I get a call from a Mr. Schimmat, the A.&P.'s industrial relations man.

"Max," he said. "Would you know who wants to meet you?"

I says, "No."

He said, "Mr. Burns, chairman of the board."

We met at the bar downstairs in the Commodore Hotel in New York. We had lunch, talked about business in general. Then Mr. Schimmat said to me, "So you're Max Block. How much money are you spending on this book you just put out?"

"Maybe a hundred thousand dollars," I tell him.

"How about that," he says. "What do we have to do to stop it?"

So I figured they're offering me the hundred thousand to drop it, because the book was very embarrassing. And they knew who I was. They thought maybe they'd pay me off and I'd take a walk.

But I looked at Burns. I told him, "I don't need it. I don't want any money for that purpose. I want to get the people in the union and get a contract. One thing," I said. "One way to stop it. Recognize my union as the sole bargaining agent."

Burns was taken aback, surprised. "Max, he said. "You know the company policy. You have to win an election."

I didn't have a single member, but I said, "Change the policy."

Burns says, "Mr. Block, we checked your reputation. You're legitimate. You don't look for anything except to get the union organized. I appreciate that."

But then he says, "What happens if you die?" Because he was concerned about the mob in New York and New Jersey seeking the jurisdiction. He figured that if I got killed, he'd have to deal with someone like Benny Macri and his brother. "If you die," he says, "then I'll have to deal with some Communist group or some of these other guys."

I looked at him. "Mr. Burns, you're right. However, you're maybe sixty-seven years old. The board members are all about the same age. Now I'm a boy. I'm in my forties. So the odds are in my favor that I will outlive you fellows—pretty good odds, in fact. And after you're dead, what do you care what's going to happen with the company, what's going to happen with this union?"

"You're right, Max," he said. And he shook my hand. "Young man, we got a deal. Deal with Charlie and work out whatever you want."

Then they asked, what's going to happen with the book?

I said, "I won't distribute it any more." That's all. They took my word. I took theirs. And that's it. Instead of fighting me, Burns decided to let me win an election. Just like that.

We shook hands, but that didn't mean we signed it that day. We'd work it out. We had to make arrangements, and it would take weeks. Months, actually, because first we moved into Brooklyn and then all over, wherever you had A.&P. shops. Also we knew there were Clerks and other characters involved who claimed the jurisdiction. But we reached an agreement.

There was a holiday weekend coming up, and I knew all

the other business agents and different organizations would run away to the country. They wouldn't be on the job. So I sat down in the A.&P. office.

The agreement was negotiated all day on a Saturday and Saturday night between the company and me and the lawyers. I wanted a forty-hour week, if possible. But of course, most people were still working forty-five or more hours all over the area, and all around the country. This was 1952, and I didn't look to knock them out of business. I'm looking to get a fair shake, settle for a five-dollar-increase, forty-five-hour week, vacations—better than they had.

They had vacation periods, but very limited. They didn't really cover it. We got them vacations, time off, sick leave. Things they didn't have before, anyhow, an increase. And the company was pretty good with the payroll.

We concluded the agreement; then we decided how and when we could get an election count, because I had to have a majority. Meanwhile, I didn't have any applications. So I instructed my business agents in the shop stores and markets to bring me applications under any circumstances.

They got them from everywhere. Just from the payroll sheets, I imagine. And some they got legitimately and some illegitimately—I don't know, I didn't ask. I'm supposed to trust my agents. And so they all brought me in applications until it looked like I had enough, the majority, a big majority.

Meanwhile, if a worker somewhere says, "Oh, I didn't sign that," or this guy says it isn't so, that doesn't mean anything—it's still a question of thirteen thousand five hundred people, and how would one know from the other? How can anybody know? But I bet I didn't have more than ten percent.

It took a lot of effort, and I had to think about some of these things to convince the company to go along, to help us with the count. But I only told the company to help, to give us time to bring in the applications.

First we went to work on the butchers, forcing the company to negotiate with me for Brooklyn and Queens, and also for the butcher departments in Nassau and Suffolk Counties, because Nassau and Suffolk had never been touched before.

When the contract was about to expire for the meat department, I began to talk to the company about getting the clerks in the union too. There was the question of the jurisdiction for the Clerks—who had been handling not the butchers, but the grocery clerks—but then I told the A.&P. that the Amalgamated would deal with the whole thing, including New Jersey. This was for all the employees in the New York–New Jersey area.

The A.&P. asked about the mob, because the mob was controlling the union locals in New Jersey. At that time it was Longie Zwillman. His real name was Abe, but they called him Longie. I knew Abe very well, because he used to come into the Black Angus in the evenings. So I told the A.&P. I'd give them a guarantee they wouldn't have any problems with the mob or anybody else. They took my word for it.

After the A.&P. signed, Abe got killed. Jerry Cantina was his partner and visited Abe's home for breakfast. And then later they found Abe hanging, so they didn't know whether Abe committed suicide or somebody killed him. But Abe liked me, and nobody bothered me from New Jersey. After we took in the whole A.&P. membership we brought in this fellow Kaplan, and he signed up the A.&P. workers for the New Jersey local. Kaplan was a student of the Longie Zwillman mob, but he was a butcher.

Local 400 had been fighting the A.&P. for years and couldn't even get close to an election. Now I called Joe Cohan, and I gave them their jurisdiction for the Amalgamated in Manhattan and the Bronx. I kept the membership from Brooklyn, Long Island, and Staten Island for 342, then I called in the Westchester County group, Local 489, and they signed the contract. The same with New Jersey. That's how we all signed. We got them conditions, and they signed with the Amalgamated.

But from the beginning, as soon as I got involved, the Clerks started reacting. Because it was a tremendous territory. There were fifteen-hundred supermarkets.

Right away one of the business agents for the Clerks in Brooklyn put out a bunch of circulars about me to make me look like a bum. Yet his shops had been working from forty-five to sixty hours a week, and he never got conditions for any of these people. Maybe the Clerks had signed up six or seven percent of the A.&P. clerks. Then all of a sudden I'm bringing in a new package, with better conditions. So they had a lot of disgruntled members.

Now a fight started between the different unions. A guy by the name of Kennedy represented Local 1500 of the Clerks. He never got nowhere with the A.&P., but suddenly he began to work at it. And the Clerks began to pay Kennedy to finance a strike in Brooklyn against the A.&P., but it was really against my union.

Schimmat called me in to sit down with Mr. Burns again.

"How long do you think they can last in the strike?" he asked.

I said, "You cooperate the way I tell you, the things I will do toward that end, it shouldn't take more than a week."

They said that's okay.

In a week, the strike was knocked out. After the first days of striking I gave instructions to my men to work on the road and bring in the leaders. Every group has a leader, the most big-mouthed guy. So then certain guys had lunch with them, and when I got through with them after one hour of lunch and after the conversation, they were on my side.

Now these guys go back, swinging their groups. Then these groups went back to work, and there were some fights, but not much.

So we broke the strike. But now the Clerks decided to fight it in the courts. They started yelling about labor and management getting together and forcing a decision on the workers. And that the workers didn't have a chance to vote. But from what I could see, there's no way the company was going to organize if the workers had a chance to vote, like that. So nothing would get organized, and the conditions would stay the same. In all my organizational activity during these years, I couldn't remember ever having more than five percent of the membership on record that wanted to organize. So we had to get a bunch of phony applications—otherwise, I figured, the workers would still be unorganized slaves.

So now we had to go to court. In the earlier years, you could start a strike without membership and carry on until you forced the company and the workers into the union. Now, with the National Labor Relations Board, part of the Taft-Hartley Law put in in 1947, you had to produce a minimum of thirty percent of the applications in order for an election to be held. And that wasn't easy, because the worker was still the hardest person to organize.

174

The Clerks continued fighting me, legally, and I sat down with my lawyers and the lawyers of the company. "Listen fellows," I said. "All I need is time and we can have an election. But I need enough time."

They said they had enough legal gimmicks to drag it out for three years, in Washington and all over.

"Get to work," I said. "That's all I want you to do. Keep dragging it."

They dragged it out for six or seven months, until finally I said, "Okay." We agreed to an election to decide whether the A.&P. workers wanted our union, the other union, or no union.

The Labor Board sent out people to all the shops, with the ballot boxes for the election. Everyone voted. Then they brought in the ballots. The count was held at the Labor Board office in New York, and we won it easy. Ten to one. After this, Jim Suffrage came to see me. Suffrage was president of the Clerks, and also on the A.F. of L. executive council. He offered me sixty thousand in cash to turn over the A.&P. clerks to him. I was kind of vague, to see what he'd say. I stalled him around for a month. He came back with an offer of a hundred thousand.

I knew where Suffrage was coming from. When you are building an organization from the beginning you're trying to build it big enough, and it's human nature to be thinking about yourself. You want to build up something for yourself. And then as you go along and this is your jurisdiction, you feel it's yours. So another guy steps in to organize it, and you don't like it. Of course, the other guy could say, "Well, why the hell didn't you organize the A.&P. yourself?"

I tell Suffrage, "Jimmy, money is not the object. I gave my word to my company that they won't have to deal with anyone else but me as long as I'm around. So I'm not going to do it for the money, to double-cross them and double-cross our own international."

I wouldn't do it. So apparently Suffrage went peddling around after that to the different mobs, offering them big money to get me knocked off.

Somehow I was lucky. In Chicago, they wouldn't take it. New York wouldn't take it. I guess my reputation with these people was okay.

But before long, this guy shows up. The girl comes in my

office and tells me, "Mr. Block, there's a gentleman asking for you."

"Send him in," I told her.

The guy said his name was Mike. I could tell he was a tough guy, and I didn't trust him. I never saw him before, and he says he's from the West Coast, but he as much as said he had the contract on me, so I could have killed him right there in my office. Or I could have called the cops and had him locked up. But that wasn't going to solve the problem. So I told him I wasn't worried about him and his people and who he represented, and let it go. I told him to take a walk.

Not long after, I was in Chicago. Then I come home late at night to New Rochelle, and I had the big dogs, a collie and a boxer. But the collie was dead. Poisoned. He was laying there on the lawn, all swollen up.

The boxer was still alive. He was a huge dog, like a bull, and my wife had let him in the house. We had the big grounds, and a fence around the house.

Four o'clock in the morning the bell was ringing, the back doorbell. I rolled off the bed automatically. I started to get up, but my wife grabbed me.

"Don't go," she said.

"Why?"

"Yesterday when you were in Chicago, the bell rang at the same time," she said.

So I realized something was wrong. Now the dog begins to bark in the back, and so we call the police. They usually had a cop sitting out there, but apparently they were changing shifts or something. And whoever was there must have known.

I didn't look out the window. If I did that, I'd kill them with my gun. So I didn't look. But my son Alvin said he heard noises and he looked through the window from where he slept, and he saw two guys running to a car. The bell was stuck, pressed down with chewing gum.

They must have stayed by the door. We had heavy doors. You couldn't knock or kick them down. So they figured they'd get me to open the door, I guess, and then shoot me.

The New Rochelle police sent a couple of detectives down. By that time, of course, these monkeys were gone.

No one came back that night. Victor Reisel reported the

176

incident in his column, and soon it was in newspapers all over the country.

The cops would follow me to the city line up in New York. Over there, the cops would pick me up and follow me to my office. It went on like this a number of weeks. So the newspapers played it up, and apparently the guys got scared. But I figured it was someone hired by Jimmy Suffrage. He offered me the hundred thousand so he could have offered the same hundred to get me knocked off.

That's what I figured though I couldn't prove it. But it wasn't something I went around talking about. Suffrage was president of the Clerks, but he was also vice-president of the A.F. of L. on the executive council. Meany was president of the A.F. of L., but I didn't complain to George—it wasn't his business.

26

The Long Island ducks were the best in the world, but conditions for the workers were the worst. We went out to organize the Long Island duck farmers, and most of the duck farms were owned by tough Poles, and they wouldn't talk to you.

This was a rough strike. We turned over trucks, trailers. We called friends of mine in Chicago, where they were sending the ducks. Joe Glimko. He still has the taxi drivers organized in Chicago. Glimko says, "What do you want me to do with the ducks?"

I said, "Dump 'em in the river." They did.

Then they made some of the drivers turn back with the ducks. These drivers were lucky. But the Polish guys, the duck owners, they said that if they catch that Jew—me—they'll kill him. And they had rifles.

But they were already in trouble, selling the ducks for a nickel a pound. They lost a lot of money in the strike, and I knew they couldn't hold out. They'd go bust.

Finally they invited me down. They were having a meeting on a Friday night at one of the plants. This is where they killed the ducks and cleaned them and packed them and sent them out. It was a big plant, but after the strike went on for two weeks they called.

So I get there, I go in and introduce myself. Before, they were so mad they were going to kill me. Now, after a couple minutes they offer me a drink, because they were drinking whisky, and they were half-loaded. They asked if I'd join them, because they didn't think a Jew could drink. They poured me an eight-ounce glass full of scotch—they figured I'd drink it down, I'd be dead.

I toasted, "Nostrovia!" and I drank it down. They were shocked. Jeez! They never saw a Jew drink that good. Before it was over, they figured if I can drink that good they'll make a deal with me. And we signed a contract.

Of course, they knew I was connected all over, and I was able to tie them up. Their lawyer was there, Irving Bergman, another Jew. They must have been trying to find a way to defeat me. Instead, we signed.

They didn't know that their lawyer was also a friend of mine. Maybe he told them to call me. So we reached an agreement. I was a tough fighter but easy to get along with. I didn't look to knock anybody out of business. I was trying to get things equalized, and the workers would benefit, because they used to work like slaves.

27

During the fifties, I started spending a lot more time at the track. There was this trainer from the South. He lived a few blocks from my office in New York, and I'd run into him occasionally. So I see him one time. He says, "Block! My horse, he'll run away!"

I said, "Let me know when he's ready."

Now he stops in one morning. "Block, I got a win today in the fourth race. Can't lose. Bet all you can." This is at Jamaica.

Okay. I called my bookie and told him to make it four thousand to win, and the two of us went to the races. After the trainer saddled the horse, he came back to my table where I was sitting in the clubhouse. Then the race is off, and the horse gets in front by maybe ten lengths.

Now the trainer starts yelling—"He can't lose! He'd have to break a leg to lose."

But you can always lose. And you can always break a leg. And you don't say that in the middle of a race.

We're watching the race. The horse was way out in front. But on the last turn, the horse hit the turn and ran out wide. He ran out by the fence—way out. All the horses passed him.

After the race I look at the trainer, and I say, "You son of a bitch! That's why the horse lost. Because you said the horse

180

had to break a leg to lose." And you just don't say that. I told him, "It lost. It went out." He didn't believe it.

Now he comes for breakfast one morning, eleven o'clock, to the restaurant where I meet him, at McGuiness's in Jamaica.

"Talk to me, talk to me," he says. "What should I do. How do we straighten the son of a bitch horse out so he shouldn't run so wide?"

I looked at him. "You know, if he runs out, there's a way to handle it. You put a little piece of lead over here," I said. I pointed to the guy's left ear. "Twist the head a little bit; then he'll stick to the track, the gate."

Now the trainer says, puzzled, "How am I gonna put the lead in?"

"With a pistol!" That's what I told him, and we had a good laugh.

In organizing, like anything else, the thing was to get started somehow. Ed Miller from the Culinary Workers international told me they went for over a million dollars but couldn't organize the hotels in Miami Beach.

If I could get him one contract, he said, he could organize the whole beach. I told him I'd try to help.

I knew Sam Friedland very well, and Sam owned a couple of hotels in Miami Beach, the Shelborne and the Monte Carlo. He was a leading man at the Food Fair Company, which we had organized through 342, and we became good friends. He had some other interests in Philadelphia, then he moved to Florida.

I get together with Sam a number of times. Finally he agreed to sign a contract with the Culinary Workers, with the understanding I'd get him some convention business from the unions for his hotel. This would help cover the expense he'd have giving better conditions to the workers, and otherwise the deal was off.

I introduced Sam to Ed Miller, and they made a deal and that was it. After that, the Culinary Workers organized the whole beach—all the hotels. Meanwhile, I set things up with Meany and Hoffa to make sure Sam got the convention business.

Sam Friedland is a fine gentleman. He's about my size. Very quiet, polite. He never got excited. He owned half of Hollywood, Florida, including the Diplomat Hotel and the whole setup there.

Later I would meet Meyer Lansky for breakfast there, at the Diplomat. I knew the Mafia depended on him, for business direction. He showed the mob how to make a lot of money. They respected him. He spent a lot of time and was connected in Florida, but he was from New York where he had homes on Long Island and in Atlantic Beach, New Jersey.

For many years, Lansky was behind the biggest bookmaking operation in New York City. The people fronting for him were Max Courtney and Frank "Red" Reed. They had lots of clubs. They had action, and betting at the track, under the table. I gave them action too.

One day I gave them some races at Belmont Park—a four-horse round robin and six parlays. The first three races, I won. The first two went off twenty-to-one, on line. The third horse, a favorite, won. The fourth horse, if it wins, I would get a quarter million dollars. That's what they told me.

Now they asked me what I wanted to do in the fourth race.

"Let it ride," I said. I was already winning about thirty-four thousand.

Meanwhile, in the fourth race I placed another bet. I gave them two thousand more to win and two thousand to place on the Vanderbilt entry, and one thousand to win on a horse called Nail.

Nail went off at ten-to-one, and it won. But the Vanderbilt entry ran second. So I wound up winning about fourteen thousand for the race. And the other horse I had in the round robin wound up third. The horse's name was Rains Came, and it was a muddy track.

He ran two weeks later at the Jamaica track and he went out at forty to one. I bet him on that one, too, two thousand across-the-board, and he came in. He won. I had a tip on him from Louisville, Kentucky. So I had the two thousand on him with Lansky. They took my action. Size of the bet was no problem. They paid me off the next day in cash, brought me a paper bag from the supermarket with money—all hundred-dollars bills. They didn't like to lose that kind of money in one shot. But I wasn't worried about them. I was worried about me.

Lansky was banking the operation, along with this guy

Heimi Siegel, his bodyguard. Siegel was maybe five-seven. He looked like an average guy. You could hardly hear him speak, but he was tough as nails. A professional killer.

Still, paying off even thousands of dollars in a paper bag here and there—Lansky or Siegel wouldn't worry that much. And if I'd won that final bet on top of the round robin, they'd have paid me the quarter million, because that's what they told me it'd come to. And I knew Lansky was as safe a bank as you had at the betting window.

So we were friends. I'd see Lansky in New York, then in Hollywood, Florida, at the Diplomat, where you had a couple thousand acres of the most luxurious grounds you can imagine —practically the biggest hotel in the world. Originally I bought into it, then they gave me my money back. But it was a tremendous deal, a couple of golf courses, lavish grounds, a lot of land. The whole setup was worth maybe three or four hundred million dollars.

Sam's son-in-law Irwin Cowan was president of the corporation for the Diplomat. I knew this Irwin since he was thirteen. I was at his bar mitzvah in Newark, New Jersey, and even after he was at the Diplomat he was still talking about how I gave him the biggest gift he ever got.

"I'll never forget it," he said. And this was years ago, because when I was president of the Amalgamated's Butcher District Council for New York and New Jersey, his father used to be a meat salesman in Schloss's slaughterhouse. He invited me to the bar mitzvah. So I gave the kid five hundred dollars, and when he opened up the envelope he was shocked. Those days you'd get five dollars. Or you get a fountain pen from your best friend. A little more from close relatives. Here he opened the envelope, and there was the five hundred. This was in the late thirties, but he never forgot it, and he still talks about it. Now Sam Friedland is in his eighties, and the last I knew the kid was still president of the corporation.

I came to Florida often, for the meetings of the Amalgamated's executive council, and also they had the track there in Hollywood. I spent a lot of time at the Diplomat, so a number of times I'd go across the way and see Lansky, and he'd be there with Jimmy Blue Eyes, a contract man, like from the Murder, Incorporated group, and supposedly the mob used Jimmy Blue Eyes a lot in Las Vegas.

Morris Kleinman, Moe Dalitz's partner from the Purple Gang in Las Vegas would join us for breakfast sometimes. Later I met Moe Dalitz, too, through Wilbur Clark. Dalitz was a big man in the La Costa development in California, by the La Jolla track, and he also had a big piece of the Desert Inn and the Stardust. And maybe Heimi Siegel would be around. I knew Lansky had a piece in the Desert Inn, and also the Stardust, and so did Morris, and they all traveled back and forth a lot. Once I bumped into Jimmy Blue Eyes on the plane, in Las Vegas. Maybe he was carrying money. But he was also a contract man. He could have been there for any number of reasons. If you're smart you don't ask, and I was smart. I didn't ask.

Siegel used to be in charge of the book in New York, the front for Meyer. Then Courtney and Reed ran the book for Lansky in New York, for the horses, and Siegel moved to Florida. Frank Reed was a high-class gentleman. Courtney was a different type. A husky guy. About six-feet and tough, but a nice guy in behavior.

In Florida, Lansky had another partner, Charlie Brud, and a couple of other guys. They ran book on the horses, and they had other stuff going. They'd work together and set up some of the legitimate players in gin and other card games. Very big games, and the suckers would drop their money, loads of it—thousands.

There'd be different operations going, and the big tough guys would back them. And these mobsters, Italians, Jews, different ones, control the games, through the agents. So you have maybe three or four people playing; it looks like they're strangers, but actually they're silent partners, and they help each other out in different ways—in the bidding, raising the stakes, stuff like that. Someone wanders around kibitzing, and they got signals set up, and maybe someone looks over your shoulder to see what kind of a hand you got. That's the way they work.

It's just what you'd expect, and that's why so few expect it. The games might start out small and friendly. They might even let you win a little at first. Then the stakes start getting higher, and you start losing. It's the same principle for the smaller game, and if the sharks can't find a big game they settle for what's around.

That was the scenario, at all the hotels in Florida. In Miami Beach, Palm Beach, Hollywood.

At the Fontainbleau, the gambling was controlled by the Italian mob, Rocky and Joe Fischette. Different guys, and you don't interfere.

At the Eden Rock it was controlled by Lansky. Him and Charlie Brud. And so on, at various places. And you got all these people with tremendous incomes coming into these games, dropping lots of cash. It's happening in all the big hotels, country clubs, all over the country. In Las Vegas, New York, in the mountains at places like the Concord, Grossinger's —big games going on all the time.

In Miami Beach, at the Fontainbleau you had maybe six, seven, eight games taking place, two, three times a week. One guy lived in the Fontainbleau a lot of the time, and he had a game twice a week. He and his buddies cleaned out a lot of people, usually playing pinochle or gin. At the end of the night, these guys wind up with four, five, six thousand dollars. Sometimes more. One guy, Ryan, a millionaire out of Texas, went for a lot. One time he got beat for a hundred twenty-five thousand.

So there's always a sucker. And with these guys working together, they manipulate the game—it's quite an edge, and it's very easy for the legitimate player to lose. Then after some people lost a lot of money, they used to start wondering. I was there. I played a long time. I noticed. Finally I put it down to them: I know so and so's the case. So they told me to shut up; I wouldn't lose any more.

Even a good player has no chance against a thief. But if the wise guy doesn't get help, it's different. They get soft. I proved the point because without help, they couldn't beat me. The people in the card games know this one guy from the Fontainbleau and from New York. I played him two nights in a row at the Beverly Hotel in New York, by Lexington Avenue. I didn't let anybody in the rooms, and we played. And he couldn't beat me. And he was very able to set up a hand. But before he'd deal, I always made sure I cut the deck nine times, and I mixed it up, too. Under normal circumstances a guy would cut it maybe once. But this way, and without help, he couldn't beat me. But I lost a lot of money before I learned.

So people get screwed in these games all the time. But in Las Vegas, especially in the casinos, it's pretty legit. Of course, there's always larceny. Some players go in to steal, and they catch them and throw them out and hurt them. But the house is run legit. Gambling is too big a business in Las Vegas. They can't fool around. And usually they don't.

Of course, they don't have to. Because if a player wins ten dollars he wants a hundred. If he wins a thousand, he wants ten thousand. So he loses. Sooner or later he's probably going to give it all back, and then some. It's a simple principle, but that's why the house wins. That's what happened to me at the races, even though I would get some good tips and I knew my way around. So over the years, I would drop maybe two million dollars at the races.

It was natural for people with money to throw around to spend time at the races, so you'd see a lot of interesting characters there. I met Carlo Gambino once at the track in Hollywood, Florida, him and his bodyguards. It was raining like mad. I went out looking for a taxi, and I see a car and someone is yelling, "Blockie!"

The Italians always called me Blockie. Sure enough, it was Carlo Gambino. He was with four other guys, and they asked where was I going. I said the Diplomat, so they drove me there.

Gambino called an hour later to invite me and my wife to dinner. There was another couple with us, a lawyer and his wife, but Gambino said that was okay, he'd pick us up with the limousine and take us to Pier 66 in Fort Lauderdale.

We get there, a very fancy, well-known restaurant. We join the group.

I look around. Right away, I see these are the top mob people from the Mafia from every part of the country. Chicago, New York, New Orleans, Detroit, Cleveland, the coast, and so on. There were about twenty for dinner altogether, and I realized that with my wife and my lawyer friend and his wife, we made a good cover for them. Because we're not Mafia people. We're Jews. But they were speaking Italian most of the time.

We were sitting in the dining room, near the fireplace. It was an elegant room. There's a lot of people around, but everybody minds their own business. They don't look who's sitting there.

Gambino introduced me to the different people. All the top mob people. Joe Proface, he's dead now. But he was a bad, bad killer. He was a well-known character from Brooklyn, and they called him the King of Oil. He was importing Italian Olive oil, and this was distributed all over the country. Proface, about my size, was maybe a couple of years older than Gambino. Gambino, in his fifties, was about ten years older than me.

Bill Tocco was there from Detroit. One of the top mob guys, from the Purple Gang, he had a lot of dealings in produce, importing bananas, and he also brought in a lot of the wine from Italy that was distributed around the country.

Some of these guys had their wives with them. They weren't worried about talking in front of their wives, especially the old-timers. The people I didn't know, Carlo introduced me to them, and they all knew I was his man or he was my man, plus they knew that my buddy was Chappy Brescia, Lucky Luciano's partner until Lucky was deported. And so they were very friendly and we were accepted. But still, after the introductions we're having dinner and I realized, and I guess so did my friend Hymie Zalato, it was like they were having a dinner of their own—the top mob people from all over the country, the Italian group from the underworld. And then us, who didn't understand a word they were saying. I guess it wasn't none of our business anyhow.

By now Gambino was becoming very respected in the movement, but he handled himself gently, all the time, and he was friendly with all of them. There was no conflict that I could see. No arguments. Nothing like that. They discussed things quietly among themselves, enjoying the meal. Gambino wasn't at the head of the table. He didn't dominate the meeting like he was president of some men's club—he didn't need a gavel to get their attention. They all respected him. So it was just the whole group there, talking among themselves.

I didn't say anything to Jean. I didn't say anything to Zalato. But Zalato was no dummy. He represented a lot of wholesale meat dealers. They used to get meat by railroad, and so Hymie was suing all the railroads and getting money for the dealers.

That was his racket. He represented me sometimes, and he wanted that I should get him a reservation at the Diplomat Hotel, and so I got him one, and we had been spending a little time there. Anyway, Hymie knew about some of these guys. And he knew what was going on. His wife didn't know anything about it, but I noticed that Jean seemed a little uncomfortable.

The dinner and meeting lasted a few hours. Everything was pleasant. Afterward, Carlo took us in his limo, dropped us off at the Diplomat.

"Gee, Max," Hymie said, "I'm surprised all these big wheels respect you so much." But I told him I just knew some of them through Carlo Gambino and that I met Carlo a long time back in the meat business in Fort Greene.

In New York, the cops were even more impressed than Hy Zalato. President Eisenhower came by the Black Angus to say hello.

It was not exactly a parade, but the cops had blocked off the street, both sides, on Fiftieth Street between Lexington and Third, and you had thousands of spectators, waiting around. Eisenhower was going from the Waldorf Hotel out to the airport. I was in front of the Black Angus, talking to a few of the cops.

Ike had to go right by my place. His car came down the street and approached near where I was standing. He had the secret-service cars in the front and back, but he was in an open car, moving along. Then, when he reached the front of the Black Angus, the car slowed and he yelled out to me, loud, "Hi, Max!" And he waved, and of course I returned the greeting.

After that, the cops that saw this they said, "Gee, Max, we didn't know you knew the President."

I said, "Yeah, I met him a few times."

So the cops were really surprised, and they'd talk about it. "Son of a gun! Max knows the President."

Originally I met Eisenhower through Dewey. Dewey and I were friends, so he came to me when he was promoting Eisenhower for President.

Dewey was a nice guy. When he made a deal, he lived up to it. And with Dewey, there was no such thing as money being involved. He was one hundred persent honest. He promoted and made Ike. Two years before the elections, Dewey told me, "I've got the next President."

I said, "Who?"

He said, "General Eisenhower."

And then when General Eisenhower was being promoted, Dewey brought him to me. So I supported Eisenhower, and I got together a few other labor leaders, and we appeared on television together. And I got the rabbinical organization and the kosher supervisors to back him.

I remember when we were introduced. We shook hands. Eisenhower winced and made sort of a joke, like I'd broken or crushed his hand—because it was true, I always had a strong handshake.

Dewey himself was very businesslike. There was a cold quality about him. I always felt the public sensed it and that was why he lost when he ran for President against Roosevelt, and then again when he ran against Truman. But right away you warmed up to Eisenhower. He seemed an easygoing, likable guy—a nice, warm guy. So I supported him, and after that we got a little friendly, and then finally, just like Dewey said, Ike got elected President.

28

Sometimes it pays to take a long shot. Take baseball, for example.

In baseball, usually I would bet only on the World Series or the championship games. But if the odds were good, I might take a long shot, because I'd seen a lot come in. And you never knew . . .

When the Brooklyn Dodgers were about twelve or thirteen games behind the leading team for the pennant, the odds for the Dodgers getting the championship and winning the Series in 1955 were given at a hundred-to-one. I thought the price too big to let it go. I bet a hundred with a good book.

The Dodgers kept winning. Catching up. I figured they had a better chance. They won the National League pennant and they went up against the Yankees, in the Series. Then they each won three games, and it got down to the final game.

I remember listening on the radio while I was driving somewhere. I think the guy that bet a dollar jumped more. But I wasn't complaining. I collected ten thousand dollars on the Dodgers. The book wasn't worried. If they lost ten thousand that day to me, they collected plenty more elsewhere. But if you bet, you catch some long shots. If you don't bet, you don't win and you don't lose.

I had the money, and money was never the most important

190

thing in my life. So I bet it. But I never bet my last dollar on a race or anything else, and I always made sure I left plenty of pocket money for whatever else I needed. You should never leave yourself short, and if you can't afford it, you shouldn't bet.

The different unions—the Amalgamated, Teamsters, Culinary Workers, Plumbers, Operating Engineers, whatever— were supposed to cooperate with each other, and also pay per-member dues to the A.F. of L. That way there was supposed to be a stronger labor voice, with joint boycotts, refusal to cross picket lines, things like that.

The main thing was to organize, but it didn't always work that way. When a new member joined locals 640 or 342, it never cost more than ten dollars for an initiation fee, even after the dollar was getting cheaper. But then you see a report of initiation fees in Chicago, under Secretary Kelly, of $113.50 for a single new member in 1926. And this was where you had thousands of poorly paid packinghouse workers at the Chicago Stockyards. A lot of this continued in later years, and Gorman would complain to me about things that went on, shaking down employers, high initiation fees, stuff like that.

So you'd get a lot of corruption, especially on the local levels. But the international couldn't do much except to withdraw the union charter. Of course they wouldn't do that because it would cut off all those membership fees, and a lot of money was involved. Even if the local was kicked out, the corruption would continue anyway. And maybe even worse where you had an independent union, because often this was nothing but a front. The workers would never see the kind of benefits you'd get from the larger international, where you had established laws.

One benefit of the A.F. of L. was the Amalgamated's cooperation with the Teamsters. For months the two leaders, Denny Lane of the Amalgamated and Dan Tobin of the Teamsters, didn't get along. But this didn't always affect us at the local level.

We had no trouble with the Teamsters since I showed our strength against Marty Lacy. The Teamsters respected us after that, and we got along. The other labor leaders respected us too, because we were tough. And if they didn't cooperate

191

with me I found a way to chop their heads off, organization-ally.

In 1942 Denny Lane died. Gorman replaced him in the top spot as secretary-treasurer, and the Amalgamated started getting along better with the Teamsters. I got to know Jimmy Hoffa better, and we helped each other out, like in the Delmarva Peninsula. There was a lot more cooperation between the unions. I never discussed with Hoffa that incident where we stopped all the Teamster trucks under Lacy. Maybe he knew about it. I didn't know. But I didn't see any point to belittle the organization. Anyway, Jimmy and I got on fine.

29

I knew George Meany from way back. He was strictly a mob character. He co-operated, and the mob pushed him in. That's how finally he got to be president of the A.F. of L. And later he became president of the AFL–CIO, the largest labor federation in the United States, with over sixteen million members—maybe eighty to eighty-five percent of all union members.

Meany used to be a plumber and then a business agent for the Plumbers in New York, and he got in tight with a fellow named Joe Fey. Fey was not an Italian, but he was a mob man, strictly rackets. He was the head of the Operating Engineers and he was taking payoffs from employers, shaking them down—everything—as long as he made a buck. And he made a buck whatever he did with them. He was a strong-arm character.

Finally, he got arrested. Tom Dewey was a special prosecutor for New York State. So Dewey got Fey convicted for shaking down employers, and Fey got twelve years. But Joe Fey is the one that made Meany. Before Fey went to prison, he got Meany into the A.F. of L.

This was in the late thirties. First Joe Fey and a couple of others from the mob in New York backed Meany to get him elected president of the A.F. of L. New York State Federation.

This was made up of all the local unions from every international, the Butchers, Plumbers, whatever—practically every local union in New York State belonged to it.

Joe Fey was the strong man. He set it up that we vote for Meany, and we were told by friends to do it. So Meany's backer was Fey. He put pressure on the different locals, and then we robbed the vaults and stuffed the ballots, and we got Meany elected. That's how Meany became president of the New York State Federation, and that's how I knew about Fey's connection.

After a couple years, the secretary-treasurer of the A.F. of L. died. There was an opening. Fey and the mob pressured Green, the president, to appoint Meany, and Meany got in as secretary-treasurer.

How it works, in an organizational chart, the internationals, the different unions, would be like spokes in a wheel. In the middle you had the president of the A.F. of L., Bill Green; around him, the A.F. of L. executive council. (Now it's the AFL–CIO, but it's the same idea.) The council is made up of members of the different unions—the Amalgamated, Plumbers, Teamsters, and so on. But not from all of the unions. Anyway, these are the groups that run the A.F. of L.

The workers elect the presidents of their own individual unions. The delegates to the internationals are supposed to get elected by their locals, but it's controlled naturally by the people that own the organization. They get them elected, and they elect them in an open ballot, but it's controlled pretty good.

Then the internationals appoint delegates to the A.F. of L. convention. The leadership of these different unions send so many people. If there's a thousand members, they're entitled to so many people. For five thousand, more. These delegates elect the president. And the council, like the President's cabinet, is appointed.

But the A.F. of L. executive council actually had nothing to do with the membership, because the members, the workers, didn't elect these people—the president of the A.F. of L. council and the vice-president, secretary-treasurer, and so on.

So Meany was appointed secretary-treasurer—forced on the organization by Joe Fey and the mob. Joe Fey contacts the different organizations, through his strength, through friends

194

and so on, and they decided to put Meany in. They figured Green was a very old man who would die pretty soon, and George would take over. That's what happened, but Meany remained as secretary-treasurer a number of years. Then Green died, and Meany automatically became president. So Meany got there, but he wasn't elected by the multitude—he was put in by the mob.

Did the mob expect something? Well, they didn't push him in for nothing. He went along for the ride. But after he got in, the mob didn't have to pay him off. They don't do things, like that. There's favors, here and there. Maybe somebody came and asked for a charter, somebody else gets in as a business agent, or somebody would get printing business or some other kind of business—stuff like that.

I was close with Bill Green while he was head of the A.F. of L. I met him through Pat Gorman, and we saw each other a number of times. I thought he was a high-class gentleman. He was about five-feet-eight, white hair, blue eyes. Very soft-spoken. A distinguished, good-looking man. I'd have dinner with Bill Green and his wife and Pat Gorman and his wife, Hattie, and with my wife, Jean. Jean was so beautiful, everybody loved her, and we all got along very well.

But Green hated Meany, because Meany was pulled in by the mob. And Green didn't like it because the mob controlled the majority of the board. The mob didn't bother with Green. They didn't trust him. But they had control over the majority of the internationals, the presidents or representatives that served on the board with him.

Every time I came to the A.F. of L. office in Washington to see Green, I'd see Meany. Apparently he didn't talk very much, because when he was sitting in the office of the A.F. of L., before the AFL–CIO merger, Bill Green was there as president. And Meany sat alone like a monkey in the corner, all by himself.

Nobody would talk to him or even say hello. I was the only guy, when I walked in, I came over and said, "Hello, George," and we'd chat, and I was very friendly with him. So they officiated. Meany was there, but they were not his friends. And during those years Meany was under Green, Green wouldn't talk to him at all. He didn't think Meany was a proper guy. But Meany developed pretty good in his way.

That was the background of George Meany. He was put in by the mob. However, I respected him a great deal. He wasn't looking for anything. He didn't need anything, personally. He didn't need anything from anybody. Then as he got old, he developed a lot of common sense. And there's no substitute for old experience. So he was active until he died. He was eighty-four years old, whatever. A lot of years, and he was a good man. I liked him as a person. He knew what he was talking about.

Of course, the mob would pick a person like Meany to put in instead of somebody else, so they could have more control. And Meany cooperated with them. And they were his friends. I had to give Meany credit. He was Fey's friend to the end. Because when Fey was in jail, George used to go visit him regularly. That's why I liked him. He was okay. A lot of people walk away.

I had lots of meetings with George. I visited him a million times.

Later, in Florida, we'd go to Sam Friedland's Monte Carlo Hotel, where the AFL–CIO counsel used to meet, after the two federations merged. The international board of the Amalgamated met there too, and I'd be staying there. So I'm going out of the hotel.

"Hello, George."

"Hello, Max."

And what's he doing while he's going in? He's carrying a load of stuff with him that he took out of the cleaners. He didn't play the bigshot.

I used to talk a lot with Meany in the sweat room at the Monte Carlo because he was heavy and he wanted to lose weight. He didn't have any interest besides the union. Nothing. I knew his wife. A nice lady. A couple of times we got together. Sometimes Pat Gorman and his wife would join us. But Bill Green wouldn't go along, if Meany was there.

We'd go out to dinner with our wives, and Meany wouldn't talk about the union. He would keep his private life separate a little bit. But when he got older, the union was mostly all that interested him. So he had a lot of hard knocks. He learned the hard way. And when he said something it usually made sense.

He became a very powerful labor leader. Number one. A powerful voice. Yet I didn't think he controlled that many votes. Because the American worker, and America, is a funny breed—they don't listen to you and me talk. So maybe Meany votes a certain way—actually it means nothing. The people wouldn't necessarily listen to him on how they should vote, how they shouldn't vote. If it made sense, they'd go along. But not just because it was Meany talking. Meany knew that too, and he didn't overestimate his importance.

One time he had a showdown. He wouldn't go along with President Nixon, who wanted him to hold wages down or something. But as for the politicians or his feelings about Nixon or Kennedy or whoever, George wasn't that interested. For him, politics was all shit.

That's the way he talked when we'd be sitting in the sweat room. He never discussed the way things were going with labor and business, because it made no difference. He knew how it worked. He knew the mob. He knew this guy, that guy, and that everybody makes a living. So he was a nice guy, and he had a lot of common sense. But he never organized.

30 Bill Green of the A.F.
of L. and Philip Murray of the C.I.O. had long been at odds
—they wouldn't talk to each other. Then both died in November 1954. George Meany became the new president of the
A.F. of L., and Walter Reuther the new president of the C.I.O.
And this would have tremendous consequences, because both
Meany and Reuther were open to a merger of the two huge
labor federations.

A year later, in December 1955, the merger took place.
Meany was elected president. William Schnitzler, from the
Bakers' international, became secretary-treasurer. The executive council brought in seventeen people from the A.F. of L.,
ten from the C.I.O.

By 1955, I had been in the movement maybe twenty-six
years. So I saw how it worked, before and after the merger.

For some twenty years, while the A.F. of L and the C.I.O.
were in competition, until the merger, the country went
through plenty of labor pains. But during this time, many
internationals—especially the locals that went out organizing
—brought in a lot of workers. And we got big improvements:
better pay, shorter hours, other benefits for the union worker.
And for other employees, too, because the non-union company
had to compete, to keep the union out. Also, the non-union

198

company had to live up to the new laws brought on by union demands. Minimum wage. Restrictions against child labor. Job security. Health and welfare benefits.

So the two labor federations went up against each other, but the conditions got better. With the competing labor federations you had unions raiding the membership of other unions, sometimes fighting each other instead of for better conditions. And you had jurisdictional issues, areas of corruption, Communist agitation, a lot of other problems. But during these years, the labor movement made great strides—a tremendous improvement in the lives of the workers.

After the two federations merged, many of the problems continued. Some of that was expected, and some progress was inevitable, in time. Only now, after the big merger, you had more contented people going to sleep, not organizing. So a lot of the workers stopped going into the more legitimate unions, with established conditions. It was easier for the larger established union to add ready-made members by merging in a smaller union, where the workers are already organized, and where you're less likely to run into problems for interfering.

Under the umbrella of the AFL–CIO, many internationals, the individual unions, also merged; part of the AFL–CIO package. The internationals were supposed to merge voluntarily, over a period of time. And the idea was to get stronger voice, more financial security, maybe more security against loss of members, and so on. But a merger could also put the internationals to sleep, the way you saw it happening with the larger federation. And it created other problems, and nothing would be done to correct these, because too often there'd be no one to provide an alternative.

I was opposed to the AFL–CIO merger for reasons that became more obvious over the years. Because, like I said, after the merger you didn't have the same competition. And the unions stopped organizing.

You have to imagine what it would be like if suddenly every major corporation in America merged together, and what you'd get—collusion, price fixing, lack of competition, poor quality, a kind of general laziness and, worst of all, nowhere to turn. To make the comparison, with a few exceptions that's exactly what we got with all the unions today, merged into one sleeping giant labor federation.

So we stopped organizing. And in many ways, for years the conditions have been getting worse. In the old days, with larger families, one man supported the household. Nowadays, it takes two or three people working for a family to get by, and a lot have a hard time at that. So it's no picnic yet for the organized worker, and there are millions of unorganized workers, many stuck with intolerable conditions.

The Culinary Workers could be out organizing, for example. You got oriental restaurants with very bad conditions, where the workers don't even get any food to eat. Lots of times they put in long hours, without extra pay. They don't get breaks. There's no holiday time. No sick leave. No vacations. No job security. In some cases they get wages—on the books—to meet certain minimum requirements, but then they have to kick back a lot of this. This happens all over.

So add it up. You got maybe a million and a half oriental workers in the restaurant field alone, all over the country, without legitimate contracts. But nobody makes a move. They're busy playing golf. Or they get paid off to stay away.

You got hundreds of thousands in the garment industry that are not organized. Many work in small sweatshops in Chicago, Detroit, Philadelphia, Miami, Los Angeles, from Coast-to-Coast, with no conditions. The pay is terrible. The atmosphere oppressive. All they got is slave labor, and maybe a phony independent union paid off by the boss.

You got millions of office workers. But nobody makes a move to organize them. It's the same thing. And when you get a number of workers in the small shops, they might be merged into a larger phony independent union. And that's all controlled by the mob.

I watched all that happening. It's happening now more than ever, because the percentage of the work force organized by the established unions is declining.

A few labor leaders in recent months have recognized the problem. John Henning, head of the California Federation of Labor, representing 1.7 million of the AFL–CIO members, noted a startling forty-five percent drop since 1950 in the proportion of organized union members to the total work force.

"If we fail to clearly understand that trend and reverse it," he said, "we (the unions) will become a relic of history."

❖   ❖   ❖

So there may have been a lot of changes, but there's still a lot to do.

I could remember when it was wilderness almost everywhere. There were no paved roads. And looking back, you realized that in those days ten miles away from home was so far—because you went by horse and buggy. By the fifties, it was already a different story. You drive a few miles somewhere in minutes. In a few hours you fly to Florida. Chicago. Las Vegas. New York. Wherever. And unless maybe you were there in the old days, you could hardly imagine the difference.

The technology got more complicated, and it became more difficult to draw the line between the skilled and unskilled worker, between the tradesman and the industrial worker. In the market, the work became much easier for the butcher and meatcutter, because the meat was now coming from the factory in smaller pieces—ten, twelve pounds, instead of the whole carcass, or even quarters, like we used to get. And you didn't have to haul heavy pieces of meat around.

At the same time, the employer was becoming less dependent on the worker. And if labor costs got too high, the employer would maybe try to replace the worker with a machine. So they put in machinery that makes things automatic. You can't stop progress.

I always took the position that you can't fight it, and you shouldn't. Instead, you fight to get the worker less hours, without any cut in pay. In the long run, the new equipment made it easier. There was the time when we had to do everything by hand—a barrel of bones, for instance, that you needed for the day's business. We didn't charge extra, but from every barrel of meat we would pull out the bones. It was a tremendous job, and when we were finished for the day we had to start sawing again, so we'd have bones for the morning, and it didn't count for anything. Those days, we just gave it away. Now, on the larger scale, every penny counts; you don't give things away.

So a lot of stuff the butcher used to prepare in the shop started coming into the stores already cut—even packaged—and this brought major changes: in packing, canning, frozen foods, warehousing, shipping, printing, advertising, marketing and distributing the products.

It became more difficult to define the membership of a particular union. Specialties overlapped. Different unions claimed the same jurisdiction. Even before the AFF–CIO merger, the A.F. of L. tried to solve some of these disputes, but they couldn't do much.

In an argument between the Amalgamated and the Clerks, for example, Meany ruled one time that if the meat was fresh the workers would be under the jurisdiction of the Amalgamated. But if there was only frozen food, then the jurisdiction would belong to the Clerks.

Pat Gorman was angered over Meany's decision, and the Amalgamated ignored it. The meat cutting was now being done more in the industrialized processing plants, and the Amalgamated wasn't about to give up control of the meat workers in the chain stores just because these workers became less involved in cutting and more involved in dispensing meat. So Gorman wasn't interested to go before Meany on these disputes. But Meany and I got along pretty good, and he let the issue ride.

Meanwhile the Amalgamated, which by the mid-fifties, had more than three hundred thousand members, now had to keep its eyes on the new technologies and the large shifts of labor. And we felt a legitimate claim to all the workers in the food industry, including fishermen, the more industrial workers in packing and canning, and related areas like the furriers.

Like other labor changes, the trend toward merging came early in the Amalgamated. In 1940, the Lamb Shearers, with limited strength, got better conditions under the umbrella of the Amalagamated. They found a more powerful voice, and the Amalgamated grew. In 1951, the United Leather Workers' International, with about five thousand members, joined the Amalgamated, bringing benefits to both groups, and still leaving some independence for the smaller group coming in.

There were other reasons for merging. In the early fifties, the fighting went on in Korea. The cold war got worse. Meanwhile, the C.I.O. was steadily losing ground, finding it too difficult to operate because of Communist infiltration or domination.

One of these unions had special interest for Gorman. This was the Furriers—the International Fur and Leather Workers' Union of the United States and Canada, a much larger group

202

than the Lamb Shearers, and the same group Shifrin came from years back, when he stabbed Silver in the chest with the knife.

The two top leaders of the Furriers, Ben Gold and Irving Potash, both avowed Communists, had just resigned over the Communist issue. And Ben Gold went to jail for perjury after signing an affidavit that he wasn't a Communist. So with Gold and Potash leaving, that cleared the way for a merger of the Furriers with the Amalgamated. Gorman, though he had no use for Ben Gold, felt such a merger promised a more unified labor field, big membership gains, more collective bargaining power, an end to the raiding of members by rival unions. Particularly, it would remove a strong rival to the small group of Furriers already affiliated with the Amalgamated.

The Furriers, headquartered in New York, had maybe forty thousand people in the fur-and-leather trade, skinning and tanning the hides of animals slaughtered in the meat industry. By now there was a precedent for bringing furriers and leather workers into a union of "meatcutters" and "butcher workmen." In 1951, Dan Tobin, then president of the Teamsters and also on the executive council of the A.F. of L., doubted there was a legitimate connection between butchers and tannery workers. The two fields seemed very far apart to him, so he was opposed to the A.F. of L. approving the merger.

But Gorman was a smooth talker. Answering Tobin, Pat explained that his father, Maurice Gorman, years back had worked at a tannery in Tipperary, Ireland. Gorman's father would slaughter the animals, sell the meat in the butcher shop, then tan the leather in the leather house in the back of the store, producing what many called the finest leather in the world. Tobin, an Irishman, like Gorman, took pride in the Irish leather, as Gorman figured he would. So Tobin overcame his objections, and the A.F. of L. executive council approved the merger of the Leather Workers' International with the Amalgamated.

The potential merger with the much larger Fur and Leather Workers' Union, the most powerful union in that trade, was not going to be so easily accepted—not by Meany of the A.F. of L., who was a lot tougher than Tobin. Nor would it be easily accepted by the Fur and Leather Workers, the Amalgamated, the businesses dealing with the Amalgamated, the National Labor Relations Board, the press or the public.

Finally, the merger idea came to the executive board. By now I was a vice-president of the international, in charge of the Butcher District Council for New York and New Jersey. I could see advantages, but I was skeptical. I had fought Communists before. I saw their tactics in the Food Workers, the Furriers, Local 400, the U.P.W.A., and so on.

But then Pat Gorman and I had dinner that night, and I asked him, "Pat, did you make a deal with them?"

He said, "Yes."

"Well, okay," I said, "We'll have to take them in and handle them."

The Amalgamated was so much larger, I didn't think it could be easily overpowered by the Furriers. But there was a lot of fear and anger everywhere about Communism. It would take plenty of work on Gorman's part, traveling from city to city to explain the advantages of the merger and to show that the other aspects were being dealt with.

It took time. It wasn't easy to convince the others. Finally, in December 1954, a merger agreement was signed between the Furriers and the Amalgamated. The Furriers would get Amalgamated cards, and finances would be combined. The Furriers would retain some autonomy but under supervision of the Amalgamated. Furrier officials would sign the non-Communist affidavit set up after the Taft-Hartley Act and required by the N.L.R.B. And those officers that didn't have to sign the affidavit by law, would still leave a signed copy with the Amalgamated.

In late January 1955, a controversial Furrier convention approved the merger, by a large majority. It went into effect on a trial basis, to be finalized by agreement in 1960. But soon after the initial go-ahead, the A.F. of L. executive council protested, calling the Amalgamated a "temporary haven" for the still Communist-dominated union.

Despite the resignations of Gold and Potash, Meany came down hard against the merger. At the Flordia meeting of the A.F. of L. council, at the Monte Carlo Hotel, Meany summoned Pat Gorman and Amalgamated president Jimmerson and told them the Amalgamated would be ousted if it persisted. The two were broken-hearted, and they left the meeting.

That afternoon I got hold of Meany. We played some gin by the pool.

After an hour or two, I said to George, "You hurt Pat and Jim very much."

He says, "Why?"

"You know. You know how we always back you up."

"But how can I change the decision of the council when it's on record like that?" he asked. "I can't turn around tomorrow and change it."

"It's very simple," I said. "I'll give you an out. You write us a letter and tell us the names of the Furriers, the Communists you have on record—the ones that are card-holding members of the Communist party. Then you request that these be excluded from the merger, ousted, and that then you'll go along with the merger. Or that otherwise the council will have to stick by its decision."

So I gave Meany an out. He said, "It sounds good." And we made a deal.

That night, about two, three o'clock in the morning, I came home from playing pinochle. There was a package. I took it to my room and sure enough, that was it: Meany's names, about thirteen people, that had to be ousted. It also gave the instructions that if we complied then everything was okay.

The next morning I called to Pat Gorman, but he didn't answer.

I called Jimmerson. I said, "Jim, where's Pat? I called him." It was early. But Jimmerson says that Pat was so down-hearted and disgusted he left for Louisville, Kentucky, his home.

I said, "Let's have breakfast." So we sit down. We have breakfast, and I tell him what I worked out with Meany.

"I knew you'd straighten it out," he said.

I asked him, "What do you mean, you knew?"

And he tells me. He was in his room by the tenth floor looking out the window, and he looked down. "I saw you playing cards with George by the pool," he said. "I knew you'd work it out."

That's how the merger got approved by the A. F. of L. It worked out, and finally, five years later, it was ratified by the Amalgamated and the Furriers.

31

Joe Fey was in jail for almost ten years. When Fey got out he moved to Florida, and Jimmy Hoffa wanted to visit him. Fey still had a lot of influence, and Hoffa had heard about him and was anxious to meet him. Jimmy and I were in Miami Beach at the time, so I made arrangements, and I took Jimmy down.

Fey lived some distance from Miami Beach, so I set it up to meet in Naples, Flordia, at a relation of Fey's, a couple of hours' drive for us. Jimmy rented the car and we went down, he drove, and then I introduced him to Joe Fey. We were sitting talking. We had a bite to eat, and we spent a few hours. That's it. It was mostly just so they could meet. We had a pleasant visit, and then we left. Jimmy drove on the way back. A Pontiac.

Jimmy was now becoming the leader of the Teamsters, and Dave Beck was being kicked out by him. Tobin, before Beck, was there for years. He had a son who later became a vice-president of the international. They both meant nothing. They were shitting in their pants, afraid of the tough guys, in case they made a move of any kind. They had no guts.

Beck made some progress in organizing, but Jimmy Hoffa made the most progress in organizing and in getting the best conditions. Later, Fitzsimmons was doing a pretty good job, organizing steady. But hardly any other union was growing.

Dave Beck was the type of guy you couldn't like. He was a cold tomato. He had icy, light blue eyes. He looked at you —cold. Jimmy Hoffa I liked, because he had a good ear. Somebody had a problem, a widow, whatever, he was always ready to listen, to help. He was a smart fellow with a high IQ. Tremendous. But he was hot-headed—he wouldn't take any bullshit.

So now Hoffa was moving in, and Beck was being kicked out.

They gave Beck his piece of the action. He was a Teamster, out on the coast, and he represented a big local there. He had spent some time in jail. So he returned to the West Coast. He messed around with real estate.

Beck was not involved with the mob, but a lot of the Teamster locals are controlled by the mob. So automatically you get involved here and there. What happens, you got a guy that's connected and he's a business agent automatically. Or the tough guys try to control him, especially if he's Italian. Or they try to kill him if they can't control him, especially if he's Italian. And so these tough guys get involved. There's a lot of pension money floating around. And so the mob latched tight onto the labor movement.

You never know who you're going to run into . . .

There was a guy who was supposed to be a cousin of the Kennedy's, and he'd come around to the Black Angus and have a drink. He had been friendly with Johnny O'Rourke, and O'Rourke was president of District Council 16 of the Teamsters. That's how I met the cousin, originally. He didn't strike me as a moocher, like a lot that came by all the time, and we got to be a little friendly.

One day I'm out at the track at Jamaica, in the Club House. I see that this fellow is with Bobby Kennedy and Bobby's sister, Pat, the one that married Peter Lawford.

The cousin introduced me. Everyone was friendly and polite, and that was all. I didn't think much of it, and I didn't try to join their group. I was concentrating on the races. Also, Bobby wasn't that well-known yet. Not like after John became president. But the group was political and outgoing.

By this time they were all planning to get John in as president. So they were cordial to me, and that was it. I was a national figure. Everybody knew me. I was president of the council for the Amalgamated, and maybe the cousin told them I represented a lot of labor votes. I didn't know what he said, and I didn't care.

Mostly the cousin kept coming up to see how I was betting. He knew I'd get some good tips, that I was in touch with some of the trainers and I followed the backgrounds on the horses and jockeys and so on. I knew which jockeys you could rely on to run a good race.

I also knew that some of the jockeys were money jockeys. They'd make a buck here and there, and maybe they'd set something up, or maybe the trainer would ask them to hold a horse back to try to build up the odds for another race, or whatever. Anyway, I told the cousin how I was betting. Maybe he followed my advice a little bit, and that was all.

So we're at the track. A summer day. They didn't run ten races then, only seven. Then about five o'clock or so the races let out. Now Kennedy's cousin comes up to me. Apparently Kennedy or one of them had an apartment or suite of rooms in the old Park Lane Hotel, around the corner from the Black Angus. So the cousin asked if I'd mind giving them a ride to the hotel from the track.

I said, "Fine."

I take the three of them and we go down to the Park Lane Hotel. It's maybe eight, nine miles. Mostly we talked about the races. Bobby and his sister were both losers for the day, so they were joking with the cousin, bawling him out, telling him he should have passed on the tips I gave him, because they found out I had four winners. But it didn't matter very much to them, that they lost. They didn't bet that heavy, or they didn't care and they weren't worried about it.

We get to the hotel, and before I go on to the Black Angus they invite me to have a drink at the bar. I said, "Fine. Okay."

I parked in front of the hotel. We all got out of the car, and I went in with them. John was there, and also his wife, Jackie, and a few other people. I didn't think much about Jackie at the time.

So we're introduced, and then we're having a drink in the cocktail lounge downstairs in the hotel, a small, intimate lounge, and we're talking, making conversation about the races and so on. After a little while, this broad comes down, a tall, attractive blonde, with a big bosom, and she comes over to John Kennedy from upstairs or wherever she was from.

At first I thought she was a relative or something like that, because of the way she came up and put her arms around him, so friendly like. But then I realized she was putting the make on him. And apparently she was drunk. You could tell, because she kept her arms around him. She was creeping on top of him, and you could see Jackie starting to get burned up. The gal was whispering to John. She had to be loaded. Otherwise, she wouldn't do that.

Jackie looked at her, and at first John tried to wave the girl away. He didn't pay much attention, but he was drinking, and she kept it up, annoying him, whispering in his ear and so on, to come upstairs, I guess. Then John was whispering back, and I figured he must have told her to go upstairs, because apparently she did. What room she was in, or where exactly, I had no idea. But then, a few minutes later, without saying anything, John walked off, apparently to follow her up. The way he left, like that, that's what I thought. And that's what Jackie must have figured too.

So now Jackie opened up her mouth. She had been quiet all this time, but you could tell she was furious. She started yelling, "You give me a million dollars, I don't have to take that kind of shit! I don't have to live with that pig! That son of a bitch!" Like that. And it was a shock, coming out of her, because she looked so elegant. And she had been quiet up until then. Not outgoing like the others.

After Jackie started, Bobby grabbed her, set her down in a corner, in the cocktail lounge, trying to calm her down. But she continued, like out of her head. A couple of others had joined the group, but Bobby kept Jackie in the corner. She was outraged. And John was gone. He may have gone upstairs to screw, to meet the broad up there, wherever she had her room. He may have had another room for her. I didn't know. John didn't return. He was gone maybe fifteen minutes or so.

It took Bobby a long time to straighten Jackie out, to shut her up. I felt embarrassed. It wasn't my business, so I went back to the Black Angus.

I was surprised, and it gave me a low opinion of John Kennedy. Because it's one thing to play around and another thing to do it in front of your wife.

There's a chapter in the book, *Jackie Oh!* that talks about the affairs John F. Kennedy was supposed to have had—with his secretary, and with some other women. This was when he was a U.S. Senator married to Jackie, and getting ready to run for the Presidency.

One couple, Mr. and Mrs. Leonard Kater, rented to Kennedy's secretary, on Thirty-fourth Street in Georgetown. They were disturbed over Kennedy talking about running for the Presidency, and his being married and supposedly seeing his secretary at the same time. The Katers claimed to have made a tape recording through the wall of Kennedy making love to the secretary. They described the recording as the obvious noises of lovemaking, except for the senator asking, "Are you ready for it?" and the secretary replying, "Whenever you're ready for it."

Later the secretary was evicted. Kennedy supposedly helped her get located in another apartment, and then the Katers said they took a picture of Kennedy coming out of the secretary's new apartment at one o'clock in the morning, with Kennedy using his hand to try to shield his face. After that the couple tried to expose Kennedy, but they didn't get very far, publicly, and the Kennedys threatened to sue the *Washington Star* if they published the picture.

According to Mrs. Kater, James McInerney, formerly with the criminal division of the F.B.I., visited her a number of times. She said he asked her for the photograph and tape, and to drop the issue. Later, after getting nowhere with the matter, Mrs. Kater said Kennedy called her up.

According to the report, Mrs. Kater said, "After he became President he called me and said the trouble with me was that I needed a good lay. Then he called me five or six times more from the White House just to be nasty. Once he called and said he was going on a campaign trip and couldn't decide which tie to wear. 'You're a very smart woman, Mrs. Kater, so you tell me what the most sincere type of tie would be. Striped or solid?' He got his kicks out of stuff like that, I guess. I don't know. I never could figure it out."

I didn't know about all that. But I knew Jim McInerney

very well. He's dead now, but some months after the incident at the Park Lane Hotel, McInerney represented me at the McClellan Hearings, and he was Bobby Kennedy's godfather. Bobby used to work in McInerney's law office because Joe Kennedy had asked him to give Bobby a job. So Bobby worked there about a year, until McInerney told the father that Bobby would never make a good lawyer. He said Bobby didn't apply himself and was too busy playing around.

I hadn't even heard about the other stuff then, about John Kennedy supposedly screwing around with his secretary, or the book that came out by Judith Exner, who supposedly was involved with the mob somehow and claimed she had an affair with Kennedy. But I mentioned the incident to McInerney about the Park Lane Hotel. McInerney just told me that John Kennedy was a whoremonger all the time, and that Bobby was too.

By that time I already knew how Bobby had been having an affair with Marilyn Monroe, because I did a lot of business with Wilbur Clark at the Desert Inn in Las Vegas. Wilbur told me the last time I was out there, before the McClellan hearings in 1958, how he used to set Bobby and Marlyn Monroe up with a suite of rooms maybe once a month or so, whenever they'd come out.

32

You can't always go by
what you hear in public. Here's an example.

Supposedly the Teamsters got thrown out of the AFL–CIO
in 1957 because George Meany was disgusted with Jimmy
Hoffa's corruption and involvement with the mob. That's what
you read, and that was pretty much what Meany said. That
was funny, too, if you knew Meany's background and where
he came from. The real reason the Teamsters got ousted was
because Meany made a deal with Bobby Kennedy.

So Hoffa was involved with the mob. Big deal. Half the
country and almost all the labor movement was involved in
one way or another with the mob. Certainly Meany was. And
so was the AFL–CIO. And that's why he made the deal with
Kennedy, so Kennedy would go out after the Teamsters and
leave Meany and the AFL–CIO alone. And of course, that's
what Kennedy did.

So Meany ousted the Teamsters, and Kennedy went out
after the Teamsters, especially Jimmy Hoffa, with a vengeance
that would go on for years. Even Joe Kennedy, Bobby's father,
thought it was strange. Supposedly, in a private meeting that
went nowhere but was an attempt at smoothing things over
between the Kennedys and the Teamsters, Joe Kennedy told
a Hoffa associate, "Everyone in my family forgives—except

Bobby." And even in the Justice Department, they would talk about the "Get Hoffa Squad."

But that was later. For starters, Kennedy got Meany to force the ouster of the Teamsters from the AFL–CIO. Kennedy needed something. He was looking to make a splash to get his brother John elected President. He needed a victory. So with the elections coming up, Kennedy started making headlines, and he went out after the Teamsters, even though Meany himself could have made headlines.

What was surprising, was that the public didn't see through Bobby Kennedy.

So I supported the Teamsters, during the move to oust them. I got others, like Pat Gorman and the Amalgamated, and Ed Miller of the Culinary Union, the Upholsterers, and a lot of others, to oppose the ouster. Later Emmett Kelly from Chicago would say that I practically threatened Pat Gorman with a gun before the Amalgamated made the decision to support the Teamsters. But that was bullshit. Kelly was opposed to the Teamsters as long as I was in favor of the Teamsters.

But the Teamsters got ousted. Meany forced it through with about two thirds supporting the ouster. But Hoffa didn't need the AFL–CIO anyway, because after the merger the Teamsters were the only ones out organizing. And this would coninue to be the case over the years. The record shows this. The Teamsters kept competition going.

So no one noticed. But those small groups are the ones most susceptible to the independent union and to mob control. These groups were all ignored by Kennedy, and usually by the AFL–CIO organizations, maybe with the feeling there's not enough members to make it worthwhile. But with the Teamsters, it's a national organization, with national laws, and so on. So these groups got conditions. Something. Before, they usually had nothing.

When the Teamsters went out, I got together with Jimmy and we set up the joint council to meet every three months to look at different ways of helping each other.

I never discussed the ouster with George Meany. I voted against the expulsion and Meany knew I influenced a lot of other unions that voted against it. He knew how I worked against it and how close I was with Jimmy Hoffa. But I remained friends with Meany. There was no personal vendetta involved. It was a thing that happened and he himself, what was he, an angel?

There was not that much pressure on Meany from the AFL–CIO to expel the Teamsters. I thought they were all a bunch of monkeys sitting on the board of directors there, the executive council. And Meany called the shots anyhow. But whether he himself felt strongly about the Teamsters, or whether it was a political thing he felt he had to do, I didn't know. We didn't talk about it.

What was I going to discuss, "Why'd you make a deal with Bobby Kennedy?" And he couldn't tell me they had a bad group and he comes from a good group. It's all the same. If you're stealing nickels, or if you're stealing thousands. It's all the same idea. The whole union setup. It was the same.

33

Bill McFetridge, president of the Building Services Union, was always trying to get a contract for the race tracks, but could do nothing. They used to come out for a week or two and picket at Jamaica, Aqueduct, Belmont. Then they'd walk away.

Pat Gorman asked me to help out McFetridge, if I could. And I got together with Frank Stevens, because Frank and Harry Stevens handled most of the catering done in the race tracks around the country. I was very friendly with Frank and his family, so I talked to Frank and got him to come down to the Black Angus, and I set up a meeting with McFetridge.

McFetridge came in from Chicago, along with the manager from his office. I introduced them and we discussed the whole thing. But before the meeting, I had explained to Frank, "Look, you're continuously fighting. There's no end to it. It's better to sit down and work out something." And I told Frank that McFetridge was a level-headed guy. Frank believed me. These were broadminded people. They made a deal and got agreements, and after that they had no more picket lines out there.

So the Building Services Union signed up all the caterers at the tracks. All the tracks around New York, New Jersey,

Connecticut, and then Florida, and so on around the country.

As a vice-president of the international, I was spending more time on other projects around the country, not only for the Amalgamated. So Jimmy Hoffa invited me to come out to Dallas because the Teamsters were having problems with the waterfront people, the Longshoremen, and he wanted me to help him settle it.

The head of the Longshoremen was a big fat guy named Captain Bradley, from New York. Ted Gleason, who later would replace Bradley as the top man, was the vice-president then. And we all went to Dallas to see if we could straighten things out, because the two groups had a lot of problems between them. I had nothing to do with it. But I was friends with both sides, so I went as a peacemaker.

It was hot and miserable in Dallas. You go into the hotel and it seems a little cooler. It goes from one hundred and ten degrees to ninety degrees. And for a while, you felt cooler. But then after an hour or so, you felt like you could have died. The air conditioner wasn't working that well. Anyway, I was in Dallas a couple of days, and we had about got the issues settled between the Teamsters and the waterfront people, when I bump into this guy in my hotel—he turns out to be Jack Ruby. This was a long time before John F. Kennedy would get assassinated, and before Ruby would shoot Oswald.

Ruby was dancing with some woman on the floor, fooling around, and somehow he made a remark to me—"You New York or Chicago?"

I smiled. You know, how the hell you going to tell?

The guy was nice. He warmed up to me. He asked again, "You New York or Chicago?"

I said, "Why?"

He said, "You look like a guy that's from the East."

I knew I was well-dressed. I guessed maybe that was how he could tell. So I figured he called the shot, and I said, "New York. But I got a lot of friends in Chicago."

We finish off the dance floor, and he's at the table next to me. We started talking. We discussed Chicago, who my friends were, and so on, and he knew them. Jackie Perno, Sneeze, and all that. So I figured he was connected someplace with the mob, because he knew some of these guys, and right away he had mentioned one name to me—Sneeze.

Ruby was about my size or maybe he was a little lighter than me then. He was outspoken, but not loud. He had a lot of friends, and he knew a lot of people. Then he invited me over to this club he said he owned, because you couldn't get anything to drink unless you belonged to a club.

The guy seemed level-headed. He drank, like I did, but he wasn't a heavy drinker. So he became friends with me, and then we joined up. I didn't have any place to go in particular, and there wasn't anyone with me except this girl I met over there, so we all spent the evening together. Then he told me about a small jewelry business he had. He gave me his card. Later I bought a few things, and so I saw him over a couple of days.

That was it. I thought he was a nice guy. I left Dallas, and I didn't think anything about it until some years later, when he shot Oswald. About a year after he killed Oswald, Ruby died of cancer. He knew he had cancer, and he didn't have anything to be afraid of—he was dying anyway. And he must have figured the cops wouldn't bother him or anything because they all knew him. And so he shot the guy.

So apparently Ruby didn't give a damn about the shooting. Either that, or Ruby was protecting somebody too. Because before Kennedy got shot and killed, there was some group from Texas that would hang out in the Black Angus when they came into New York. They'd come around lunchtime with some other guys that had an office in the neighborhood somewhere and they'd spend a few hours drinking at the bar and eating lunch.

They were big guys. One of them, about six-four, an insurance man, was asking me questions before Jack Kennedy was elected, whether I thought the Jews would vote for a Jew like Goldwater and against Kennedy because he was Catholic. I told him I didn't think it mattered, because nobody controlled the Jewish vote. So unless there was some special reason, it wouldn't matter that Goldwater was Jewish or that Kennedy was Catholic.

Then John got elected and became President, and some time after that he said he was going south to campaign. This big guy came into the Black Angus again, so I told him, "I see the President is going to be out your way." And he said to me, "I don't care—he's not going to come out of it alive, anyway." Then a little while later, when John Kennedy went there, he got killed.

So that was a big statement that guy made to me. When someone tells you something like that, it's easy to say they're full of shit. But I listened to those guys. I heard them talk. I saw the hatred. And when Kennedy got shot, I wasn't shocked.

I didn't know who. I couldn't say why. But the same people, the same organization, they were pretty sure. And the big guy said, "He ain't gonna live it out." They used to come, about four or five of them, have a drink at the bar and invite me over, and I used to bullshit with them. Maybe they wanted to feel me out some way. So you can't tell, what's going to happen . . .

34

In my business, I never knew who I would come into contact with. Howard Johnson was a Swede. A big, husky man. Smart. He built up a huge organization. Tremendous. He told me he had about five hundred of his own places and about five hundred more franchised. He used to come visit me a lot, at the Black Angus, and later at the country club, the Deercrest. He was trying to get me drunk all the time.

I had a big strike against him. Originally we pulled a strike on his warehouse in Jamaica, that's all. Meanwhile, he would come to get me drunk in New York, because he wanted to make a deal and pay me off. He wanted to "get this Jew-boy drunk," he'd say. And then he would wind up stiff, and I'd take him home. He had a suite of rooms at the Waldorf-Astoria, and I had a suite on the floor right above him.

So he used to take me out, and we were drinking champagne at all the best clubs in New York. He had all kinds of gimmicks, but I wouldn't take any money from him. We became friends. At the same time the strike was going on, he'd come to the country club in Connecticut on a Sunday. He wanted to prove to his lawyer that he could find me, and he'd stay and talk to me at lunchtime.

The strike lasted maybe five months. We gave him a lot of

trouble. He said he went through a lot of money, maybe a million dollars.

So he says, "What do I have to do with you, Max? Pay you off?"

But I wouldn't do it. I told him, "I won't take your money —from you or anybody else. You got to organize or I don't want it."

"But I don't want to organize," he said.

The strike was against the warehouse. But Howard said that if I'd get this organized, eventually it would force him into signing with us for the restaurants and everything else. The hotels and so on. I said I wouldn't interfere.

"You wouldn't do it," he said, "until somebody else comes around, and then you'd be forced to cooperate."

So I struck him on and on.

Meanwhile, Howard would come to pick me up with his chauffeur and take me to Billingsley's place, the Stork Club, in New York. We'd have dinner there, and we'd be drinking down martinis. Then later he'd take me to the Copacabana. And he'd order champagne. And I would drink with him whenever he drank.

And while we were out drinking together or while he was visiting me at the country club, his lawyers would still be out looking for me to serve the injunction papers to stop the strike.

It went on like that. But we were drinking too much, and I told him so. "In the long run," I said, "you'll go by the way-side."

"No. I don't drink just with anybody all the time like this," he says. "I'm only drinking like this with you because I want to see how you can take it, because I didn't think you could." And he said, "I figured I'd get you drunk, you'd shut out, and maybe you'd make a deal and walk away from me. But you never got drunk."

I didn't. I was cautious. I was eating well. I didn't just gobble it down, and I was healthy and strong.

So the strike continued. But finally, after about five months, I walked away from him. I would destroy him, but I didn't want it. He became so friendly with me, and I figured I didn't have the manpower for the other places. And here he gave me the right answers. Also, I had been tipped off by Howard himself that the McClellan Committee was investigating me, and so I figured I had to be a little careful.

Howard was older than me. He was married to his second wife. She had a son, and the son went to college, and they were breaking him into the business. Later, Howard died, and the son became president of the company.

So the McClellan Committee was investigating me, and they were supposed to be looking into union corruption. I could have pointed them in a few directions, but they never asked.

Meanwhile, I knew how it worked. I watched it happening. Almost without notice, without any publicity, it had been going on for years. It affected millions of workers, and millions more could fall into line. It's what happens when you don't organize legit—the worker gets picked up by the independent, and the mob steps in.

The independent union is usually strictly controlled by the mob. The tough guys, they got the cronies, and they see a company has trouble with the union, or has been approached by a union. So the mob guy finds out, or maybe the employer goes to see them, to see if maybe they can help. Or the boss gives them money, to pay off whoever is bothering him. Okay. So the wise guy from the mob asks the union to take a walk, which he does.

Next thing, the mob or its front people sit down with the boss, and they tell him, "Now look, you're gonna have a problem every day and every week. You never know. Here, you sign this contract with us, and we set up an independent union. Give us the applications. Pay the dues for the people, and maybe some welfare and insurance. You'll be protected. Anybody comes around, you got a union contract.

The guy that heads the phony union is also in the mob. So they can put the muscle on anyone trying to organize legit. If there's some characters that don't want to pay attention to that, you can still fight them with the labor board. So you use the government to beat them down. Because the boss knows that if he goes to the labor board, the board will say the independent is the same thing as the more legitimate union. It shows you got an agreement going. Three years, five years, ten

221

years, whatever—it doesn't matter, because in a few years they just renew the same lousy deal, and the workers have to live with it.

That's how they run the racket. And they get thousands of dollars a day, or a week—whatever's coming in. And the ones paying are the people working there, because they're not getting a legitimate union, with a legitimate income or pension or job security or welfare.

Sometimes the independent might connect up to a larger international, or to a labor federation like the AFL–CIO to make it look more legitimate, but it's still run on a local level, and there isn't much the international or labor federation can do. So maybe you get a deal where the employers pay off the mob, then they do what they want with the employees.

The employer doesn't think there's anything bad, only that he can hire more freely than he can through a legitimate organization. He can operate any way he wants.

All of a sudden they come with a new contract when the old one expires. They give the workers a five-dollar raise. Maybe a legitimate union would get him a forty-dollar raise. And the pension and welfare is set up. Whatever they get, the pension is set up for themselves. But the mob uses all that money.

So these people have a setup. They operate, and nobody touches them. Because if anybody touches them they get told to take a walk. They don't take a walk, they'll get knocked off.

35

One time my wife and I were out driving somewhere in Long Island, and I was wearing dark glasses because I knew the McClellan Committee was investigating me. That had been going on for weeks or months, and I didn't want to make things easy for them because I think they were looking to give me a subpoena then. So Jean and I are out driving, and I got the dark glasses on and I stop for a red light. Now some car pulls up alongside me, and someone yells out, real loud but friendly, "Hello, Max!"

It was some guy I knew—he recognized me right away. It was funny, because everywhere I'd go, there'd be people that knew me. And it's like I was supposed to be hiding. And my wife asked me, after this car pulled up, "You think you're traveling and nobody recognizes you. You're supposed to be hiding?"

When the McClellan hearings finally came up, what was supposed to be the senate's big investigation into union corruption—the "investigation of improper activities in the labor or management field"—I wasn't incognito anymore, if I ever was. Because they built me up as a star witness.

Before it was over, they would have me on the stand almost a full week. Like with the Teamsters, the story would make headlines all over the country, with Bobby Kennedy doing most of the questioning and me giving Bobby a hard time and a lot of people enjoying the show.

223

The hearings were held in the spring of 1958, in the caucus room of the U.S. Senate Office Building in Washington, D.C. You had the senate committee there and the legal staff and all the assistants. Several hundred spectators were jammed in, plus reporters from all over, photographers and TV people, and all their equipment.

Senator John McClellan, the Democrat from Arkansas, was the presiding officer of the senate committee. The other committee members were Senator Sam Ervin, Jr., the Democrat from North Carolina, and then the Republican senators, Barry Goldwater of Arizona, Carl T. Curtis from Nebraska, and Senator Irving M. Ives from New York.

Bobby Kennedy was chief counsel. The chief investigators were Walter May, George Martin, and John Cheasty. They had a number of legal people, like George Kopecky, who went over some of the union contracts and paperwork. And then all these guys had their assistants. So that was a lot of high-powered people. They had the resources of the U.S. government; they investigated for months, and they spent at least a couple million dollars to see what they could come up with —which I figured was mostly a lot of bullshit. But still, when I came up to take the stand, I would have to face all that— and Bobby Kennedy.

The public was given the idea the McClellan hearings would be a widescale investigation into union corruption. The senate committee could have done that, because like I said, you've got these phony independent unions, thousands of people in every city, and all kinds of stuff going on all over the country. And Kennedy knew about that. But there wasn't much mileage to be gained by knocking down a phony union with a dozen members, or thirty or forty or even three or four hundred. So Kennedy turned the spotlight on a few large international groups, like the Teamsters, where you had thousands of truckers involved, and to the Amalgamated, which supported the Teamsters, and to a few international figures like me that had backed some Republican presidents.

If I hadn't pushed so much and built so much, Kennedy never would have bothered me, because it wouldn't be important to him—I would amount to nothing, and it wouldn't be headlines. But I was an international vice-president, and I had organized thousands of union members. I was organizing plants like the Grand Union or the A.&P., the biggest chain of supermarkets in the world. So I organized the biggest food chains, the biggest packers.

Eugene Debs had written about how I was the first one to get a union-shop contract in the packinghouses. Then too, I was friends with Jimmy Hoffa, who Kennedy hated. I had supported Eisenhower. I had made some enemies in the A.C.T.U., the Catholic Trades Union, because I had moved in and organized the A.&P., which was heavily Catholic, and the A.C.T.U. was close to Kennedy. Also, I knew Kennedy had gotten inside information, from the A.C.T.U., which recently came into the Amalgamated, and from Emmett Kelly, who was involved with the A.C.T.U. and who wanted to get me out of his way in the Amalgamated. So it was no surprise when Kennedy started putting together a case on me.

The information from the A.C.T.U. and from Kelly was about me and about Locals 342 and 640 of the Amalgamated. Mostly little bullshit, but if you're not careful, the committee could still hang you on perjury charges, and other charges could come after the hearing. I wasn't that worried. I wasn't going to stick my head in a noose and give the committee fast, easy answers just to please them. And I figured Bobby Kennedy was playing a game. He wasn't worried about corruption —he wasn't out to accomplish anything except his own purposes.

So my lawyer was Jim McInerney. Hy Zalato had introduced me to him. McInerney was godfather to Bobby Kennedy, and Kennedy called him Uncle Jim, since he used to work in McInerney's office. McInerney was a Washington lawyer, who used to be assistant to the Attorney General Tom Clark. So Jim told me that he liked me, but he couldn't take the case until he first cleared it. He went to see Bobby, to ask whether he should represent me. So he went to see Bobby and then he told me that Bobby said, "Take it. It's a clean union," and that it's okay, because I was legitimate. So McInerney represented me.

A lot of the early witnesses were questioned with an eye toward me and the Amalgamated, to see what information they might come up with that could be used against me. And some witnesses didn't handle themselves too well, creating problems, because I didn't want to agree with them and I didn't want to contradict them. Then some witnesses were just plain dumb.

There was one guy, who was testifying, and Senator Ervin asked him, "How much did you declare on your income tax?" And the guy said, "Well, I made six hundred dollars a year for the last five years."

The guy had Cadillacs, and he was working for lawyers and the labor unions and doing very well for himself. So Sam Ervin said, "You could do the country a great service, if you would explain in this time of high living and inflation how you can get by with six hundred dollars."

The guy looked at Ervin and said, "Well, I eat very little, for one thing." And then he added, "Your investigator—he's seen me fishing. I eat a lot of fish. I could eat fish six nights a week."

So he's funny. But he's stupid—a stupid ass. Guys like this had no brains. With me, first of all I had a big income legitimately. I paid my taxes. But if they'd ask me how much I paid, I would tell them I don't remember. You better ask my accountant. I wouldn't say it. They would have a hard time getting anything out of me, but I would be very polite and kill them with kindness.

I tried to tell Jimmy Hoffa that was how he should handle himself. But he was too hot-headed. This time Kennedy wouldn't get him for anything anyway.

On Monday, they started on my brother. Louie was not as calm as me. He tore into them. Louie is a bright guy, and sharp. But Kennedy tried to prove Louie was on the payroll of a medical clinic that 640 and 342 had set up for the local membership but that Louie wasn't really involved and was just getting a phony paycheck, because Louie had already retired as president of Local 640 a couple of years back.

Kennedy kept trying to get Louie confused, because he thought Louie wouldn't understand anything about the medical setup. Louie didn't go to college. He didn't go to high school. But he's smart—he knew more than Kennedy about all the medical stuff. So Louie took him apart.

So there was Louie and this guy and that guy from different organizations, and it was all built up. And in the street, people with questions and all that, they waited for me to testify with the answers. And the people in the mob that I would see, they weren't worried about anything, because they knew I wasn't going to talk about them and that I could keep my mouth shut.

For weeks, they questioned a lot of people. But after Hoffa, I was the star, and everything was brought to me. Now they tried.

When I was sworn in, I said I was in favor of them investigating all the unions and I was under the impression they would start from A to Z or go from Z to A, right down the line, investigate everything and everybody. But instead, I said, they picked out only a few unions, and that I was a good target. All I know, I told them, is that I didn't do the wrong thing. I ran a legitimate organization. I spent my money a lot of times out of my own pocket for organizing.

So Kennedy asks me the first question, I don't answer at all. I'm sitting five minutes maybe. It's a long time, and after I think it out, I give him the answer, real emphatic—"Mr. Kennedy! I don't understand the question!" And they were shocked, because they were waiting, and waiting, and they didn't know what was going on. Maybe they figured I was sick or something. But I just wanted to think back over the question. They took pictures, and I was thinking and thinking. And the investigators and the committee, about ten or eleven of them, they all burst out laughing. Later, McInerney told me why.

Because they all had warned Kennedy in advance, "You ain't going to handle him so easy. He's tough to handle." Kennedy said, "Leave him to me." So they left me to him, and they saw that with the first question, he fell apart.

So Kennedy would ask me a question, but maybe he'd be off on some detail. Like he'd ask me about my involvement with a company, whether I bought stock in it, but he wouldn't have the name of the company quite right. He didn't know, for example, that the Food Fair Company and Food Fair Properties were two different companies, and he kept getting the names wrong.

I told Kennedy I didn't know how to answer, that I didn't understand the question. And when he repeated it, he never said it the same way. So I could say I didn't understand, because the way he put things was constantly changing. Then he'd either drop the subject and go on to something else, or I'd try another answer and he'd make out he was only interested when I came up with the answer he wanted. So I would correct him, but I'd direct it. Not right away. Because I had lots of time.

Meanwhile, it made headlines. And they played the games.

Bobby Kennedy asked me a question, and it was ten different angles for ten different things. He didn't give me a general question, so I told him I didn't understand it. It went on this way until lunchtime. Then it was more of the same, with long silences between the questions and answers.

Block: Would you please repeat the question, Mr. Kennedy! I did not get the question.

Kennedy: Did you receive any stock rights from Mr. Louis Stein in connection with the Food Fair Properties?

Block: I don't understand what you mean by stock rights?

McClellan: Let me help you. You are pretending to be the dumbest labor leader I ever heard of. You know what the right to buy stock is, don't you?

Block: Yes, sir.

McClellan: All right. Did you get any rights from the Food Fair Company to buy stock, on a new issue of stock it was putting out?

Block: I don't think it is a proper question, sir.

McClellen: I don't care what you think. I am asking it, and I am asking you to answer it.

Block: I don't get the question. I want to answer it.

And it continued like that. Finally I explained: I read the paper and I also heard the Food Fair Properties was being formed, so when I met Mr. Stein somewhere in New Jersey, I think it was in Deal, I asked him about that and he agreed and said yes. I also advised him that I wanted to invest some money in it; I think it is going to be all right. He agreed to that. The only thing he asked me was how much I would want to invest.

"Oh," I said, "around twenty thousand or twenty-five thousand."

"Don't you think it is going to be a gamble?" he asked. "Why so much?"

"I have confidence that it is going to be all right," I said.

After that I got a notice from the stock firm, asking me for two thousand dollars for two thousand shares of common stock, and I sent them a check. Then I called Stein to ask about the balance I was supposed to invest, and Stein said he thought twenty-five thousand dollars was too much of a gamble.

Then it goes on some more and McClellan says to me: "Did you pay Stein or the Food Fair company anything? That is the question."

Block: I haven't bought anything . . . I never paid for . . .
McClellan: Whatever you got from them was given to you?
Block: Whatever I got I paid for, sir.
McClellan: How did you pay for it?
Block: Whichever way I was able to pay at the time I got it.
McClellan: Well, which way was it?
Block: I don't understand the question again.
McClellan: Did you ever pay Stein in cash or check or any other way for anything you got from Food Fair?
Block: Anything I received from Food Fair or any other company I paid for.
Finally McClellan says, "Unless you say you paid and make some statement about it, the record is going to reflect that you did not pay, because they say you did not pay anything."
Block: Who is "they"?
McClellan: Stein, Food Fair.
Block: I don't understand the whole question.
McClellan: you don't understand the question. The question is simple: Did you pay Stein or Food Fair for the rights you got from them to buy this stock?
Block: Food Fair or Food Fair Properties? Which?
McClellan: Well, Food Fair Properties.
Block: It is two different companies, that is why.
McClellan: You what?

Now I explained about the two separate companies, but I drove them crazy. McClellan, Kennedy, the whole bunch.

Finally McClellan asked me did I receive twenty-five thousand shares of stock, and I tell him I did. He asked how much did I pay, and I told him one dollar a share. So McClellan asked me, was it worth four dollars a share and I paid one dollar a share? I told him I thought the company robbed me out of ninety cents a share, because when I committed myself all the company had was a seal, a corporate seal and papers. They didn't have any income, they didn't have any property, they didn't have anything. Besides, I paid the same price for the stock as everybody else. Everybody that was a stockholder. And they all got the same deal, for a dollar a share. So then it's a year later and the market price is four dollars. So what has that got to do with it?

Then they bring in Kopecky, who had examined the contracts for Local 342 and retail food chains in the New York area, and Kopecky said that the Food Fair stores and another small retail chain didn't have to make per capita payments of two dollars a week into the pension fund until June 1958, while other retail chains had been paying since June 1956. So they picked this out, even though we negotiated different contracts with different groups—usually according to the area and what the situation would bear, and sometimes according to what we could get. Looking at everything, we had a good contract with the Food Fair stores. I figured he knew that, but he picked this out anyway.

Kennedy: Do you have any comment on that, Mr. Block, when you signed a different contract with Food Fair, giving them a saving of some fifty thousand dollars during the same period of time that you received these stocks and bonds from Food Fair Company?

Block: Are you asking me a question or telling me something?

Kennedy: I asked you if you had any comment on it.

Block: I can tell you quite a bit on that. I know your staff, how it works. I know you know how to investigate. But you know that this contract is the highest rate of every one in the city and is the best contract, and there is other unions, too, dealing with the same company in the same markets that don't have our type of conditions . . .

Kennedy: The only question is why you gave Food Fair this special agreement.

Block: I didn't give them anything. We don't go to an employer to give him something. We go there to get something for our people. And we get the most we can, under the circumstances. We have always obtained the best conditions for our people. The one thing you cannot talk about, is conditions in our area, because we got the finest of anybody in the country.

Kennedy: That still doesn't answer the question. Why did you give Food Fair a special arrangement, as far as this pension was concerned.

Block: We don't give. I told you we don't give.

Kennedy: You said that.

Block: A union doesn't give; it takes, and it gives it to its members.

Kennedy: Why didn't you take that two dollars from Food Fair then?

Block: Because they didn't want to give it to us.

McClellan: I see. All right.

McClellan was a smart fox, smarter than Bobby Kennedy. He stopped because he saw Bobby wasn't fooling me, and McClellan knew he couldn't get anywhere either. But sometimes McClellan would take me on, and then he would get a little hot. And Senator Ervin, when he wasn't interjecting a wisecrack, would sometimes get a little hot too.

Block: I can only say what I know and what I recollect. I can't just find an answer that would fit the program. I just answer to the best of my ability as I see it.

Senator Ervin: If I might suggest, it is not necessary to find an answer that will fit a program. All we want is an answer which will fit the truth.

Block: Senator, I am trying to tell the truth to the best of my ability.

Senator Ervin: You said you could not find an answer that would fit the program, which is a rather peculiar kind of an answer, according to my way of thinking.

Block: Well, I guess it is how you think. I mean well.

McClellan: All right.

I wasn't just playing games up there. I knew I had to be careful. By now I'd had plenty of experience talking before large groups, and I wasn't that nervous. Still, I wasn't taking any chances. So mostly, I gave Kennedy a hard time.

Kennedy: Who is Nathan Math?

Block: A lawyer.

Kennedy: Does he have any connection with the Food Fair Company?

Block: I think he does some work for them.

Kennedy: Do you discuss contracts with him, with the Food Fair Company in New York?

Block: Usually they have a man that negotiates the contracts in Philadelphia, and he comes in and takes care of the contract negotiations.

Kennedy: Would you answer my question? Do you discuss the contracts with Nathan Math?

Block: Which contracts are you talking about?

Kennedy: The contracts of Food Fair Company.

Block: I beg your pardon?

Kennedy: The contracts of the Food Fair Company.

Block: You mean the contracts of the Food Fair Company and the union, 342.

Kennedy: Mr. Block, you are not that dumb.

Block: I am not, but I don't want to answer something that I am not sure what I am going to answer to.

Kennedy: You know what the situation is. You know you have had discussions with Nathan Math, you know he is the attorney for the Food Fair Company, and you know he signs the contracts. Why act like that?

Block: I don't want to act like that.

Kennedy: Listen to the question. If you understand it, answer it. If you don't understand it, say you don't understand it. Just answer the question: Haven't you had discussions with Nathan Math in connection with the Food Fair company contracts?

Block: When?

Kennedy: Any time?

Block: I did many times.

Kennedy: All right. That is an answer to the question. The answer is "Yes"?

Block: Many times.

Kennedy: He has also signed the contracts for the Food Fair Company, has he not?

Block: I can't say that. I am not sure of that.

Kennedy: I can show you this.

Block: If you show it to me, it is so.

Kennedy: We will go along much faster, Mr. Block, if you will try to answer the question.

Block: I would like to, but I want to make sure.

Kennedy: We have a lot of things to go over with you.

McClellan: Here is what purports to be a copy of the contract between the Food Fair Company and your union. I present it to you and ask you to examine it and state if you identify it as a photostatic copy of the contract.

They hand me the document, and I confer briefly with McInerney.

Block: You don't want me to read the whole thing, do you, Mr. Chairman?

There was another spurt of laughter from the audience. Now the chairman responded with emphasis.

McClellan: No, I sure don't! Just state if you identify it. Read enough to satisfy yourself.

I read a little bit, then I confirmed that I signed the contract. But after that I gave them a hard time, because I told them I didn't know what was in the contract—I only saw my signature, and I didn't remember the contract.

On another subject, Kennedy asked me about the union's welfare fund.

Kennedy: Where did you get the money, Mr. Block, to take this mortgage from Mr. Raddock, to take it from the welfare fund on Mr. Raddock's Worldwide Press?

Block: We borrowed it from the bank.

Kennedy: So the welfare fund was having difficulty with the mortgage; it was in default. The union took it over, and the union had to borrow from the bank in order to take it over. Is that right?

Block: Well, I will give you an explanation of that.

Kennedy: That is correct, is it not?

Block: But I think it needs an explanation.

Kennedy: You can give an explanation, but that is correct, is it not?

Block: The union had—

Kennedy: Is that correct, Mr. Block? Then you can give any explanation you want.

Block: I forgot the question.

Kennedy: The mortgage . . . Oh, give an explanation.

Now I confer with McInerney, and McInerney asks me not to be so hard on Kennedy.

Block: I am sorry.

Kennedy [he appears to have composed himself, but I know he's frustrated as hell]: I will ask it again. Isn't it correct that the mortgage was in default of the welfare fund, the mortgage that was held on the Worldwide Press by the welfare fund was in default, that the union took it over and when it took it over it had to borrow from a bank in order to put up the money? Isn't that correct?

Block: It didn't have to, sir.

Kennedy: It did borrow—wait a minute. They did borrow from a bank?

Block: We did, yes. That is correct. But we didn't have to. That is what I tried to explain. We did it from a business standpoint, because the union has made money on the deal. We paid the bank all of the money by now, and we are making a full profit on the mortgage. It is a safe mortgage.

Kennedy: But they were in default for the first year.

Block: If he is in default again he will lose the building, and the union will make a lot of money.

Kennedy: He was in default in the first year and you had to pay six hundred fifty dollars in interest to the bank in that period of time.

Block: The union made money on the deal all the way. If you check the record, I am sure Mr. Kopecky knows that. He is a good man.

Now another committee member joins in.

Senator Curtis: What I would like to know, Mr. Chairman, is what rate of interest did they pay the bank and what rate of interest did Worldwide Publishing pay on this mortgage to the union.

Mr. Block: From my information, we got the money for about three percent and we got about five in return. That was for a short term. We paid the money back to the bank after a few months; as we got our money in the bank, and in our own banks, we paid it back, and now we have the mortgage with five percent interest payable every month. Our union is making money on the deal all the time. The building is worth about three hundred or four-hundred-thousand dollars. The whole mortgage is sixty thousand dollars.

So that was it. They let the subject drop.

Bobby tried to confront me with different things other guys said. So my secretary, Billy Casale, he had no business staying there, because they had already questioned him a little bit.

But he hangs around. Finally, they questioned me on something—a thousand dollars for the Republican party and a thousand dollars for the Democratic party, which we donated.

They wanted me to tell who I donated to. But they couldn't get heads or tails out of me. I said, "No. I don't remember." And one of the senators was sitting there on the committee, the senator from New York—he was shitting in his pants, because he got the thousand. But I didn't say anything.

Then we went out for lunch. I was with my lawyer, and the senator came over.

"Hello, Max. Hello, Jim." And he looks at Jim, and he says, "This guy you got here [meaning me] is a solid citizen."

But I told the senator, "That's more than you can say for yourself. You sit there like a mummy, with your mouth closed."

"Well, I can't stand up there," he said.

"I know you can't," I said. "But I have to for you."

So he got the thousand. I passed it on through Ray McGovern, controller for the state of New York under Dewey. I gave it to him, and he handed it to the senator.

I gave it to him, but I didn't squeal. No matter how they tried, I wouldn't say. Then they grabbed Billy again and put him on the road, alongside of me. They asked him. But apparently he wasn't listening while I was answering. Otherwise, he would know the answer. He was busy bullshitting. So they asked him, "But who did you give the money to? The two thousand dollars?"

"To Max Block," he says.

He could have answered like me, "I don't remember. You're talking about things that happened years ago. How do I remember what happened those years?"

Just like that, that's how I answered. And they couldn't get me who, what, and when—I wouldn't tell.

So, Billy's gone. Now I'm supposed to explain the two thousand. They didn't want no more Billy. They say to Max Block, "Who did you give the money to?"

"What are you talking about?" I said.

"The record here shows that you gave a thousand dollars to the Democratic party and a thousand dollars to the Republican party."

"So?"

"Who'd you give it to?"

"I don't recollect."

"You heard what your secretary said?"

"Well, I'm not saying he lied," I said, "He's entitled to his opinion. And that's all. He said he gave it to me, and what's wrong with that? Nothing wrong. I didn't say he didn't. But I don't remember the whole story."

So I don't remember anything. And the records showed, on a blank page, a thousand dollars to the Republican party. A thousand dollars to the Democratic party. That's all. But there was no proof of anything.

They were so frustrated, they took it off the records.

Meanwhile, I still might take four or five minutes just to answer one question. Or not to answer it. But I know who I gave the money to. The senator on the committe. And the other fellow, in the Democratic party, Carmine de Sapio, was the secretary for the New York State Democratic party. He did time a few years back. I gave him a thousand. And I gave to the others from upstate New York. Anyway, I didn't want to squeal. I wouldn't tell. I gave money to others, too.

So the committee asked about strike expenses and convention expenses. We go through more of the same routine—interrupted here and there by outbursts of laughter from the audience.

Kennedy: . . . There is this withdrawal of sixty-four hundred dollars, which is the total amount left in the bank account. I am trying to find out what happened to the money.

Block: Well, the delegates used it up.

Kennedy: Did you just give it to the delegates?

Block: Yes. How else are you going to do it?

Kennedy: Did you pass it out?

Block: I didn't.

Kennedy: Who passed it out to the delegates?

Block: The secretary of the union.

Kennedy: Mr. Lippel passed this money out to the delegates?

Block: That is how it works.

Kennedy: Is that what happened in this case—Mr. Lippel passed this money out to the delegates?

Block: Who else would?

Kennedy: Just answer the question, Mr. Block.

I took my time, then I answered him again.

Block: I imagine so.

Kennedy: Is that what you know happened? Do you know what happened in this case.

Block: Well, it can't be any other way.

Kennedy: Just answer the question. Is that what happened in this case?

Block: I imagine so.

Kennedy: Well, Mr. Block, I am asking you if that is what happened. Do you know or don't you know?

Block: That is the practice.

Kennedy: Now, did that happen in this case?

Block: I suppose that is the way it happened.

Kennedy: Do you know what happened in this case?

Block: I didn't stay there and watch. I don't know.

Kennedy: You knew the money was being withdrawn?

Block: Who drew the check? Do you have it?

Kennedy: Just answer the question. Did you know the money was being withdrawn?

Block: Of course.

Kennedy: You did?

Block: I had to know, and I didn't draw it, and I went there and lived there.

Kennedy: You knew the six thousand four hundred dollars was being withdrawn from this special convention fund?

Block: Well, that was the fund for it.

Kennedy: Just answer the question, Mr. Block.

Block: Yes, sir.

Kennedy: You knew the money was being withdrawn from this special convention fund?

Block: I knew it was going to be used, and there is the special fund for conventions.

Kennedy: Would you just listen to the question?

Block: Yes, sir.

Kennedy: Do you want to relax now and listen to the question? You knew at this time that the money was being withdrawn from this special convention fund, is that right?

Block: I imagine I knew. But I just couldn't exactly give it to you the way you would like me to answer. I would like to answer you properly, but I am not definite on the exact issue.

Kennedy: You don't recollect now?

Block: I do recollect, and I mean I don't have to recollect.

That is the way it works, and there is a convention fund, and the money was for that purpose.

Kennedy: Why was the money withdrawn at that time when the delegates already had their expenses paid and the checks issued to them in the regular way? Why was this extra money withdrawn?

Block: I imagine I must have told them to get some more money because the fellows were running short.

Kennedy: Why didn't you just make checks out? They have such things as checkbooks, and you could make out a check to the man who is running short.

Block: These fellows need cash at the bar, and they need forty dollars or twenty dollars, and how are you going to let them down, the rank-and-file members? And you must realize they got paid for their week's pay, which they lost also, in their jobs.

Kennedy: This was just for you to pass out to the delegates.

Block: It is not for me, and I did not use it.

Kennedy: You and Mr. Lippel to pass out to the delegates!

Block: Whoever needed money got it, that is all.

Kennedy: You had sixty-four hundred dollars in cash to pass out to the delegates, is that right?

Block: I imagine so. I don't know.

Kennedy: That is the purpose of the money?

Block: Well, it couldn't be any other purpose.

Kennedy: Just answer, Mr. Block. Was that the purpose of the money? Yes or no?

Block: Well, I imagine so.

Kennedy: You know, Mr. Block, and you gave the instructions to have the money withdrawn.

Block: Yes, you asked me a question if I gave instructions, and I said that I imagine so. How else could it be?

Kennedy: Now, the purpose of the money was to pass out to the delegates; is that correct?

Block: Naturally.

Kennedy: Did you keep much of this money yourself?

Block: Beg pardon?

Kennedy: Did you keep much of this money yourself?

Block: I don't recall having any money when I was on my way home.

Kennedy: Did you keep much of the sixty-four hundred dollars yourself?

Block: I imagine I got less than the delegates received.

Kennedy: Did you keep much of this sixty-four hundred dollars yourself?

Block: On my way home I didn't have any money.

Kennedy: Did you keep much of the sixty-four hundred dollars yourself?

Block: How could I keep money if I didn't have it? I don't know if I kept anything.

Kennedy: What is the answer to the question, "I don't know?"

Block: I didn't keep any money.

Kennedy: You did not?

Block: I don't go to a convention to make a profit.

Kennedy: Then the answer is "No."

Block: Of course not.

Kennedy: Is the answer "No"—that you did not keep the money yourself?

Block: Definitely not.

Kennedy: You can answer those questions?

McClellan: I don't know whether he has answered definitely he didn't keep any money.

Kennedy: Perhaps I should ask him again.

McClellan: Let me ask him once more. You answered the question that you definitely did not; and now do you mean by that you definitely did not keep any of this money?

Block: I may have kept it temporarily, but not for good, sir.

McClellan: You may not have any of it now.

Block: I didn't have it on my way home, either.

McClellan: When you left the convention, you didn't have any of this money?

Block: No, sir.

McClellan: All right; proceed.

Meanwhile, there'd be bursts of laughter from the audience.

36

My daughter came to Washington for the hearings and she sat next to Ethel Kennedy in the courtroom. So Ethel told my daughter, "Iris, tell your daddy to cooperate a little bit. Bobby doesn't sleep nights. He's gotten nervous. He's pulling his hair out."

When Iris told me that, I got slower. Lots of times I'd take four, five minutes, just thinking, before I'd respond to a single question. Then after a couple of days elapsed. I walked out. I told my lawyer I was going to the men's room, and I went. I wasn't in a hurry. I came back in maybe twenty minutes. And everybody's waiting, the whole committee and everybody else. So then my lawyer went looking for me but I was already walking in.

"Jesus!" he said. "What'd you do, you took so long?"

"I'm a union man," I said. "I'm supposed to take my time."

He laughed like hell. So they got all the live mikes, and the T.V. cameras out, and all the high-priced legal talent, and there's supposed to be a big story. They're all in a hurry. But I wasn't in a hurry. I figured what the hell—I got plenty of time.

At the end of the day, we'd go over the minutes, and there'd be nothing in the minutes that McInerney was worried about.

240

Because the committee's questions weren't answered except when I wanted to clear something up. So we had a good laugh at the whole thing.

McInerney cautioned, "Don't laugh so much. It'll be different in the papers. The headlines will run just the questions."

The next day, before we went into the hearing, I asked McInerney, "Well, how is the meeting you had with Bobby Kennedy last night?" because McInerney went to Kennedy's home every night and they discussed the issues.

And McInerney would kind of wave it off.

Then after being questioned by Bobby some more, I said to McInerney, "What the hell do they want? Kennedy knows it's a legitimate organization." Because that's what Kennedy told McInerney in the first place, when he told him it was okay to take the case.

Now Jim said to me, "He's not interested in that. He's interested in only one thing—to instill the name of Kennedy into the minds of the public and to elect his brother president." And McInerney told me how when he would go over to Kennedy's home, after the hearings and our own sessions each night, Kennedy would have half a dozen people looking over all the articles in the newspapers and marking off how many times the name Kennedy was mentioned.

So I wasn't worried, because I knew that's what Kennedy was really interested in—selling the Kennedy name to the voters. Then after a couple of nights McInerney tells me Kennedy wanted me to say yes on certain items and that Kennedy agreed that nothing would come of it.

"Fuck him!" I told McInerney, "I'll tell it as I see it."

I got back on the stand, and they wanted to know more about finances. McClellan asked, "What did you get from the counsel as president?"

I looked at him. "Headaches!"

Everybody broke up. I gave simple answers. A lot of times the committee would be shocked. They went to college, but they couldn't seem to get anywhere with me.

So they'd wear out one subject and move to another. They wanted to know about the country club.

* * *

Kennedy: Mr. Block, did you . . . approach some of the employers to become members of your country club?

Block: I don't own a country club, sir.

Senator Goldwater: Well, the Stanwich Crest Realty Corporation, which owns the country club, the country club that is on the Stanwich Crest Realty Corporation ground. Did you approach any employers to become members of the country club?

Block: I don't think I would ever approach anybody.

Senator Goldwater: Did you?

Block: They can become members as well as anybody else.

Senator Goldwater: Did you approach any employers to become members of that country club?

Block: I don't recollect any of them.

Senator Goldwater: You don't recollect?

Block: No, sir.

Senator Goldwater: How about Mr. Breslau? Did you approach him?

Block: I did not approach him or anybody else, I don't think.

Senator Goldwater: You don't think? You can't deny that you did.

Block: I can't remember it. I told you I don't get along with Mr. Bresleau to begin with.

Senator Goldwater: How about Mr. Barney Lubeck, of Grand Union Company? Did you approach him about becoming a member of your country club?

Block: No, sir.

Senator Goldwater: The answer is what?

Block: No, sir.

Senator Goldwater: You did not?

Block: No, sir.

Senator Goldwater: Did you approach any other employers?

Block: I just don't recollect any of that stuff, because I don't do any of those things.

Senator Goldwater: We had two employers who testified before the committee who said they became members of the country club and hardly ever use it, and they don't even live in the vicinity. Would you explain why they became members of the country club?

242

Block: You should have asked them that, sir. I don't know.

Senator Goldwater: I am trying to get help from you on this.

Block: I am trying to give you all the help I can, but I don't know what it is.

Senator Goldwater: One employer said he visited the country club once last year, and it cost him a thousand dollars for one visit. He said he visited approximately three times the year before, and he said he never plays golf. The other employer didn't even live in the vicinity. What I am trying to find out is this: Here you have this country club, with this investment by the insurance agency, the investment by the insurance company, the investment by the four employers, the investment by the international union, and then the membership by employers. I am trying to get an explanation. We find on the other hand that some of these employers have not had their contracts enforced. It creates a very peculiar situation to say the least, does it not?

Block: That is how you put it. I don't interfere, and I am not mixed up in any business. But it is no crime in this country to have invested a few dollars in something, in the stock market or anything else. I would rather do this than go out and stick up some employer or shake him down.

Senator Goldwater: Well, if that is your choice, maybe you are right.

So I told the committee that we didn't force the people in the trade to join our club. That it wasn't so—we were fussy. It was a privilege to join our club. We had a beautiful place, and we did a tremendous business. About one hundred fifty members. There was a thousand-dollar initiation fee and five hundred dollars a year for membership. They got a bond for their money.

When the committe would get nowhere in one direction, they'd try another. They asked me about the union's pension fund.

Kennedy: What about Mr. Breslau? . . . According to the testimony, the contract, as far as the pension fund is concerned, has not been enforced with his company, and over the period of the past four or five years, this has amounted to a saving of between twenty-five and thirty thousand dollars.

Block: Well, wait a couple more years and it will be more. However, he signed a contract like everyone else did, and only last January, when I discovered that he was behind in his payments, I called the president of their association, and they were at the office with their lawyer, I think there was a lawyer with them, and they wanted to settle with me for half payment—I mean, to begin to pay from that date.

I insisted the contract reads 1957, in March, that is what everybody owes, or else we will go to arbitration and get the thing straightened out from that angle.

Kennedy: Has he paid it yet?

Block: He hasn't paid it yet. He is still in business. He is not going away. They are a rich outfit.

Kennedy: Why has it lasted over a period of four or five years at a savings to him of some twenty-five or thirty thousand dollars, and it wasn't until after our investigation began of your union that you called him in and started to try to collect?

Block: Well, that is only your statement. I haven't said that.

Kennedy: Say something, then.

Block: I will. I am not interested in what happened twenty years ago.

Kennedy: This isn't twenty years ago. This is in the last four or five years, a savings of about five thousand dollars every year, by the fact he has not had to pay on his pension and welfare.

Block: He had a contract with C.I.O. without any pension. That part I don't know if you were told about. After all, you go according to the information you obtained, but you have not been told that. He had a C.I.O. agreement prior with him dealing with Local 640, and he never had any pension. The pieceworkers—I was not interested in that. When we had a strike about in 1957, March, I think it was, and I have all the records here, as an assocation, we had the strike and the whole industry was tied up and we settled it. He was part of it, and the contract was signed.

Kennedy: Mr. Block, that still does not answer the question.

You have a contract here calling for pension-fund payments, amounting to two dollars per employee.

They were never paid up until the time our investigation started. This was a saving to him of about twenty-five or thirty thousand dollars.

Block: You must figure from last March he owes that amount of money, and he will pay. He still didn't pay. He claims he shouldn't pay, and the contention of the union is that he pays.

Kennedy: He signed a contract. I can't understand why you don't enforce the contract. Here you have him investing five thousand dollars in the Deercrest Country Club.

Block: What do you expect me to do, go up there and shoot him with a gun? I will take him to the proper place and he will have to pay, according to the contract. I will take him into court and the labor board.

Kennedy: That is one situation. Then you have Mr. Steinman. Here is another employer that made a five-thousand-dollar-investment, who also has a contract with your union and who has not paid on the pension fund. What is your explanation for that?

Block: It is very simple. You have a lot of employers that are not paying, that have not bought any bonds from any place. When you negotiate a contract—I don't know if you ever were familiar with negotiating contracts—you negotiate and try to obtain all you can for your people, and at the same time you must look out for the industry. You don't just put them up to the wall because you want to. We are not a bunch of Communists or mobsters, putting them up to the wall. We get fine conditions and if we have a pension set up a year later, we are not worried about that, as long as the people are satisfied. That is the way it works. We did not get our pension twenty years ago. The pension is only in existence a couple years.

That's what I told them, but I wasn't going to educate Bobby Kennedy on the ins and outs from the witness stand. So some people had put off paying into the pension fund, and for others it was not in the contract for them to pay until later. The worker was still covered, I explained, out of the general fund, and the worker got conditions. We started a pension fund. Before, with the C.I.O., they didn't have any pension fund at all. I figured Kennedy probably knew that anyway.

I discussed it with McInerney, and he told me I was doing fine, and not to worry about it. Because he was still going over to Kennedy's house every night after the hearings, and he knew what was going on. And nothing had changed there.

I covered myself legally, hedging and qualifying and saying how I didn't remember this or that. McInerney had a lot of influence, and he managed to keep some of the TV coverage to a minimum somehow. But I felt a lot of stuff in the press got twisted up and was accomplishing Kennedy's purposes.

Meanwhile, my family and friends were all behind me, and my daughter was saying, "Gee, I never knew Daddy was so smart."

The committe raised a number of other issues. But as far as I was concerned, they were getting nowhere, they had nothing on me. My attorney said that if every client was like me, he'd never lose a case. So they questioned some strike expenses, other general expenses that I had over a two-year period, the fact that a chauffeur, Danny Beatson, claimed he would take me to the track and I spent a lot of time and was gambling heavy at the races. I figured this guy, who had been my chauffeur for a while, was looking to get ahead fast somehow. I said that if I spent as much time at the races as they said I did, instead of concentrating on the union, then how come I was able to organize more than all the others?

Meanwhile, Bobby Kennedy was getting more and more frustrated. And ever since Ethel Kennedy asked my daughter to try to get me to go faster and be more cooperative, I kept getting slower. At times it practically drove him up the wall.

Even so, Bobby could be sharp, I had to give him credit for that. He got on as chief counsel because of his brother John, who was a senator then and originally was supposed to be on the committe, and to my knowledge Bobby didn't have much experience. As far as I knew, it was only after he started taking on Jimmy Hoffa and the Teamsters, and me and the Amalgamated, and used all this to campaign for his brother, that he started making a name for himself.

I didn't know much about John Kennedy then. Although I

didn't like the way I had seen him act in front of Jackie, I didn't think he was such a bad guy. Teddy was younger then and not much involved in politics, and he seemed a pretty good kid. But Bobby I didn't trust, least of all from where I was sitting. He was looking to trip me up, so I was always on guard with him. It wasn't just to be funny that I took my time answering.

Now Bobby got an idea on how he was really going to screw me up. He asked about expenses for a hotel suite in the Beverly Hotel in New York. It didn't take me long to figure out what he was getting at. I knew it wasn't me that he was trying to make President of the United States.

Kennedy: Do you have a hotel suite at the Beverly Hotel?
Block: Sometimes.
Kennedy: Is that paid for by the union?
Block: Yes, sir.
Kennedy: Is that near the Black Angus Restuarant?
Block: It is about a block away.
Kennedy: How much money have you paid to the Beverly Hotel for that hotel suite?
Block: I don't have any steady suite. We use the hotel when we need it.
Kennedy: The union does, or the members of the Black Angus Restaurant.
Block: Oh, please. It is strictly used from the union standpoint.
Kennedy: Don't you have a room at the union that you could use?
Block: We use a lot of rooms.
Kennedy: Why do' you need a hotel suite at the Hotel Beverly, which is close to the Black Angus Restaurant?
Block: I just happen to know that hotel. It is a nice, clean hotel. Last Saturday we used—and we must have spent about two, three thousand dollars—the Shelton Towers.
Kennedy: How much money have you spent, has the union spent, in payment to the Beverly Hotel?
Block: I couldn't give you an exact figure on that. What period?
Kennedy: 1952 to 1957 shows $9,301.82.
Block: I think that is not too much.

Kennedy: All paid for by the union?

Block: Yes, sir.

Kennedy: Why couldn't you use the union offices?

Block: I use the union offices too.

Kennedy: We found a number of people who stayed in that hotel, with bills amounting to eight hundred or nine hundred dollars, at least, had nothing to do with the union, and their hotel bills were paid for by the union.

It went on like this. Then Kennedy mentioned the name of Betty Marshay, that there were some items, one thousand or two thousand dollars, and the bills were paid to the Beverly Hotel in New York for Betty Marshay.

And I was thinking, because now I figured Kennedy was trying to trap me. Betty Marshay used to be the wife of Wiley Post, the famous pilot. Wiley had a patch over one eye, and he made a lot of headlines because he had flown around the world a couple of times, piloting his small plane. He was killed with Will Rogers in a plane crash in 1935.

After Wiley Post was killed, Betty Marshay became a girl-friend of Pat Gorman's, and Pat kept her in Chicago. His home was in Louisville, Kentucky, and he had his wife, Hattie, there. And Pat used to go home every two weeks or so and spend a couple of days with Hattie and the family and then go back to Chicago, and Betty Marshay. Chicago was also the headquarters for the Amalgamated.

I could see that Kennedy was trying to trap me. Because after all, I'm a married man, and probably he figured I'd say that Betty Marshay was Pat Gorman's girlfriend. Then the headlines would read that Max Block squealed on his boss. And if I didn't explain, it would look like maybe Betty Marshay was *my* girlfriend. So either way it would be embarrassing. And I know Kennedy knew who Betty Marshay was.

This time I figured Kennedy was pushing too far. I looked at him. He could see I was angry. "Mr. Kennedy," I said. "This wasn't a nice thing that you brought up. However, I could say a few things too." I opened my book, a little book I had with me.

Now Bobby got scared. Because he knew how close I was to Wilbur Clark, how easy it would be for me to have gotten the dates from Wilbur of all the times Bobby and Marilyn Monroe were in the hotel suite together at the Desert Inn in Las Vegas.

Right away, Bobby backed down. "I'm sorry, Mr. Block," he said.

Bobby almost had to figure that if I was going to lay anything embarrassing on him, it would be that. Because he knew that I knew about Marilyn Monroe meeting him at the Desert Inn. And he was asking for it, the way he was trying to set me up. He knew also that I was at the Park Lane Hotel when his brother John and Jackie had that scene. Maybe he figured I would embarrass his brother John. But I wasn't going to say anything. It wasn't my style. There was nothing in the little book but blank white pages. Only Bobby Kennedy didn't know that. So he got nervous and backed away quickly.

Kennedy dropped the issue.

37

The senate committee spent months accumulating information, and they wanted to go into all of it. Before I was through they would accumulate more than a hundred pages of printed testimony.

I didn't contact Pat Gorman or the others at the headquarters of Amalgamated in Chicago. I didn't call them to help me or to hold my hand in Washington. I didn't meet with anybody during the hearings. I was in the hotel, with my staff, my secretary, Billy Casale, and some boys, and my lawyer. My wife was at home in New Rochelle, and my daughter Iris had flown down to attend the hearings.

I told Louie to go home, because I didn't want him to be called for additional questioning. And the others from the Amalgamated, they were all scared to death and shitting in their pants. They all had skeletons in the closet. But no one from the mob was nervous about my maybe slipping up or saying something. They had confidence in me. I ran into some of them later. All they had to say was they respected the way I handled Kennedy.

On the stand, Kennedy and the others asked me a barrage of questions about the mob. Did I know this guy? Did I know that guy? Did I know Carlo Gambino? Did I know Chappy Brescia? Did I try to give the union's business for insurance to

George Scalise? Did I try to help this guy out? That guy? In the end they got zero from me on that.

They showed me a picture of Carlo Gambino when he first came to the United States—a long, thin nose. Very skinny. I said I don't remember this guy at all. I wasn't going to say I didn't know Chappy Brescia, when I saw him every day. So I said, yeah, I know him. And they talked about how he was involved with the mob, and this and that, and I said, "So what? That's his business." And I said the same about the others. They asked me about a lot of people. The live ones I didn't remember too well. The dead ones I did.

The committee questioned me at great length about my son's use of a union auto that was involved in an accident and about the insurance reimbursement and about the use of union cars. And Kennedy wanted to know if I used my influence from the union to help obtain business from the A.&P., Food Fair, and other companies for my son-in-law in the cellophane business.

I asked Kennedy how he got his job. He jumped! He didn't expect me to say that.

Then Kennedy wanted to know about some other places.

Kennedy: . . . Did it happen that you threatened Waldbaum, the officials of Waldbaum?

Block: No, sir. Definitely not.

Kennedy: What about Grand Union? Did you approach them about giving your son-in-law some business?

Block: No, sir. I don't remember anything like that at all.

Kennedy: Do you deny that you approached the officials of Grand Union about giving your son-in-law some paper business.

Block: Mr. Kennedy, if I would approach all these people, my son-in-law would have done a very big job. But for three years he starved, with all these connections.

Kennedy: I think he has done very well, as I understand.

Block: He has done lately on his own. You know the records, I am sure, Mr. Kennedy. So they dragged that out, and it went nowhere.

The committee questioned the union approving expenses for my wife on a trip to Florida with me, and they questioned some general expenses on my trips to Florida.

Kennedy: You got $2,607 from the international as advances to go, and another $1,007 from Local 342, and then above and beyond that your hotel rooms, pool, the solarium, the masseur-oil boy and the cabana were all charged to the union. Do you have any comment on that? That is on those four trips to Florida, above and beyond the other expenses you had, they amounted to $9,372.65, the trips to Florida.

Block: In most cases this was business trips. In all the cases I may have had a little pleasure with it for a few days.

Kennedy: You must have had a good deal of pleasure on that last one.

Block: Very little.

Kennedy: How could you spend so much money?

Block: You don't have pleasure with money. You can have pleasure without money.

Kennedy: You are the one that has pleasure with money.

Block: No; I have more pleasure when I don't spend money.

Kennedy: You were able to fight it off this time and have pleasure anyway, because you spent over four thousand dollars; it is around one hundred sixty-five dollars a day.

Block: It must have been—you know . . .

Kennedy: Beyond that, Mr. Block, there is $6,491.35 which is charged to disbursements for flower bills, photographs, cigars, and telephone calls from your home, all charged to the union.

Block: I don't understand that.

Kennedy: I will give you some examples: $180.81 charged to Local 342 for cigars; $81.37 for photographs; $160.11 for lingerie; $180—

Senator Ervin: Maybe that is a union suit.

Block: I will explain that.

Kennedy: And flowers are $5,048.10.

Block: Do you want me to explain it? I would like to if given permission.

Kennedy: I am bringing out all of these things so you can explain them.

Block: Please, Mr. Kennedy, I would appreciate it very much if you would allow me.

McClellan: Go ahead.

Block: The way you read it off here, of course, is as you have it; I appreciate that. But it does not sound right. When

252

you talk about cigars and lingerie; lingerie, I will tell you what it was, if you look up the dates: It is at Christmastime when we have all the girls in the office getting gifts. We buy them one year lingerie, another time maybe a bag, another time stockings, and down the line. That is where the lingerie comes in. I guarantee you it was not bought for my family. It was strictly for the office and office girls. You talked about flowers. What could I do as an individual with that amount of flowers? It is worked through the office, and it is sent out to different members or employers that may have an occasion, either a birth, death, or something, and that is where we send them (The cost of the flowers was also for a number of years.)

That sounds big, but you must realize the size of the organization, but we have a lot of people we are dealing with, and we have a lot of organizational friends. And the cigars I will answer, too. This year, apparently, they bought for me cigars for the year for Christmas. I didn't know anything about that. They are drying up in the office anyhow. I don't have too much time to . . . smoke them.

However, that is the way it is. It doesn't sound right when it is read off the record about lingerie and all of that, but this is all explainable because it is so.

Now Kennedy would accept the explanation about the lingerie but he would question the sending of flowers to my daughter's wedding. Then he took the combined union salaries of me, my brother, my brother's brother-in-law, my sister, added it all up over a three-year-period, and said it was a lot of money. And they questioned some other expenses.

My attorney would still say to me, "You chopped 'em up, but wait till you see the papers."

The issues came out, and it became more apparent to me that Emmett Kelly was involved, working with the A.C.T.U. from New York, ratting, making up stories, and so on.

That was Danny Beatson. So now Kennedy had testimony from him, and he asked about a big strike we had.

Kennedy: Mr. Block, once again, Mr. Beatson said that you did not spend the money out there. We are trying to find out what happened. You got ten thousand dollars, and he says that the most you spent was twenty-five hundred dollars, and he was in charge of the strike.

Block: He said so? I can't believe it!

Kennedy: Will you tell me what happened?

Block: I know how big the strike was, and I thought we spent more than that.

I figured Kennedy knew how you had to pass money around sometimes to get things done. But now Kennedy was telling me how I should be shocked. So we continued the game, back and forth.

Kennedy: . . . Is there any other explanation you want to give on it then? What I think is the thing to explain is the checks to cash. I think that is what needs the explanation.

Block: First of all, Mr. Kennedy, I did not sign the check. I am not the bookkeeper.

Kennedy: You signed a letter asking for the ten thousand dollars.

Block: There is nothing wrong there. I didn't ask to send it to me. It was not made out to me. I did not put it in my pocket. It was sent to the organization. I think the organization spent more than ten thousand dollars at that time.

We'd exhaust one issue, and then Kennedy would have another.

The senate committee started comparing a forty-hour week on the one hand to a forty-five-hour week we settled for with A.&P., and the committee overlooked that the Amalgamated contract with A.&P. was stronger in all other areas and that where you had the forty-hour week they got paid by the hour anyway. Then there was the most important thing, that you've got to scale the work to meet the competition, so nobody gets hurt. Otherwise, if you organize only the one shop and get too much, you're destroying your own jobs for your people—the way the A.C.T.U. did with Safeway.

But the committe wasn't interested in how many hours they were working in the surrounding areas, or that we had the best of all the contracts in the area. They wanted to pin down that I made a secret agreement with the A.&P.—to continue a forty-five-hour week—and that I knew about phony ballots in the A.&P. election.

But I wasn't about to be pinned down.

Senator Ervin: Mr. Block, when I was a small boy, I used to go to carnivals, and in all the carnivals they had down in my county they had one operation where a man would charge you a nickel and give you three balls and you could throw the three balls at an employee of his who stood about forty feet away and stuck his head through a hole in the canvas. It was his business to dodge those balls. Now, if you happen to hit him with one of those balls, the man who operated this concession had to give you a prize. If you missed, he didn't give you anything and he kept your nickel as profit.

From having observed you as a witness and seeing how you dodge questions, I would like to make arrangements to get you to be my dodging man in the carnival, because nobody would ever hit you and everything would be clear profit. I have spent a large part of my life in a courthouse listening to witnesses being examined, and I have never seen a person who resorted to dodging process to evade a simple answer to a plain and simple question, who possessed the skill which you have demonstrated in that respect to this committee this morning.

Meanwhile, Kennedy was still adding up figures.

Kennedy: You have a special insurance policy, don't you, the officers of the union.

Block: I don't understand the question. I don't understand the whole procedure there on the policy.

Kennedy: You have a ten thousand dollar policy while the rank and file have two thousand dollar policies, and that has cost the Local 640 $4,223.14.

Block: How many years?

Kennedy: In the last ten years.

Block: I knew it was very cheap. That is why I could not understand why the thousands were in there.

Kennedy: But you knew, then, that you had a different one than the rank-and-file members?

Block: I did.

Now Kennedy makes a report to the chairman about my responses.

Kennedy: Mr. Chairman, we have added up Mr. Block's

statements of "I don't recall," or "recollect" or "remember," which totalled one hundred eleven times, and he equivocated in his answers eighty-eight times.

So what does that prove?

McClellan: The counsel for the A.&P. stores requested that this question be directed to you. Do you know of any other labor–management contract in the New York retail food business from 1952 to 1957 that could match the A.&P. contract in advantages for butchers and clerks?

Block: In my opinion, this is the best in the country.

McClellan: Your opinion is it the best?

Block: And to my knowledge it is surely the best in the eastern area.

Some of the questions dragged on, and they didn't always get fast answers. I hadn't come to help Kennedy. I wanted to help myself. When Kennedy raised questions about whether I misused money from the pension fund, or pocketed other union money or got free stock from the Food Fair Properties or the A.&P. in return for supposedly soft contracts, he had the wrong guy, and he knew it. He didn't come there to prove anything about me. He was looking to get the name Kennedy in the headlines.

So I got some stock in the A.&P., and they asked about that.

Senator Irvin: The question is whether, when you purchased stock in the A.&P. Tea Co., if you purchased it in the open market at the market price on the stock exchange?

Block: Yes, sir.

Senator Irvin: Through your broker?

Block: Through the broker, yes, sir.

So it was like I told them. Any stock I got, I paid for, at the market price, same as anybody else.

The only fact, I knew that the A.&P. was going to split ten to one, and it was one hundred sixty dollars or one hundred sixty-five dollars a share. I figured at ten to one, automatically it'll go up. So I bought some, and I told some friends to buy, and the reason I knew the A.&P. was going to split was because the president was retiring, or about to die, and new ideas were coming in; they had been very conservative. So I remember, the guy I negotiated with most of the time, Charlie Schimmit's assistant, a fellow by the name of Hamburger, mentioned to me that they were going to have some changes in the structure, in the stock, and that they were going to split it. That's how I knew. So I went ahead and bought some stock for one hundred sixty or one hundred sixty-five dollars a share.

They split the stock ten for one, to about sixteen dollars a share. After awhile, it went up to fifty nine. That meant five hundred ninety dollars, from about one hundred sixty-five. So I sold it. I was right. Originally I bought about twenty-five thousand dollars worth. I sold it for four times that and made a lot of money. But like in any business, you hear something, you have to move. It was nothing special.

So I was making a big income. I didn't have to pocket the union's money, but Kennedy would lump things together, sometimes adding expenses up over a period of years. He knew better, but to keep getting the headlines he implied that I was misusing expense money. And he kept coming back to stories he got from my former chauffeur, Danny Beatson.

Kennedy: During the period 1955 and 1956, Mr. Block, there were expenses to you for that two-year period of $26,705. That is above and beyond the salary. There are no records at the union supporting that. According to the records we have here, it was not reported to the Labor Department on the records that we have examined there, which are supposed to list expenses. Can you tell us anything about that money? According to Mr. Beatson, who stated that he was with you continuously for a long period of time, you were out at the racetrack all the time spending large sums of money. This is $26,000, or more than $26,000, in expenses during this two year period. Can you tell us how that was used? There are no vouchers in the union.

Block: I don't know how you got those figures. That is why I couldn't answer. I get a certain amount of money with expenses on a check, and I don't know about any other way how you got it figured. That is why.

Kennedy: This is the expenses during the period of time in which there are no vouchers. I expect if I show you these checks you are going to give the same answer that you did on the five hundred dollars, that it is small amounts and therefore you have no explanation.

Block: You give a figure of $26,000 for two years.

Kennedy: I thought that was more to your liking. You didn't like it when I brought up just the five hundred. Now I am trying—

Block: When you put it together it sounds bigger. However, it isn't bigger.

Kennedy: During the period 1955-57, there are $86,507.02 checks drawn to cash for which there is also no explanation. We are getting higher.

Block: It sounds pretty big, but if you check the records of our organizational problems we have been through in the last four or five years or six years, we had tremendous expenditures. You can't attribute that to me. I mean, I just receive salary and expenses, fixed, and very seldom additional.

Kennedy: I am trying to get the facts from you, Mr. Block.

Block: It is a big organization.

Kennedy: We examined the books and records of the organization, and there are no vouchers whatsoever. If there were vouchers of any kind on this, we could discuss it. But there are no vouchers, but just the checks, and checks drawn to cash: $86,507.02, and your expenses above and beyond that were $26,705, for which there are no vouchers.

Kennedy went on at length, too, about the five hundred dollar item, where the records were unclear concerning payment for Israeli Bonds.

Kennedy: Where is the five hundred dollars.

Block: Whatever the record shows—

Kennedy: The record traces it to you. That is why I am asking you the question.

Block: And if it traces to me, I could swear on a bible that it was legitimate, and I used it for the purposes that it was intended.

Kennedy: Where?

Block: I don't know. It is in 1955 (three years earlier). It is put to me. I mean, it is not fair, Mr. Kennedy. It is a small issue for our type of organization, and I am not hungry for a dollar, or five dollars. I would not do that. I would not lower

258

myself to do anything like this. That is why I am surprised with you confronting me with stuff like this.

Kennedy: It is just petty?

Block: It is not in my class.

Kennedy: If you were going to take money, you would not take just $500, right? Is that what you mean?

Block: I never was so money hungry that I would do anything like that. I would rather spend out of my pocket than take an extra dollar from the union.

Kennedy: Mr. Block, all I am asking you to do is explain the five hundred dollar transaction. The union is out five hundred dollars.

Block: Mr. Kennedy, I appreciate your efforts, but you must appreciate my position. You know I just can't give you an answer on something like this that I don't recollect in 1955, a transaction like this.

Kennedy: This is pretty important. You are president of the union. Somebody has taken off with five hundred dollars. It appears to be you. I am trying to get an explanation of it.

Block: You know I wouldn't do that.

Kennedy: Frankly, Mr. Block, I don't know that.

But of course that wasn't what Kennedy had to say about me when McInerney asked him if he should represent me.

So I couldn't account for every five hundred dollars, especially after a period of a couple years, and neither could any other union president, and Kennedy knew that. If you were going to steal five hundred dollars, there were easier ways to do it than to have it show up on the books, and Kennedy knew that too, or should have.

Of course there was a lot of stuff that went on in all the unions. There's always going to be somebody making a buck. It was the same as in a bank. So in a bank, the manager or the president or one of the vice presidents, or one of the key men in position, suppose he may be charging you one point under the table, and he allows you the loan. The money he makes he splits with somebody else on the board. But you pay in cash, it's not something that goes on the books so someone like Kennedy can have an easy shot at you. It doesn't work that way.

In the bank they may take five points, and they may take ten, and you may get a better deal. You're entitled to a hundred thousand dollar mortgage; maybe they give you a hundred fifty thousand dollar mortgage, sometimes close to the full amount of the whole property. However, with the union funds and elsewhere, at the rate everything was going up, nobody lost anything. Everybody made a lot of money, including the funds—whatever they made.

Kennedy and the investigators should have figured that out. At one point they questioned the auditing by the international.

Senator Curtis: What was the nature of those audits?

Kopecky: Similar to that prepared by the C.P.A. They accept the books and records as prepared by the local unions, and made an extremely limited investigation.

Senator Curtis: Well, I think the whole procedure is a fraud upon the members of the union.

Kennedy: Someone could take thousands of dollars out of the union and it would never be detected by this method of auditing.

Kopecky: That is right. As far as the international union is concerned, they attempt to train and educate rank and file members and union members who show an interest in records and bookkeeping and accounting, and attempt to explain to them what should be done. But these are not trained accountants.

So what did they expect, that the international was going to try to indict itself in the investigation? Kennedy might have better pointed out that when someone makes a buck it's usually done in cash, on the side, and doesn't show up on the books anyway. Or that if you wanted to smooth over anything illegitimate on the books you wouldn't rely on poorly trained accountants to do it.

As to Kennedy challenging the way I passed out money at conventions, or strikes, or in organizing, we didn't just pass out money. We passed out what the members were entitled to, what we agreed upon for them to use. And if the members ran short, we had extra money. We cashed a check, and we gave it to them anyway. But we didn't give it to just one. We gave it to everybody. All the business agents and delegates alike. They would be rank and file members, too.

So they had nothing on me, and as for getting stock in the Food Fair Properties for a dollar a share and later selling it at four dollars a share, I bought it for the same price as everybody else. I bought A.&P. shares too. It wasn't a crime to invest a few dollars in stock. Of course I also sold it and made a profit. But wherever I made a profit, I paid tax. And whether I paid for the stock by check or by cash, they tried to make it look funny. But I didn't buy the stock all at one time, so I didn't recollect how much was check, how much was cash. I said I didn't remember. And I told the truth. I paid for it, and they knew it was legitimate, but it sounded good for their case.

Naturally there's a fine line as to how you do favors in business when you're dealing with friends. But almost all the people I dealt with became my friends. Even my enemies became my friends, most all of them. So you can benefit, the way Bobby Kennedy probably got his job on the committee with the help of his brother, or the way John benefitted from the headlines his brother was making during the hearings. We're human beings, and it doesn't matter that much whether you're a banker, businessman, labor leader. The only thing, all the so-called tough guys that are supposed to be from the mob happen to have done more than the characters sitting around doing nothing.

Then according to the constitutions in the labor movement, in order to hold office you have to be a member of the union. So a truck driver drives a truck. So who is he. He's not a little sissy. He's a big strong man. He feels tough. Now he's selected to be a business agent. Then he grows in the union a little more, and he's a tough man, and he can fight, and maybe he did something and maybe he didn't. And that's how it happens, and how it works. It's nothing unusual. It's the same with the plasterers, or the bricklayers. They're tough men, because they do tough work. And this is how it develops. And then this guy happens to have a neighbor who somehow is a little shady with the mob, and this guy's got an uncle or a nephew somewheres, and that's the connection. But it's the same thing with any other business.

❖   ❖   ❖

261

By the end of the week, late Friday afternoon, the committee still had gotten nowhere with me. Kennedy wanted to continue. There was a holiday weekend coming up; they were trying to decide whether to go into a night session, and they were in a huddle. Meanwhile, Kennedy forgot to turn off his microphone. So their conversation came over the mike. McClellan said to Kennedy in his long southern drawl.

"You let that son of a bitch go! You ain't gonna get nothin' out of him!" And Kennedy, hearing the echo in the Senate chamber, grasped at the mike, but it was too late. Everybody in the room was laughing.

So they let me go and that was it.

38

Some things take a long time. Seven or eight years before the hearings, I had applied for a two-hundred thousand dollar life insurance policy. I already had a few small policies and the tests always showed sugar in my urine. Because of this they charged me more for the premiums. So what does that mean—I'm a sweet guy?

Now to get the new policy, the company wanted me to take a more extensive examination. So I go down to their offices on Seventh Avenue, across the street from the Penn Station. They had this Doctor Hershey, in charge of the whole examination. They still found sugar in my urine. That's all they said. But they wanted me to see this doctor that was supposed to be a heart specialist from Austria.

I go see the guy. I'm in the office, and he makes me run up and down a ladder, real fast. After this, they got me in a dark room, and they had this thing, a fluoroscope, like a screen they looked through. They put it up against my chest. Sort of a live X-ray, like television. So they see what's going on inside you. And my heart was pumping fast, after running up and down the ladder.

Now they use the fluoroscope only in special cases, because of the high exposure to X-ray. But those days, they would use the procedure a lot more. So it was dark, but it was like he was looking through me. The technology was really something.

"Doc, what are you looking at?" I asked. "Something wrong with my heart?"

"Yes," he said, "You've got an enlarged heart."

I says, "How can you tell?"

And he told me, "Because you have a large heart."

So I said to him, "Doc, I also have a large cock. A size-nineteen neck. I have a big chest. I'm built big. What do you expect me to have—a little heart?"

It must have shocked him. He says, "What did you say?" So I told him again.

Then we went out, and he repeated what I said, to Doctor Hershey, because possibly he didn't quite understand me. So Doctor Hershey says, "Maybe Block has got something." Then they called in some other specialists, and they checked me some more. Finally, they decided. My heart is perfect—I just had a large heart. Meanwhile, the bum can give you a heart attack, telling you you got an enlarged heart.

I got the two-hundred-thousand-dollar policy. They didn't tell me anything else, except that I had sugar in my urine, and they charged me a little more for the premiums because of that. That was the same thing they would always tell me, so I didn't think anything of it.

Then, a few months before the senate hearings, I was at our country club, on a Saturday night in Greenwich, Connecticut. I was drinking screwdrivers, and after a while I felt funny and I didn't know what it was. I walked outside for some air. About a half hour later, my wife came out after me. She was looking for me in the dark, and she found me lying there stretched out, unconscious.

The next thing I knew, it's like Jean woke me up. I went inside and had a glass of milk, because I drank too many screwdrivers. After that, I went to our doctor in New York, and he gave me some pills to take. But he didn't really explain anything to me.

I had started feeling a little funny during the hearings, and soon after that it was like my body wasn't acting quite right. I was always strong as an ox. It wasn't anything severe, but I just didn't feel good. And all that drinking with Howard Johnson didn't help any. We used to drink a bottle of gin and a couple bottles of champagne every other night. And Pat Gorman was always a heavy drinker, and I'd drink with him.

Most of the guys on the board were drinkers. And people would come into the Black Angus, buddies, and I'd join them for a drink.

But no doctor or medical person ever told me anything, except that I had sugar in my urine—they didn't tell me what that could possibly mean or that I should watch my diet or cut down on my drinking, or anything else. So the condition would go on for years and years.

Meanwhile, there was a lot of pressure on me. I had the minutes of my testimony at the senate hearings sent on to Jimmy Hoffa, and we discussed it together. Mostly I wanted to give him an idea how to handle things, because he was being called back to testify at the hearings. But Jimmy was too hot-headed.

Beck ran off, when they subpenaed him. Now Jimmy had to answer to the committee. Yet he felt he didn't have to take any crap from Kennedy, so he would argue. Sometimes it would get very heated. And Kennedy grew to hate him. Hoffa beat the case—they couldn't hang anything on him from the hearing—but he made an enemy. And Kennedy would hound him for years.

That kept some heat on me. And I was waiting for the follow-up to the hearings—the proceedings had been forwarded to the Treasury Department and the Department of Justice and to the District Attorney of New York County for "appropriate action." I wasn't worried. McInerney was still close to Kennedy. He knew what was going on, and I figured they didn't have anything on me.

But the Amalgamated worried about Kennedy. Now pressure to force me out came from the A.C.T.U. and that group, working with Kelly. Kelly had organized some of the butchers on a small level, but he still didn't want to organize the chains. He was involved with a lot of stuff, making a buck where he could. So if there was too much heat, his own operation might surface for inspection.

Mostly, I gussed, Kelly wanted me out of the way so he'd have a clearer path to calling the shots at the Amalgamated, which he felt he should have inherited from his father.

Then I was notified by the district attorney's office. They were ready to hand down three indictments. I still wasn't worried, I figured my actions were legitimate and they didn't have anything on me. I had received a two-thousand-dollar check from the insurance company for the car that was wrecked in the accident my son had, and the check remained in my desk a while. At the hearing, Kennedy implied I was going to just keep the money. But the dealer, Herb Kaplan, a big Buick dealer located in South Brooklyn, told me to wait until the new cars were out. I waited; eventually the check was deposited in the union's bank, and we got the new car. The other two possible indictments were actually part of the same case, but I felt they got the indictment in order to create problems for me or to force me to resign and make Kennedy look good.

Lansing Shield, the president of Grand Union, was a fine gentleman. He was friendly with Frank Hogan, the district attorney from New York County, and he spoke to Hogan about me—what a good man I was and so on. So Lansing arranged a meeting between Hogan and me, and the two of us went for lunch at the Addison Hotel, on Fifty-third Street near Park Avenue.

Although I had never met Hogan, four or five of his assistants from the D.A.'s office had questioned me before the senate hearings started. They wanted me to tell what I knew about the mob, about the mob's influence in the unions.

"What are you going to do," I told Hogan's men. "Tell this guy, 'You have to stay out of the union' because he's involved with the mob? How can you do that? They'll say you're nuts. They'll take over the local and maybe even knock you off. And for what? There's no record of any kind that they're even in the union. So how can you take this guy's name off a record that doesn't exist, tell him he can't have anything to do with the union? You just can't do that."

Finally, I said, "All the questions you ask me—if you think you got a lot of work to do, why don't you go out and do it? You kept me over here and wasted my days."

"You know what you told us all day?" one of them said then.

"What?" I asked.

"Look." And he took his thumb and finger and made a circle, a zero.

"I'm not working for you," I told him. "I'm not working for the city. I'm not working for the police department. That's not my job. I got my own headaches. But if you know all these things that you asked me about, then you got a lot of work to do. Go do it."

So now I went to lunch with Hogan, the D.A.

We talked about a million things. Then he said, "Max. What do you need it for? You don't need all this business now. You're in good shape. You make a good living." And he kept telling me, "Why don't you resign and we'll drop everything? We won't bother you because you won't be a headline any more."

"It isn't a question of being a headline," I said. "It's only a question of not being guilty of anything."

But I weakened anyhow. I told Hogan I'd think about it. I felt sick. I was a little scared because I didn't know what was happening with my body. I'd get sleepy or drowsy. I was starting to lose weight, even though I still ate a lot. I didn't have much energy.

It was diabetes. But in those days I didn't understand it, and the doctor didn't tell me. They didn't know about it, how to control it, like now. Finally I sat down with Jack Lloyd, president of the Amalgamated, and Harry Pool, a vice-president, and another vice-president. We made a deal, that I may as well go instead of fighting—they would have had to fight like hell to get me out, otherwise—and I resigned and took my retirement. That would take some of the heat off the Amalgamated.

39

I thought I could use a rest. After the McClellan hearings I went to Canada for a couple of weeks, and I get a telephone call from Louie. Pat Gorman's wife, Hattie, came to the Black Angus, and she insisted that Louie get hold of me. Pat had gone off to Europe for vacation, but Hattie kept saying that if he was around he'd be against my stepping out.

I knew that. Pat supported me during the hearings, and he would continue to do so. After he came back, I still called the shots as far as he was concerned. Any time I called or wrote a "love letter," whatver I wanted he did anyhow. And it would go on like that for years.

So I had Pat behind me. And if it wasn't for my being sick with diabetes, and not knowing what the problem was, they'd never get me out, because I still had four or five years left on my term of office.

There was only one guy at the time who was familiar and capable of handling Local 342—the others considered were too inexperienced—so I suggested him to Pat Gorman, and he took over after I left. But still a lot of membership and power shifted. Local 640, which I had been running since Louie retired, was merged into Local 174, under Frank Kissel. After a while, so was Local 400, because now it had all the A.&P. members.

Officially the three top leaders of Local 174 were Kissel, Harry Stubach, and Karl Muller, Stubach was president of the Local, but he didn't say much. Kissel ran the operation, fronting for the mob. And Kelly would give directions to Muller. So Muller and Kissel, working with Kelly and the A.C.T.U. group, and some of the others in the mob, now controlled the largest local and the central organization in the Amalgamated. But you had a lot of jockeying going on, with people seeking to fill the spots after I left. I had a lot of titles—now they had to distribute the jobs.

Meanwhile, Kaplan assumed more leadership in New Jersey. But I had helped build his local, from a handful of members to thousands, when they got all the A.&P. members. Originally, in his younger days, Kaplan was a lieutenant of the Longie Zwillman mob. Longie had been put in by Lucky Luciano.

And in New York, Kissel, Stubach, Muller, I knew these guys from before they were born. I figured they were no good. Not killers. Just bad eggs with no balls. Time would show they were involved in a lot of rackets.

A pattern began to emerge. They stopped organizing, leaving the shops to be signed up with the independents that were strictly mob controlled.

Since I left the Amalgamated they must have given up at least a thousand butcher shops that I had under contract. They did not renew when the contracts ran out. These shops signed up racket groups. And the monkeys would be afraid to move or to open their mouths. But with me, these other characters couldn't move in.

When they came for a sit-down, they were told. And then if they didn't like it, they got killed. I didn't kill anybody. But Little Augie Pisano, George Scalise's godfather, all of a sudden you read in the papers that Augie and Scalise put Louie and me into the butcher's union originally, in the early thirties. Little Augie never called the shots, despite what they said in the papers.

There was a fellow, Marcus, a labor lawyer. He was testifying against George Scalise, a mob guy. And George Scalise was vice-president of the international for the Building Services Union. Bill McFetridge was the president of the international. Scalise was also in the same mob as Little Augie. They were all from different Mafia families.

So I knew Augie, and Scalise. In the late twenties and early thirties my sister worked for Scalise in the union offices of the Building Services International, and so I ran into him a lot. Later, a fellow named Sol Cilento, who was close to Augie, used to hang around me. So that was another reason I would sometimes be identified by others as associated with Scalise and Augie. In 1955, Cilento was indicted with Scalise and Little Augie on charges of a three-hundred-thousand-dollar kickback scheme involving insurance funds from the Distillery Workers' and Liquor Salesmen's Union.

In the early thirties, Augie and Scalise tried to start a local for the butchers in New York, but they got nowhere with it, except maybe a reputation for being involved in a butchers' union. So I knew these guys for years. They'd say hello, but that's about the size of it—I had nothing to do with them as far as their business was concerned. I'd see them, but I didn't pal with them. We had our own crowds. But that wasn't the story you read in the papers.

The story kicked around for years. George Scalise—"Poker Face"—went on trial in New York in 1940 on charges of grand larceny and forgery. He was charged with stealing millions of dollars from the Building Services Union and other unions he was supposed to control. They claimed he was shaking down employers and padding the union payrolls. Tom Dewey was the district attorney, and Marcus, who had been a lawyer for the mob, was now the key witness against Scalise, ratting to save himself. So that's how my name came up.

Muray Gurfein, who later became a federal judge, was the prosecutor under Dewey.

Gurfein: Did you have any further contact with any other union at the instigation or direction of Scalise?

Marcus: I did . . . He told me that he would like to get a charter for the non-kosher butchers in the Borough of Brooklyn. At that time I represented the butchers' union in New York, and I told him that I would get a charter for the non-kosher butchers in Brooklyn, providing I know who was going to be in this union, because I told him that the butchers' organization will not have anyone but butchers in the organiza-

270

tion. He mentioned the name of Max and Louis Block, both of whom I knew to be butchers; and I said, "That's very good. I will get you the proper applications and you will fill them out, and I will do all that I can to get this charter." I asked him who, if anybody, was going to finance this proposition, because I told him that the butchers' international would not advance any finances for organization, and he said, "Augie and myself."

Gurfein: Augie and myself?

Marcus: That's right.

Gurfein: That was—was that the same man you referred to as Augie Pisano?

Marcus: I believe so.

Gurfein: Now, was a charter obtained for this non-kosher butchers' union in Brooklyn?

Marcus: It was.

Gurfein: . . . Did you ever have any conversation with respect to any bosses' association of butchers at or about that time, with Scalise?

Marcus: Yes. I believe several weeks later Mr. Scalise again called me to his office . . . and told me that he would like to form an association of Italian–American butchers.

Gurferin: Employers, was that?

Marcus: That's right.

When it was over, Scalise was convicted and then spent years in jail during the forties. And the conviction may have suggested to some that Marcus was correct in saying Scalise and Augie were heavily involved in my operation.

But the local that Scalise and Augie tried to form before I came on the scene got nowhere. When we did organize, it was not an association of Italian–American butchers. And a lot of people forgot, but Louie and I were in the butcher business since we were little kids, long before we ever met Scalise or Augie. So they didn't back us and we didn't look for their backing, and they didn't give us any money to operate anything because we financed our own.

I worked. I operated my two butcher shops and financed Local 640 until it got on its feet. Later on, I beat my case, my murder conviction, and so I couldn't go into anything at the time. In 1935, the case was dismissed. I waited until 1936, and then I sold the butcher shops and got into the retail organizing fields. And the charter for 342, that was established in the Ridgewod area of Brooklyn in 1905.

But it got in the paper, because of Marcus—that Scalise and Augie were behind my operation—and so over the years you forget, or you get confused, and maybe Augie started to believe it himself. Or maybe he just figured I was going out and so he would move in and pick up what he could.

So Little Augie, who was supposed to have put me in, read the newspaper clips and they sounded good and he forgot that he wasn't in charge, because he decided to put his claim in, and he must have been out of line.

Little Augie was a small Italian guy, about five-five, five-six. He used to wear high heels. He's stand up with his chest out. He was on the quiet side, a serious character, but a bad son of a bitch. So he got too big for his shoes.

One day he was out with this girl he spent time with, a blonde who used to be Miss New Jersey. Supposedly the two went out for drinks at the Copacabana with Anthony "Tony Bender" Strollo and Strollo's lady companion. Then Augie had dinner and after that he stopped somewhere in Queens with the blonde for a couple of drinks, and then they left and went to the car, a new Cadillac.

Somebody was sitting in the back seat, and killed both of them. He was shot three times in the head. She was shot twice. Later, Strollo, too, who had been with Augie ealier, would disappear.

So that's what happened to Little Augie. Normally the mob wouldn't kill the girl, unless maybe she was involved some way. Or maybe they had to kill her because she was a witness.

I didn't know which ones ordered the killing, because I didn't talk to anybody and nobody talked to me. But apparently Augie went to the mob, or one of them, and spoke about it at a meeting. And he must have been told to stay away from Max Block. And that was it. Apparently he didn't obey orders—so they killed him. Meanwhile, the police didn't know what happened. And a lot of people couldn't figure it out, because Little Augie was saying he was in charge.

40

The Kennedys sold themselves to the public. Every day you'd pick up the papers and read about the Kennedy family. You see this. You know that. You got the Kennedy look. And here Kennedy is on skis. He's skiing. Now you see, Bobby Kennedy is next to a tall guy above him. But I know Bobby's shorter. So I look down. Bobby's on his skis, and the other guy is without skis. They're on the snow by his feet. So I saw them as phonies, but they were fooling the public, and John got elected.

The father, Joe, was a no-good bum. As ambassador to England he supported Chamberlain on appeasing Hitler. He admired Hitler. Now John was supposed to be the gentleman, but everyone forgot how the old man made his money. You can't blame the son for that. Joe was just a worn-out old man by now, and I remember when I used to see him on Central Park South, he was in a wheelchair and getting weaker. So I'd say, "Hello."

What was I supposed to do—tip his wheelchair over? He was no good. During the election campaign the Kennedys hid the old man. The rumor got out, and they started it, that John didn't get along with his father and that his father didn't bother with them. But after John was elected President, all you saw was Joe. His father's kisser was right on T.V., and I

273

looked and I told some of my friends who voted for him, "See? Now he says to the public, 'He's still my father.' And the apple doesn't fall far from the tree."

When John was running for office, some reporter asked him, "If you get elected President, would you put your brother Bobby in as Attorney General?"

And John said, "No. That would be unethical." So the next thing, John gets elected, and he makes Bobby Attorney General.

So I'm walking with Maxwell C. Raddock of the Worldwide Press. We were at LaGuardia Airport in New York, in the terminal on the way to catch the shuttle plane to Washington. And who's alongside of us? It's Bobby. And he says real loud, "Hello, Max Block!"

I looked at him and I said, "Why don't you go fuck yourself!" And I felt good about it, because it wasn't every day you got to tell that to an Attorney General.

Kennedy walked off—what was he going to say?

Meanwhile the F.B.I. guys were there with Kennedy.

"Jesus, Max. Those F.B.I. guys might have killed you," Raddock said. And he looked at me, like I ought to be more careful. So I told him, "What are they gonna do to me—kill me for telling him to go fuck himself?"

And what else was Kennedy going to do? He didn't have anything on me, or else he would have used it. In the end I was never indicted for anything. So I saw him as a phony bum, and I couldn't tolerate him. The McClellan hearing was over now, but I didn't think anything was any different. I saw him as too eager to hurt people to get ahead. And I figured that people don't change. Maybe they get a little smarter, but that's it.

So that was all. Nothing more came of it. And Maxwell C. Raddock was always talking about how he could write books about me, if I would open up. But that was one story Raddock never ran in his Worldwide Press.

41 For years I watched what was happening in the food industry, the changes in technology and labor that had so much impact on the kind of food we eat.

In the early days, the trade unions tried to keep out the chains, to keep them from moving in on the territory of the small meat market. Now the small meat market was going out, while the big chain, the big industrial plant, brought large numbers of union members. So everything changed.

When I was a kid, the stuff we ate came from around where we lived. It didn't have to be stored in large central warehouses, preserved for months or even years. In the small shop, the butcher or produce man or baker or dairy man had a better understanding of the product. Usually he knew the people he sold to.

Today you got cashiers and clerks dispensing goods from the large chains. They have little opportunity to learn about the product, and no real contact with the people waiting in line to buy it. As working conditions improved, because of the unions, many changes were unavoidable. Some even helped keep the price of food from going up more than it has. But as time went on, the situation took its toll on the food we eat.

You really need a Ph.D in chemistry to know what's going into your food today.

Before, if someone was cheating the public, at least he knew it. And word got around, and the public usually found out about it too. But now, even the butcher in the chain store rarely has that kind of understanding. Maybe he suspects a lot of products today aren't so hot. But he also figures it isn't his business.

We still had the Black Angus Restaurant and the Deercrest Country Club. And I kept up to date on the Amalgamated. In 1959 I accepted a five-year contract with the American Kosher Provisions Company as first vice-president in charge of sales, selling provisions—salami, bologna, frankfurters—for kosher departments in supermarkets. So I was very conscious of what was happening in the chains, especially the increasing use of canned goods and prepackaged foods.

You take a can of sweet peas. You add sugar, and the people become a little hooked because it suits their sweet taste. That's not the main reason for using so much sugar, but the industry doesn't mind. For the extra sales they can tolerate decaying teeth, hypertension, overactive kids who can't concentrate in school, and other possible problems from diabetes to an overweight population.

If the food isn't loaded with sugar, it's loaded with salt. The spices make it almost impossible to taste the food, but that can be a blessing. Take that away and you discover a lot of stuff is tasteless. Or you can't eat it. But the main thing—you take that can of sweet peas, or most any of the canned goods, and you got to fill up the can. The can is half juice—water and melted sugar and other kinds of garbage. So you use the juice. Otherwise, you got to fill up the *whole* can with peas.

The sugar preserves. Instead of fresh peas, like you used to get in a produce stand, now you get them in a can that's been kicking around for years. Salt is a preservative, and it also retains the water, to fill up the can or increase the weight.

As it goes along, more canned and packaged goods get used, so that's a lot of extra labor. And the public wonders about its grocery budget. Instead of paying for food like in the old days in a produce market or a bakery or butcher shop or dairy, now you pay for all this other stuff. Instead of buying more natural fresh food and vegetables, which you can still get in the supermarket, you pay for triple profits—for the packaging, the labeling, and the food you're not getting because half the can is nothing but water with a little sugar and spice.

You don't get this only in canned goods. It's the same with meat. For instance, bologna, instead of weighing four pounds it weighs six—it's like lead. And in the bologna factory, when they chop up the meat, they throw in a lot of ice cubes instead of water. The ice cubes are chopped up with the meat, but they also put in salt to retain the water and the weight. The same with patties.

In the chopped hamburger you don't have veins to hold the water so you use salt to retain the moisture, and it's frozen. On the package they advise you to put it on the fire right away, frozen. And of course it'll burn, but it's maybe twenty-five percent water. Wait till it thaws, you'll see the water run out. Only you're not supposed to wait. Cook the stuff and burn off the fat, and you got almost nothing left; but that's what you started with.

If it's warmer than thirty-four degrees, the water drips out. You see a lot of "juice" on the bottom, that's a sign that meat hasn't been properly refrigerated or isn't fresh; it's been kicking around too long and started to thaw. Maybe a shopper put it in a cart, carried it to the other end of the store before deciding against using it. Sometimes it gets laid down anywhere and stays that way for hours. The meat spoils, but the manager just puts it back where it came from. So you think it's nice and juicy. You take it home and cook it, and maybe you get sick.

The wrapping is supposed to be for cleanliness and health. But that's bullshit. That's like saying the salt water preserves the meat quickly, which is why the federal government tolerates it—but the main reason is to retain the water and the weight, so you pay more for it.

It's especially that way with the corned beef and pork products, stuff like that that you get in the supermarket.

There's veins all through the body. Every piece of meat has one, a couple. And they got a certain short pump, like for a tire. So there's a nozzle, and they stick it into the vein. We used to do it by hand. Now they use a pump. You just open the vein and shoot the salt water, or brine, in fast. It protects from spoilage. It'll lay a year. And you turn five or six pounds of meat into maybe eight or nine pounds. They just shoot the brine through like the animal was a junkie, but it's the consumer that gets the junk.

The federal government says you're allowed to use only a little salt water, but nobody cares. It's not carefully controlled. The guy that's doing it knows the thing doubles in size—he pumps in as much as he feels he can get away with; usually, whatever he wants. Lots of times he has to make up the weight, to replace what he's stealing. In some places, where they manufacture provisions and have only state supervision, they get away with murder, I've seen a five-pound brisket in a supermarket that began as a two-pound piece.

The Jewish people buy a lot of corned beef. They use the brisket, which has more fat in it. But in the supermarket it's full of salt water anyway, the same with the round, the top, bottom, eye, shoulder.

In any good delicatessen, kosher or not, a guy wouldn't buy anything pumped up like that. He knows and he sees. So he wouldn't do it. If he has to cook it himself and serve it, it'll wind up one-third the size and he'll lose money.

Occasionally an inspector issues a summons. But the inspector can't watch everything in a big plant with hundreds of workers. He may be a friend of the owner, or getting paid off. He walks the other way. So in the supermarket, the corned beef is soaking and the tongue is worse.

All the corned beef is loaded with saltpeter. You put in a lot. It makes the color look good. But for years they've been using saltpeter in the meals in the prisons to reduce the prisoners' sex drives. So when you get *corned* beef, that's supposed to mean its been pickled in brine, to preserve it. But that's not all you get—they rob you on the weight, they screw up your sex life with saltpeter, and it's so loaded with salt it gives you high blood pressure.

They also put saltpeter in the provisions they make in the bologna factory. So you get it in stuff like bologna, salami, pastrami, and sometimes in chopped meat, or certain filler meat, to gve it the red color, so it looks good. But it knocks down your sex drive.

In the market, you used to know what you were getting. Today, maybe you don't want to know. You take the meat from an old cow, and to the consumer it might look good because it has a lot of fat, or marbling. A fat cow, the meat is delicious, but still tough. You have to cook it a long time. But with a lean cow, it's like a rock. You use it for bologna, frankfurters, hamburgers.

Today, since the meat is fabricated, coming in in smaller packages, the butcher doesn't know because the only way to tell whether you got a young steer or an older one is when you see where the animal has been cut into halves, where you split the spine into two pieces the long way and then look at the tips of the small bones sticking out.

With young steers, at the end of the little bones you see where it's white and gristly. If the steer is an old one, the tip of the bone is on the pinkish side, like the rest of the bone, it's all about the same color. Then it's a rough bastard. But if you see a little white gristle, the soft cartilage that hasn't hardened into bone yet, then it's one to three-year-old, a young steer, and it's tender. But to look at it in a supermarket, less than one butcher in ten could tell.

If the meat is tender in a restaurant that doesn't mean anything, because they usually tenderize it. There's a pail, with tenderizing juice. You throw the meat in, let it lay a moment. You take it out, keep it a half-hour or so. Then you put it on the broiler. It's very tender. It doesn't matter how tough the meat was before, because the tenderizer breaks up the sinews. It also breaks up the sinews in your belly.

The color of meat should be between red and pink. You cut the meat, and the color doesn't look so good, it's a little on the dark side. But after a while the color gets beautiful. As the meat ages it gets darker on the outside and it gets a little on the moldy side, but then it's trimmed all around. So if the meat is dark, it's been sitting around too long. If it's prepared meat, sliced, and it's dark, the meat is already getting spoiled; maybe it's been a week or so since it was cut and it wasn't sold.

In kosher provisions, the quality of the meat may be better, or more carefully checked, though it's still pumped up with water, because they also have to compete. But apparently the questionable quality of our meat and other foods was becoming more obvious to many people, and this had a lot to do with increasing sales of kosher foods in the markets, to both Jews and non-Jews.

When I started with American Kosher provisions, they were doing maybe a half million dollars a year. Before long, as kosher foods became more popular in the chains, I got it up to about thirty million a year. Another thing that helped push the kosher foods a lot was Jayne Mansfield.

The public relations man from the company suggested Jayne. She came in to help with promotions, and she was a pleasant lady—smart and very cooperative and willing to help. We went up to the Catskills on some promotional deals. Hyman Kleinberg put her on as second vice-president under me. After a while, they put her on the board of directors.

The fellow that represented that outfit, Nathan Math, was the same fellow whose name came up in the McClellen hearings. Originally he was an assistant district attorney in New York, a handsome, tall guy, able and well-known, and he got me to take the job. I got a thousand dollars a week plus expenses, and I stayed on about six years.

Eventually the company went on the stock market, as the American Provisions Company. When they issued the stock, I got forty thousand shares. Jayne Mansfield did all right too. She helped a lot with the promotions, and in addition to the quality of the kosher foods it didn't hurt any that Jayne Mansfield had long legs and large tits.

"Ignorance is bliss." And the customer gets ripped off. As things get more complicated, you have to live more by faith in what you're told. You may doubt. But a lot of the time you go along anyway. Because what are you supposed to do? You have to eat.

You hear the ads. They got something new. Now the big chains like Safeway, Market Basket, and Kroger have started advertising that they are grading their own meat. Safeway says this way you'll get lean meat cheaper. To listen to the ads, by their not having to pay to have U.S. inspectors grade the meat at the slaughterhouse (the slaughterhouse pays the inspectors' salaries), they're supposed to save the consumer money. Who are they kidding? The chains will make a fortune on this, and the customer gets robbed.

And the chains can get away with it. If the meat is from the same state, it doesn't have to be U.S. government inspected. It's not that the meat is bad, but this way the customer doesn't have to get what he's paying for. That's the idea.

The chains still have to use and pay people to grade the meat. So who are they bullshitting? And the cost of the U.S. government grading at the slaughterhouse is nothing. Cheaper than in the chainstores, because the U.S. graders got a roller with a stamp, and they cover the whole carcass. One man can grade maybe two hundred cattle a day, maybe a couple hundred thousand pounds. So it costs maybe a penny to grade twenty or thirty pounds. But the chain may make twenty or thirty cents a pound, before it gets through, by upgrading the price of its meat.

If it's ungraded, and not graded cheaper, the chain actually may pay a penny or two more per pound at the slaughterhouse for the same meat. But they'll still make a fortune by upgrading the price.

The quality of U.S. graded meat is more reliable than when the chains grade their own. Where it's U.S. inspected, the grading is close to perfect. Except where there are payoffs, but these you can find in every industry.

When stuff comes in from out of the country, it's very tough to catch anything with the usual spot check, one tiny piece of meat in maybe one out of every ten cans, but sometimes you do. So authorities just found about thirty or forty thousand pounds of horsemeat coming in from Australia to one of the suppliers for the Carl's Jr. hamburger chain, and the supplier was put out of business. About the same time, I hear some Safeway and Market Basket stores advertising specials on "New Zealand lamb," but I handled lamb for years and I know a leg of lamb when I see one. So apparently the consumers got kangaroo legs, marked as lamb. I know it wasn't lamb, not only because it's too stringy and tough, but because you could take a whole lamb and it wouldn't weigh as much as one of those legs, which went up to maybe twenty pounds. The store owners probably didn't know, and maybe the buyers didn't know either. But someone knew, and without the U.S.D.A. grading, who's to question. Never mind the "leg of lamb," it's the public's leg that's getting pulled.

After the chains started with this latest grade-your-own gimmick, I walked through some of the markets to take a

281

look. I saw certain cuts marked "prime," the top grade, and "choice," second, but in many cases where they graded their own meat the quality was mediocre and the meat tough, rough. If the chains can convince us the consumer is saving money by the chains grading their own meat, then the chains can sell the public just about anything.

I remember once I bought a load of ungraded meat somewhere in Florida. It wasn't the best, but it was okay. I sent it in to the wholesaler in New York, ungraded, but he couldn't sell the loins and ribs, because the good restaurants wouldn't buy it. They were scared. The meat was cheaper and the wholesaler could price it for less, but he still couldn't sell it. Under normal circumstances, graded, there'd be no problem selling loins and prime rib.

The reason the slaughterhouse didn't let the inspector grade the meat in the first place was because the inspector told him he wasn't going to give a "choice" grade. The inspector said the cattle were a little poor, and he'd have to put a "commercial" grade on it. Once the inspector puts a "commercial" grade on it, the slaughterhouse has to sell it cheaper. So the owner says to the inspector, "Don't put any grade on it." So usually the only cattle not graded are the ones where you figure the inspector is going to mark it a cheaper grade.

Ungraded meat is nothing new. But it's a new one for the chains to buy ungraded meat, then grade it themselves. If it's ungraded, the quality is likely to be a little poorer to start with. And every piece will probably get the benefit of the doubt when the chain grades it, because there's a lot of money involved. The thought of it could give you indigestion.

According to a report in the *Atlantic Monthly* about five years ago, Federal Trade Commission figures indicated that the nation's supermarkets steal about two and a half billion dollars every year from their customers, not through their cashiers but through false weights and other shady methods. If this figure hasn't doubled since then, it isn't for lack of trying.

42

Some of the conditions in the food industry were hard to swallow. I also knew that where the mob was involved, sometimes you could consider yourself lucky if the food didn't kill you. And the union had a role to play in all this, too.

The Merkel and Trunz families were both fine families of German immigrants, and they built up big companies and made good names for themselves. They both handled good meat and ran legitimate operations.

When I dealt with Merkel, the family was entirely on the up and up. Then the old man died. Times changed. Costs rose with inflation, and they had a hard time. They had to compete and pump a lot of salt water into the meat like everyone else, yet one reason they had a hard time was because they still sold more meat than water.

But other problems, too, became more apparent with Frank Kissel, Harry Stuback, and Karl Muller, of Amalgamated Local 174, organizing the meat-processing plants—including Merkel and Trunz—and then taking over the other wholesale shops that had been organized by Local 640.

Merkel had fifty or sixty retail shops, which had been signed earlier by Local 342. Now under Local 174, Merkel was forced to meet the biggest share of the payoffs to the union and the mob—up to ten thousand dollars at a crack. Along with Trunz, Merkel had to collect the payoffs for the union from the smaller companies around. Along the way, the Merkel kids sold the business; and the new owner, William McWilliams Industries, of Texas, soon discovered unexpected problems, as happened all too often in the industry. It seems that a number of the Merkel employees had their own private sales operations going on, with a free supply of Merkel meat. Bill McWilliams had plans to improve the Merkel business with efficient management but found he couldn't manage very well. Local 174 of the Amalgamated apparently wouldn't let him fire the employees who were stealing him blind.

When they figured out how deeply the mob was involved, and that they weren't likely to change things, McWilliams decided to sell out. About this time, 1963, "Tino" de Angeles, a mob guy, began talking to Nat Lokietz, another front for the mob, about buying out Merkel Meats. That was how Lokietz eventually got into it.

I knew Tino and his friend Charlie, another mob guy, the connection for the meat that would be sold to Merkel, but I didn't know what Tino was into at the time. Everyone was impressed when they heard later, because in 1963 Tino cornered the salad-oil market by selling some four-hundred-million dollars' worth.

The Merkel Company would have gone bankrupt over all this, it turned out, because the day before Tino was to come up with the down payment to buy Merkel for Nat Lokietz, the news got out. All of Tino's "salad oil" in those storage tanks in Bayonne, New Jersey turned out to be water and air. A lot of people went bankrupt.

Merkel would have gone down with them, but at the last moment Lokietz came up with the eight-hundred-thousand dollar down payment from other sources. The full price was said to be about two million dollars.

Merkel, under Lokietz, was able to undersell the other meat provisioners and greatly improve its share of the market. I knew Lokietz had a reputation for selling meat provisions with a very high water content, but that was nothing new. To pull the company up, they had to do better than that. What gave Merkel the edge, helping them to become a leading company in the field now, was buying cheap from the mob and selling huge quantities of horsemeat, kangaroo meat, and "stinger meat" including meat from diseased and dead cows processed for mink farms (because the minks are raised only for fur and not for eating), and meat treated with small doses of formaldehyde which is normally used in embalming to cut down on the stench and discoloration.

By paying off the inspectors, using counterfeit government-inspection stamps, and buying off the meat buyers in the supermarkets, the new management ran Merkel successfully for quite some time. But Lokietz didn't know his doings were being bugged by a few detectives from the New York D.A.'s office, part of an investigation into Frank Kissel and his group at Local 174.

At first, the officials didn't want to reveal the bug, which was intended to lead to information on Kissel's connections to the mob, so no action was taken. But eventually authorities impounded some forty thousand pounds of horsemeat, kangaroo meat, and stinger meat from the Merkel plant, while the shop foreman from Local 174 expressed surprise. He talked about the careful "quality control" program at Merkel. Then the impounded meat was stolen somehow right out of the warehouse where it was placed, but the authorities were later able to trace the meat again, with the help of the bug and supposedly by following the stench.

The story broke in December 1964, and the front-page headline in the *New York Daily News* read: MOB FLOODS U.S. WITH FAKE BEEF—Find 20 Tons in Queens Plant.

Supposedly the meat had been coming into Merkel for at least a year, since Lokietz had taken the company over, and maybe a million pounds had been distributed to the city's schools, the army, the air force, hospitals, prisons, supermarkets, and so on. Quite a bit apparently went to the A.&P., where a number of meat buyers were on the take. Of course, Merkel wasn't alone in selling horsemeat or kangaroo meat—but mink meat with formaldehyde, that was stretching it some.

The long investigation that eventually swept up Merkel got underway, originally, after one of the A.&P. buyers was charged with taking payoffs and upgrading meat. The buyer was fired, but his wife complained. She sent an angry letter to A.&P. officers—why pick on her husband, she asked, when payoffs were still going on? Apparently her husband was the only one paid by check. But as a result, a vice-president of the A.&P. went to the district attorney's office.

After the story broke, the markets commissioner, Albert S. Pacetta, who according to the bug was to get a ten-thousand-dollar bribe, defended the new Merkel company as an innocent victim.

"This is probably a one-shot situation," he was quoted in the paper, after the horsemeat and other stuff was found. "I know that none of this shipment, not even one ounce, has got out of Merkel's warehouse." Of course, what the commissioner knew was one thing—maybe he wasn't too bright. Apparently the sale of the low-grade meat had been going on for at least a year.

At a press conference, the commissioner said his inspectors received "full cooperation at the Merkel plant" and that "no effort was made to hide anything." And standing next to Pacetta at the press conference was Karl Muller, president of Local 174 of the Amalgamated, one of the guys that along with Emmett Kelly ratted on me when the investigation was underway for the McClellan hearings.

Before I resigned the talk by these guys was that my staying on would give the Amalgamated a bad name. Before it was over they would all go to jail—Kissel, Muller, and Stubach, from Local 174, for extortion. The leaders who followed me in 342 also would be jailed, although in one case it would be for income-tax evasion. And Kissel, Muller, and Stubach would be played against each other, and the sizable payoffs from Merkel and other places would backfire. Because after the Merkel story broke, a bug was authorized in the headquarters of Local 174. Their day was coming.

43 As time went on, it became obvious that the mob was expanding its activities in the business world. Perhaps less understood was that in those areas where the mob was always known to exist, like boxing, the mob influence became even stronger, especially since the 1950s.

In February 1962, a twenty-two-year-old two hundred ten-pound heavyweight boxer, Cassius Clay, won the championship title in Miami Beach from thirty-year-old Sonny Liston. Cassius Clay (now Muhammad Ali) didn't know it, but Sonny Liston apparently had made up his mind—he was getting a little old for that stuff, and he was ready to retire. So from the looks of it, he threw the fight, and he picked up a bundle, and so did the mob.

I discussed it with Barney Felix, the referee, a good friend of mine. Later I discussed it with Rocky Marciano, because he came into the Black Angus after that and I figured he saw the fight.

I saw the Liston–Clay fight on television. Then I talked to Barney, a pretty good fighter himself, along with his brother. Barney was telling me how he kept pushing Ali, wouldn't let him quit, because it was like Ali kept running from Liston and wouldn't fight.

Barney went up to Ali in between rounds, he told me, and he said, "Don't quit, don't lay down. You'll be suspended for life."

Apparently it was a setup. Ali didn't know, and neither did Barney. But Barney wanted a legitimate fight—he's a good boy. And so he kept on Ali, because nothing was happening in the match.

Barney was right there; he could see what was happening. The way he finally figured it, Liston was supposed to lay down —but only after so many rounds, and of course he was supposed to take a few blows. But Ali didn't know that, Barney said, so it looked to him like Ali wanted to quit after one minute when he got hit in the belly by Liston. Because Liston was a hard hitter.

Maybe Liston was afraid he'd accidentaly knock Ali out; and Ali was just dancing around. So Barney kept on Ali, he said, and finally he told him, "You son of a bitch! If you quit, you'll be crucified for life. You'll never fight in the ring again."

After that, Barney said, Ali came out swinging. He hit Liston, but not that hard—because Liston you could hit with a hammer and you wouldn't knock him out. He was tough as nails.

So Ali threw a left and a right, and Liston went down. But you could throw a hundred punches like that and it wouldn't knock Liston down. Barney was right there. He could see, and he knew what was going on.

"Shit!" Barney told me. "You couldn't knock out a cat with that." So he figured Liston was taking a dive, that the guy saw an opportunity and he went down, and he didn't get up.

This was in the seventh round. Everybody was surprised, because Liston was the big favorite—a powerhouse. And you couldn't tell me anything but that the guy laid down, and Barney confirmed it.

All the big money went down on Liston. I guessed he made up his mind to quit, so it looked to me like he made an arrangement with the mob. If he wasn't ready to quit, he probably wouldn't make a deal—but going out, he could make a bundle to retire with. He was in close with the boys, and that was the way I read it—a funny match, with Liston trying to lay down and Ali not wanting to fight.

Tunney was definitely not involved with the mob. Neither

288

was Dempsey. The mob got into it later on. Marciano tried to keep away, and he was successful at it too. And Barney Ross tried his best to keep away, and he did.

But the mob influence was getting heavier in the fight game as time went on. And for a fighter to get anyplace nowadays, you usually have to fall in with them, and they make the matches. Otherwise, you might not get into the ring. And they get stiffs to lie down. Frankie Carbo was involved for a long time. He was in that, and he was a kingpin in the mob. Now the younger ones most likely have to deal with the black mob. The fighters are mostly black, and it's a little different.

The mob doesn't care. They find a boxer with a little class and they bring him up fast, so they can make money off him. But you put a kid like that up against a tough fighter, like Sonny Liston, if he's really fighting, and the guy's going to get killed.

They bring these kids in that don't have that much training. You watch a match today and it's like a street brawl. They don't know how to fight, and they're not that tough. They can't handle themselves against a tough fighter, so a lot of them do get killed. In recent years, most of the boxers who did die got killed because of that. You get hit in the head too hard, too solid, and you get a concussion on the brain, and goodbye!

I saw too many boxers die that way. So maybe Ali knew how tough Liston was. Maybe he felt he wasn't ready yet but got pushed into it. Maybe he backed off for that reason. But this time he didn't have to, because Liston would hardly lay a glove on him.

If looks can be deceiving, this is especially so in Las Vegas. I started spending a lot of time in Las Vegas. I'd see different people around, but I'd mind my own business. I didn't always know who was who.

So there was this old guy in the Desert Inn, probably in his late fifties, I figured, but it was hard to tell because he needed a shave. He looked like he had about two dollars in his pocket.

It was Howard Hughes.

I was sitting with Wilbur Clark, the owner who started the Desert Inn in Las Vegas, and Howard came by, and Wilbur introduced us.

289

"Howard, I want you to meet Max Block. Max—Howard Hughes." We shook hands, and Howard mumbled hello. I gave him my usual strong handshake, and he took notice.

Then Wilbur said, "Howard, you better make arrangements to move out, because I need the rooms." Hughes had the whole top floor of the hotel tied up.

Howard looked at him and said, "How much do you want for the fucking joint?"

"Do you really want to buy it?" Wilbur asked.

"Sure."

And that was it. They started bullshitting.

They made a funny twosome. Wilbur Clark, who had the most publicized name in Las Vegas, with his picture on silver coins, ashtrays, gambling chips, matches, and menus, and Howard Hughes, the recluse.

Wilbur, the "good will ambassador of Vegas," whose wife was Catholic and who had been presented to the pope in two private audiences and who was listed in *Who's Who*, wanted the world to know he was around. With his diamond accessories glittering even among the bright lights of Las Vegas, Wilbur was twice voted among the ten best-dressed men in America. And in Las Vegas, he was practically the only hotel owner without a criminal record.

Howard Hughes, on the other hand, looked like a bum. He was all right. Alert. He didn't appear to be on drugs at the time or anything like that, but he still needed a shave and looked like he had no more than two dollars in his pocket. And that was how he walked around the hotel all the time. Of course, Hughes could buy Wilbur out many times over. So the two negotiated, and Hughes and his group ended up buying out the Desert Inn, Hughes's first entry into the hotel business in Las Vegas. The figure, I recall, was about fourteen or fifteen million, but Wilbur Clark saw only a part of that.

Next to the Sands, where you had Frank Sinatra and Dean Martin, the Desert Inn was probably the most successful hotel on the strip.

Wilbur had started the Desert Inn in 1947 with his brother and a couple other investors, with a few hundred thousand dollars. Then they ran out of money, and building came to a standstill. A few years later, Wilbur met Moe Dalitz, of the Detroit Purple Gang, and soon after that Wilbur had a deal.

He got the additional financing he needed from Dalitz and Dalitz's partner, Morris Kleinman, and there was some other money involved, including large loans from the Teamsters Pension funds.

Of course, Meyer Lansky was also involved in the Desert Inn, and later, along with Wilbur, Dalitz, Kleinman, they also had a big piece and the controlling interest in the Stardust.

Moe Dalitz owned the Desert Inn Country Club in Las Vegas. He was also the big man in the La Costa Hotel and Country Club, usually called La Costa, a five-thousand-six-hundred-acre luxurious resort complex north of San Diego, by La Jolla and the track there. They got about fifty or sixty million dollars in financing for that out of the Teamsters. The Teamster Central States, Southeast and Southwest Areas Pension Fund, had about $1.4 billion in its kitty—the largest private pension fund in the country then. Along with the hotels in Las Vegas, La Costa was a pretty good bet to make money.

I was at La Jolla when they were building La Costa, and I bought two houses there. I got them, sold them fast and made a little profit. But I should have hung on, because they're worth maybe a half million dollars now.

Kleinman, Moe Dalitz's partner, spent a lot of time in Miami. That's where I would see him, with Jimmy Blue Eyes, at the Diplomat. Kleinman used to pick up money for Meyer Lansky.

Wilbur usually stuck close to Las Vegas, but of course, no-body came from Las Vegas. Originally Clark was from Illinois. He hitched out west as a kid and spent time around San Diego, Reno, Palm Springs. Like Hughes, Wilbur was an interesting character. Once he was on the Edward R. Murrow show, "Person to Person" kind of an American success story, because Clark had worked his way up from the bottom, wash-ing dishes, working as an elevator operator, bellhop and so on.

So he had a colorful career. Years back he worked on some of the gambling boats along the California coast. After that he operated a couple of small bars, with gambling in the back, and then he bought a small hotel in San Diego. Later he bought into El Rancho Vegas, a big hotel on the Strip, and then got into the Desert Inn.

Dalitz and Kleinman were also involved with gambling in-terests, and it went from there. In the early sixties Wilbur was on the books as the largest owner, with about seventeen per-cent, with Dalitz and Kleinman getting about thirteen percent each. Somehow they worked it all out, when Hughes came in.

By this time, in the mid-sixties, you couldn't find a major hotel in Las Vegas that the mob didn't own or hadn't bought into. Hughes was not involved with the mob. He had his own empire.

On one occasion some years earlier, Wilbur went before the Kefauver investigation. The committee was trying to investi-gate mob influence in Las Vegas, but they got about as much out of Wilbur as the McClellan Committee got out of me.

Wilbur said he didn't know the names of a number of people in charge of the different departments in the Desert Inn, which he was supposed to own, and Senator Tobey of New Hamp-shire, one of the guys on the Kefauver Committee, interrupted him.

"You have the most nebulous idea of your business I ever saw. You have a smile on your face, but I don't know how the devil you do it."

"I have done it all my life," Wilbur said.

And it was true. He always had a big smile, and he was a jovial guy, and people liked him. So we were close, and we got on well together. I wasn't involved with Wilbur with the hotels in Las Vegas, but we had some other deals set up on some other hotels.

Wilbur originally came to see me in Miami Beach, after a guy from Philadelphia in the mortgage business suggested he see me about arranging some financing. So then Wilbur came down and told me what he had in mind—he wanted to arrange a loan, five million here and a million-and-a-half there, and I was supposed to help him get the financing from the different unions, the Teamsters and so on. And after we spent some time I told him I could handle it, and I did.

So I spent time with him. I went out to Las Vegas to his hotel, and after that he got himself a brand-new hotel across from the NASA complex in Houston, Texas. I got him the first mortgage on that hotel and another in Anaheim, the Wilbur Clark Crest Hotel, and he took that over and he began building in La Jolla, by the golf course, the first high rise on the eighteenth hole.

He got involved with a partner, Bill Ward III, and Ward

also lived in La Jolla. Bill Ward apparently came up with the idea about building some new hotels, involving some millions of dollars, and we had already gone into it and I was going to get the money, but it was promised from the Teamsters.

We met in La Jolla, at Wilbur's high-rise by the golf course. We talked about adding a hotel in Austin, Texas, and by this time the thing was worth maybe fifty million dollars. We got together, and Wilbur was there with his wife, Tony, and I told him I could handle it, because I had already been promised the financing, and we worked out an arrangement. My son was going to front it.

This was on a Tuesday and Wilbur wasn't feeling too good. We were supposed to get together again in a few days. So we worked out the deal that Monday I'd meet him in Las Vegas and we'd go to the lawyers' and draw up the papers and I'd be entitled to the ten percent, and I was supposed to get one hundred twenty-five thousand cash, for arranging the financing.

"I'll see you next Monday in Vegas," Wilbur said, "and I'll have the lawyers draw up the papers and we'll get everything in black-and-white." And Wilbur had about a seven-million-dollar statement on his net worth that was being used as collateral.

Thursday I got a call in my home from Alvin, my son.

"Dad, you up?"

I said, "Yes."

"You better be up."

"Why?"

"Wilbur died," he said. "He had a heart attack and died."

So nothing was down yet on paper and I lost a lot of money on that deal. But Monday I came to Las Vegas as planned, only it was to Wilbur's funeral.

44

Some people think of the Teamsters as a crooked union, especially after it was ousted from the A.F. of L., and Kennedy went after them. But the Teamsters are in better condition than all those others where various people shake down the employer. The Teamsters didn't give away anything to sell out the worker, like some of the established unions and most of the independents.

The Teamsters get contract agreements, and they're equalized industry contracts, and they can't get away from those. They have to stick by them.

Jimmy Hoffa's mother, a young widow, used to wash clothes that Jimmy carted home. Then they moved from a small town in Indiana to Detroit, where it wasn't much easier. As a kid, Jimmy chopped and sold wood. He hauled ashes, a phrase to later generations. To pick up a few dollars, Hoffa would hang out by the factory gates and pass out leaflets for patent medicines to the workers.

At fourteen, in the seventh grade, he quit grammar school to work full-time. Like his father, an unsuccessful coal prospector who died when Jimmy was four, Jimmy had hopes of a better life.

When he was seventeen, not satisfied with the conditions, for himself and for others, he organized his first strike. Hoffa's son would play tennis and become an attoney, but Hoffa fought his battles in the street, where you had to make up the rules as you went along.

Nowadays, new organizers don't often realize what's going on. They think it was always this way. It was always a snap. They don't have to bring in the members. Today unions are like a registry, collecting money from the payroll.

Hoffa was railroaded by the Kennedys. Bobby wanted him, and Bobby finally got him.

Hoffa was no angel but he did a great job for his organization. And he was more honest than a lot of guys that convicted him.

Hoffa wasn't a gambler. He wasn't a high-liver. He was a guy with simple tastes. But he had an amazing memory, and no matter who you were, he knew your name and what your problem was. He was always ready to listen to you and you didn't get phony chatter from him. He paid attention. He was interested. That's why I liked him.

Bobby Kennedy got hold of a drunken bum, a convicted dope pusher who was a member of the Teamsters to set Hoffa up and testify against him. And supposedly Hoffa said it was worth fifteen thousand dollars to beat the case, a mail-fraud charge. He could have said it was worth a million. What difference did it make how much it was worth? So does that convict a person?

They tried to prove Hoffa said it to this guy, in order for this guy to pay fifteen thousand to a juror. This money was nothing. But they grabbed this guy and arrested him and threatened him, and he testified against Hoffa. So Hoffa was convicted of jury tampering in Tennessee. But four of the nine Supreme Court justices voted against the conviction.

Chief Justice Earl Warren called the conviction "an affront to the quality and fairness of federal law enforcement." According to Warren, "Here the government reaches into the jailhouse to employ a man who was himself facing indictments far more serious, charges including perjury, than the one confronting the man against whom he offered to inform.

"It employed him not for the purpose of testifying to something that had already happened," Warren said, "but for the purpose of infiltration, to see if crimes would in the future be committed. The government in its zeal even assisted him in gaining a position for which he could be witness to the confidential relationship of attorney and client."

New York Teamsters leader Barry Feinstein was quoted in Steven Brill's book *The Teamsters*: "Sure he was guilty. But they could put you in jail, too, if they did that number on you—investigating every detail of your life. Who isn't guilty of something?" And Brill's report added, "'Sure we had a vendetta,' one member of the 'Get Hoffa Squad' conceded . . . 'But you have to understand how terrible this guy was . . . We weren't Nazis . . . But I guess in this day and age (some years later) I'd have problems if other people organized a squad like this specifically against some other guy or group.'"

So a lot of people outside of Nixon had their "enemy lists," and it's too bad if you were on the wrong side. In early 1967, in Hollywood, Florida, Jimmy Hoffa presided over his last meeting of the Teamsters executive council.

The day before he went to prison, Jimmy introduced me to Frank Fitzsimmons, and he said to Frank, "Whatever Max wants, he's a good friend. I know Max for thirty years." And right there, in front of Frank, Jimmy said to me, "Anything you need, talk to Frank." And Fitz said, "Sure." And so Jimmy gave me an okay with Fitz to do anything I wanted.

Hoffa picked Fitz to replace him, because they were friends and Fitz had been with him for years and he trusted Fitz. Then Hoffa went off to jail.

45

A lot of stuff catches up with you. In August 1967, Frank Kissel, Karl Muller, and Harry Stubach of Local 174 were indicted for extortion. The charges involved payoffs of sixty thousand dollars by Lokietz, from Merkel Meat and Trunz and other meat dealers to prevent Local 174 from striking at a crucial time in 1964 just before the Fourth of July.

Of course there was a lot of other stuff going on and I got the report back how these guys said, "Jeez! Max must have made millions." I didn't, because we didn't operate that way. But at Local 174 and the Amalgamated some of these guys, they couldn't believe it. They figured I must have made millions. So now they would try. And they found it wasn't that simple.

After long delays the three finally went to trial. To stop the union from retaliating against the shops for testifying about payoffs to Local 174, the district attorney's office arranged to have *all* the meat dealers testify. They'd get immunity from prosecution, but those who refused to cooperate were threatened with perjury charges.

The evidence was so strong, the defense didn't deny the

payoffs but argued only against the extortion charges—they said the dealers tried to bribe the union bosses. But apparently the demands from the union were so excessive, this time, that the dealers hadn't even offered.

The first key witness was Lester Levy, president of the Plymouth Rock Provision Company that was doing some thirty-five million dollars-a-year volume. Levy, a relation of Kissel, claimed he had a small profit margin while employing about six hundred workers, almost all of them members of Local 174.

Levy told about a negotiating session of the Meat Trade Institute in the Belmont Plaza Hotel in Manhattan in early 1964. Frank Kissel pulled him aside, Levy said, and told him that in order to prevent a strike—the union's first strike in the processed-meat industry since 1930—he wanted sixty thousand dollars.

"It was just before the Fourth of July, which is one of the busiest weeks of the year," Levy explained. "We had two, three hundred thousand dollars of perishable inventory and no freezers." So Levy went to Karl Muller, he said, who he had known some forty years, to complain about the high demand set by Kissell. But Muller told him, Levy testified, "Whatever Frank Kissel does is okay, and Muller couldn't 'make any changes.' " Levy's share of the payoff was set at six thousand, he said, and Kissel was supposed to come around to collect.

After that, another witness explained how it was all set up to make the bribe tax deductible.

Fritz Katz, owner of Stoll Packing and several other companies handling ham, bacon, and pork products, employed maybe two hundred fifty butchers and was signed with Local 174. Katz testified about his conversation with Frank Kissel.

"Frank, what do I hear? Sixty thousand dollars? That's ridiculous! What kind of figure is that? And I was angry and he was angry," Katz said. "Kissel brushed me aside . . . and he says, 'Stop chiseling. You get away cheap.' And he walked out of the room. That was it."

Katz testified that Kissel met again with him, along with Charlie Trunz, and Buddy White of Plymouth Rock Provision Company. Katz said Kissel wanted the sixty thousand "in one lump sum . . . before the contract is signed," and Katz was supposed to collect it. But he said, "Frank, I don't want to collect this."

Katz explained that after going around, because Charlie Trunz didn't want to collect from the others, and neither did Buddy White, they finally told Kissel, "All right, we'll see what we can do."

According to testimony, Katz and White then listed the pork dealers, estimating their various sizes and shares each would have to pay. Merkel Meat and Plymouth Rock, the largest packers, would pay ten percent, or six thousand; Stoll and White, four thousand, and so on.

Katz told then how the package didn't go over with the other meat dealers. "If a doctor says cancer, you must learn to live with it," Katz said he told the dealers. But immediately, he said, Kissel, who was also present, interrupted. "I resent being called a cancer."

Fifteen dealers testified at the trial, including Nat Lokietz and Sam Goldman of Merkel Meat. One bragged he shorted Kissel a thousand. Another, Charlie Trunz, Jr., said Kissel got an extra thousand from him. Supposedly Kissel told him, "Charlie, I think you can do a little better."

Then a number of dealers testified that after the investigation started Kissel contacted them, trying to prevent their testimony. Afraid of perjury charges, the meat dealers testified anyway. But later they sent on letters telling how Kissel and Muller and Stubach were good guys and solid, upstanding citizens.

Meanwhile, according to wiretaps, before the trial the investigators supposedly learned about a new collection system —called "baseball"—by Kissel and his group. The sixty-thousand-dollar figure would remain the same for the bunch, but each month a different company would pay, on a rotating basis, its share of the three-year contract.

The "baseball" story was not brought out in the trial, but the judge felt he had enough anyway. All three were sentenced to state prison. Kissel got seven and a half to fifteen years, Stubach got five-to-ten. Muller, who cooperated with the D.A. and was in ill health, three-to-six years.

A few weeks later the three were ordered freed. Another judge said there was probable cause the appeal would be upheld. But then the district attorney's office issued a new indictment against the three, claiming eleven other meat companies were forced to pay off sixty-five thousand. Meanwhile, the appeal was denied—the three went back to Sing Sing. Before they were paroled, Muller served two years, Stuback about three and a half. Kissel served four years of hard time, then went on a work-release program.

46

One time I was in the Desert Inn in Las Vegas, playing blackjack.

All of a sudden, I heard a guy say, "Max!" I looked up, and I saw Kopecky and May, the two chief investigators that worked for Kennedy at the McClellan hearing.

I realized how much time had gone by. It was ten years since the hearing, five since J.F.K got shot in Dallas.

"Hello, how are you?" I said. It wasn't like with Bobby Kennedy—they had had a job to do, I figured, and that was all. So now we got together very good. I told them to invest some money with me, and I'd play for us. They gave me a few hundred dollars, and I added some more, and then I played.

I won about twelve hundred, and we split it up. Then we sat down and ate and talked.

Kopecky's a gentleman and smart. "Max," he said, "Bobby'll be our next President."

I said, "Can you see hair grow here?" And I showed him the palm of my hand.

He said, "No."

"That's how he's going to be President," I told him. "The bum—he ain't gonna be anything. He'll be lucky if he doesn't get killed like his brother. He hurt too many people. And even if he doesn't, I think it's not going to be anything.

301

"And if he does become President," I went on, "what do you think—he's gonna make you Vice-President? You broke your balls for him, and you lied and everything else," I said. "Did I do anything?"

And Kopecky said, "Max, we love you. You know that we really like you. Out of nine investigators, nobody we talked to said a bad word about you." And they were amazed, because for the months they had investigated not a single person ever said that I shook anyone down. They didn't hear a bad word about me.

So I said, "You didn't say a bad word, but you didn't say a good word either, you son of a bitch." But I wasn't mad. They had made a report at the time of the hearing, and it was read to me. The government spent fifty-two thousand dollars for an impartial audit of Locals 342 and 640. At the close of the hearing, McClellan read the findings of that report, and he said there wasn't a dime out of order. And I said, "Yeah, I didn't know I was so honest."

They didn't argue with me. It was all friendly, but I still wanted to tell them. "You know goddamn well I'm loose with a buck. But I wouldn't sell myself for money." And then I said, "What do you think now? Bobby's brother had been President—Bobby was in a position to do something for you, but you're still in the shithouse. You're still on a payroll, doing your job."

And Kopecky said, "You're right, Max."

The next day, seven o'clock in the morning, there was a knock on the door. It was Kopecky and May. They said they wanted to tell me goodbye and to thank me for everything, because we won a little bit and we had a good time.

Then about four weeks later, Bobby got killed. He got shot at the Ambassador Hotel in Los Angeles.

I had told Kopecky and May how Bobby's assassination wouldn't surprise me, but of course, I was shocked, like everyone else, when it happened. I didn't know anything about the shooting, but because of what I had told them I thought maybe they'd come around. But I never heard from them after that.

So Bobby got killed, too. Campaigning for the Presidency was a gamble.

❖   ❖   ❖

I spent a lot more time at the racetrack. This trainer, Frank Kearns, his horse lost a couple times, and he couldn't understand it. Finally he found out what the problem was and he told me—the horse was jerking off.

The horse is lying down on the hay, and he gets a hard on. He starts moving, against the hay or the straw, whatever he's lying on. I'd seen it happen before, with other horses. They start moving, until they come.

That's what Kearns told me. So apparently the horse was weakened and not paying attention to the racing. Of course, I figured horses were never too smart anyway, and I had already written the horse off.

Then the trainer says to me one day, "I'll fix that son of a bitch!" And so he cut the horse's balls off. He had him castrated, so he could pay attention to business.

Now Frank came up to me a little later and he said, "If he stumbles out of the gate, he'll win." And Jesus! the horse stumbled out of the gate, and he won—he won by about five lengths. He went off at terrific odds, about thirty or forty-to-one, and I had a bundle riding on him.

47

Once in a while, some of the people you know make it big. In the late sixties, Carlo Gambino became the godfather for the whole Mafia, the boss of bosses. But he remained, to me, an easygoing fellow.

He had a bodyguard who lived next door. And he still had the big, beautiful house by the water. He made a remark to me how lucky he was to be able to outlive Charlie Lucky, Joe Adonis, and some of the others. By rights they should have knocked him off, he said. So he thought he was lucky. As the years went on, some of the people died or got killed for one reason or another. Others, like Charlie Lucky, got deported.

Gambino was against dealing with drugs. He felt strong about it, and if the family didn't obey, they'd get killed. Young ones would come up, and if they'd get out of line they'd get knocked off. That was the way it worked in the mob—it didn't matter if you were a brother or an uncle.

I was in the mob without knowing it. They considered me one of them. Because after all, any killing that was going to happen in the area they made sure I stayed out. I didn't know. I didn't ask.

The Saturday before Joe Columbo was shot, they sent word to me. Maybe they considered me as one of their comparés. I was at the races, and an old-timer told me to stay away from

New York on Monday. So they told him, if he saw me at the track he should give me the message—I shouldn't be around.

This was 1971. Joe Columbo was about thirty-seven, thirty-eight, a little on the chubby side. He was always with the mob, and then he got a contract to knock off Joe Bonanno. But instead of knocking off Joe Bonanno, he went and squealed to him, and after that Bonanno made him a big man in South Brooklyn. That was where he came from.

Columbo was involved with numbers, bookmaking, shy-locking, all the illegal stuff, and he developed his own mob. Then he was harassed by the Internal Revenue Service, and he started making complaints. The authorities were taking advantage of the Italian people, giving them a bad name, he said. He tried to copy the Jewish organizations to make a good image for the Italians, and he organized thousands of pro-testors. Probably he figured out a way to make a buck out of that too.

Finally he was told by the mob, different people, to lay off the F.B.I., because he was creating too much heat in the city, and maybe they also figured he was getting too powerful. He was a pretty bright guy, but not bright enough. Because when the mob sent word to Columbo to lay off, not to continue his war with the F.B.I., he went ahead anyway. He called an open-air meeting at Columbus Circle, on Columbus Day.

The mob had a black man shoot Columbo as he went up to the stand to talk. And as the black fellow shot him, there was another guy right behind to kill the black guy. Columbo didn't die. He was badly crippled. After that he didn't cause any more heat.

Over the years, the same problems come up. I hear a discussion on television about abortion. But they'll be fighting the abortion issue forever. The whole argument against abortion I never liked, because if you outlaw it it will still be done on the black market. Only that way it costs more money, and it's not handled as safely for the woman.

The law probably never stopped abortion. So I don't listen to positions about "right to life." You often kill both the other way, when it is done illegally.

There are plenty of cases of illegal abortions. I know. My cousin Joe used to do it, in the back of a butcher shop in

Shelton, Connecticut. Young girls, and he'd put them right up on the butcher block, and stick in the wire. I remember they used to do it in a barbershop in Richmond Hill, too.

I told Joe he was crazy. It was easier to kill a cow and make money, I said. So they'd get twenty dollars or twenty-five dollars, but I told him he was nuts. I wouldn't do it for a million.

The same thing with prostitution. The law never stopped any prostitutes from doing business. It only created an industry for pimps and the underworld.

I didn't go looking for the guys in the mob. They came to me. That's the way it's done all the time. When they see somebody they can use, they warm up to you. The question of killing is already a last resort. They usually only kill each other. Murder Incorporated was an exception.

With an outsider they're cautious. They don't kill so fast. But of course, you never know. And the mob had ways of dealing with certain rats, like Jimmy Doyle. So Doyle, an uncle to Johnny Dio, had a bad reputation even with the tough guys.

Doyle used to come in by himself to the Black Angus, and I had a friend who used to come in all the time. And one day Doyle came in with this friend of mine, a Jewish fellow from downtown. So later I see my friend in the back. "What are you doing with him?" I asked.

"He's my partner."

"What do you mean, he's your partner?" I said. "He's a low-down, no-good guy." The guy was a sharp guy, but I knew he was no good. But my friend assured me it would be okay, that he could handle himself. Apparently he figured Doyle was going to help him develop his business into a bigger operation.

A few weeks later, my friend was dead. He had some kind of clothing business. Manufacturing. So maybe the others figured they didn't need him. They knocked him off, and they wound up with the business themselves. They'd get a lot of businesses that way.

If you're going to hang around with some tough characters, you have to know how to keep your distance and to take care of yourself. Even a tough guy can get into trouble. A few years elapsed, and Jimmy Doyle was found dead. He was strangled with his own necktie.

306

48

The times goes on and you raise your family. For ten years I played softball in Great Barrington, Massachusetts, where the kids went to summer camp. I'd get moving, and the others would see me run and they'd be surprised.

I was a good runner because I used to do a lot of roadwork when I boxed, and my legs were in good shape.

It was beautiful country, and Jean and I would take the kids to the concerts in Lenox. Jean used to fix a box lunch for us and we'd go out on a picnic in Lenox, and the place would be full of people enjoying the concert in the warm spring evening.

The kids were young, growing. My son Alvin would go there every year from the time he was five until fifteen, and my daughter Iris and our adopted daughter, Danielle, also went to the same camp for years.

So the kids grow up and the parents get older.

I remember when Jean told me she wasn't feeling well. It went on like that for a time, and it didn't improve. After a while she went to see the doctor. Then she had some tests taken, and they told her she had cancer.

It was a shock. She had always been healthy. We thought

the cancer hadn't advanced very far and we were optimistic. They told her she needed surgery, so she went. After that, they told us they thought she'd be okay. But it turned out the cancer was still there, and a year later, 1971, she died.

So my Jean was gone. There was a big emptiness. You remember the past and the things you shared and the things that you built together, but it's not the same. After a while you learn to live with that, so you go on because that is the only thing you could do.

Then I almost died too, from the diabetes.

I was visiting my brother and his wife, Sylvia, in Connecticut. Sylvia said to Louie, "Max is in bad shape—if Max refuses food, there's something wrong with him." Anyhow, Louie called the doctor, and the doctor told him to bring me in to King's hospital in Portchester, New York, near the Connecticut line, so I could get a checkup. But as we walked out of the house— we were on the steps and I was holding onto Louie—a police car drove up and the officer said, "Mr. Block, do you need help?"

That's all I heard. The next thing, I opened my eyes in the Greenwich Hospital, in Connecticut, in the emergency room where they'd taken me. The nurse was looking at me.

"What's your name?" she said.

"If you're asking me my name, there's something wrong with me," I answered. "How long was I out?"

I was in a coma for two days and all the doctors thought I was finished. They kept working on me, but they told me they never thought I'd come back to life.

I learned that when you're in a coma like that you don't know a fucking thing.

They kept me in that Greenwich hospital for two weeks. I came out and I was glad to be alive. I wound up getting the insulin shots in the hospital. I had been advised some years earlier to take insulin, but I was afraid to take the injections —now I was afraid not to. Right after I started taking the injections I felt better.

49

Jimmy Hoffa was still in jail, and I didn't think it was right. Because Hoffa was a good man. He didn't look for a buck for himself even if Bobby Kennedy had tried to convince the public that Hoffa was a thief. A thief of what? What'd he steal?

He was a hell of an organizer. He brought in maybe a half million Teamsters. That's why the union got so big. And they gained so much, from the time that Hoffa got into it. He got the workers really good conditions. If he was still there, there'd be a million more members.

The whole idea to get Hoffa out of jail was my idea. I thought Jimmy Hoffa was framed by Bobby Kennedy because he had it in for him. And Hoffa fought him, insulted him while they had the hearings going. And as far as I could tell, Bobby had a deal with George Meany to knock Jimmy out of the box. Meany would have got satisfaction out of that because he had been fighting Hoffa organizationally, constantly arguing back and forth. And like I said, that would be a way to turn the searchlight away from Meany, who also had plenty of bones in his closet.

So I thought Hoffa got a raw deal. Because I had been a long-time supporter of Tom Dewey I went to Dewey. I talked to him about getting Jimmy out of the can.

So Dewey said, "I'm going to go talk to the President and see."

Dewey used to visit Nixon all the time. So he came back one day and I met with him in his law offices on Broadway in New York.

He said, "Okay, Max," and he gave me the name of a lawyer to see, a young lawyer, an Italian, from the office of Secretary of State Rogers. Dewey told me I should go see this young lawyer, that he'd follow through. But then a day later Dewey called me back. "No, Max," he said. "Forget about it. Don't bother with him."

"Why?"

"It would be a conflict of interest," he said. "It wouldn't be good."

So I said, "Who should I hire?"

"Nobody," he said. "I'll tell Mitchell to handle it, the Attorney General."

He worked it out, and that's how it came about. While this was in the works, I didn't visit Hoffa in prison. I figured it wouldn't be a good idea. I didn't write, either. Letters would be censored, and I wouldn't take the chance. I never even called on the phone. But I used to go to Washington and talk to Fitzsimmons.

The way we worked it, Dewey gave me the instructions to have Fitz call a meeting and have the board give the resolution that the union backed Jimmy one hundred percent, and so on. I told Fitz and he went ahead and did it.

Finally, I get called by Dewey. He told me to have Fitzsimmons call up Mitchell. So I go see Fitzsimmons at his office in Washington. We had lunch at their restaurant on the fourth floor. Then I told him, "Fitz, call the Attorney General."

"Who, Mitchell—that cocksucker?" he says. "I don't want to talk to that bum."

"Why?"

"He never returns any of my calls. Not for the last year, year and a half since he's in office."

I said, "Call now."

So he did. He called and he got through to Mitchell right away. Then he turned to me. "Look at this son of a bitch."

Mitchell comes on and he says, "Hello, Frank." And he invites him up. So Fitz went up there to meet with him, and

Mitchell put his arm around him and said, "Now you come in through the right door." And then Mitchell took Fitz into where Nixon was waiting in the next room.

I wasn't there, but Fitz told me that's how things went. And Nixon told him they were looking into it and working on it.

So I expected Hoffa to be out. But then Dewey died on a golf course in Florida. That delayed things some months, because otherwise Hoffa would have been out right away.

Finally, in time to affect the 1972 elections, because there was a lot of votes involved, Nixon approved a plea for clemency. So Hoffa came out in December 1971 but would be under parole supervision until March 1973. One of the conditions of his parole was that he not participate in union activities.

After Hoffa got out, I went to see him at the Blair House, a condominium in Miami, where he had a penthouse apartment.

Jimmy complained to me about how Frank Fitzsimmons double-crossed him, but I told Jimmy he was crazy. I told him how Frank worked it with me, how originally I went to Frank and said I was going to work on it, to get Jimmy out of the can, and how Frank said, "Fine." Then I told Hoffa how Frank had followed through on all the requests I had passed on from Dewey and that everything they wanted, he did.

But Jimmy was convinced Fitz double-crossed him. Hoffa was still pissed off because his wife, Josephine, and maybe a few others, had steamed him up. And Josephine, I knew, had a problem like Martha Mitchell. I figured she was drinking a lot then. She would stir things up. She used to work in the office and carry on with the telephone all over the place. Fitzsimmons couldn't take it; she was still getting a paycheck, but he told her to stay home. So she kept instigating bullshit.

So Jimmy got excited, but I told him, "It isn't so."

Then when I came to Fitz, I said, "What's going on? What happened? Why is he mad?"

So Fitz tells me, "I don't know why he's mad." But Jimmy said Frank had promised not to run again, that he'd step down when Hoffa came back. But I knew that before that, Fitzsimmons said in person that he planned to run for reelection.

"I don't want to run for reelection if it's not permanent,"

Fitzsimmons told him. "If you come out and you want to go back, then I'm not going to run now." So they made a deal, and I told Jimmie, "You're wrong."

That was the deal they made until later when they made the agreement on the pension, $1.2 million or whatever it was, and they got a million dollar tax break. They made the deal for the separation, and that's all. But then later, when the Teamsters election came up, all of a sudden Jimmy wasn't satisfied with the earlier deal with Fitzsimmons. He wanted to get back on top, and he just couldn't do it.

I didn't go into details. All I said to him was, "Listen, Jimmy, you made a deal with him, didn't you?"

He says, "Tell them it's full of shit."

After Hoffa disappeared, nobody could say anything about what happened because nobody knew anything. What can anybody say? It's all guesswork.

Did he get killed? Did he get buried alive? Did they take him to a different country? Common sense tells you, if you're going to take away a guy, you're not going to let him come back. And Jimmy wouldn't sit still. So it would be easy to figure you got to kill him. Otherwise, he wouldn't go along.

So I can't tell you who, what, when, and why. It was too late for Jimmy Hoffa to pick up where he left off.

50

On more than one oc-
casion, my life was up for grabs. A little Italian fellow, an old
friend, called me long distance on the telephone. I hadn't
heard from him in years. When he called, he heard a little
mumble and it was like I dropped the phone. So he knew there
was something wrong with me. Right away, he called back
the switchboard.

"You better go in and check to see what's wrong with Mr.
Block."

But the girl didn't want to disturb me. "He's sleeping," she
said.

"Forget the sleeping," my friend said. "He didn't sound
right. He don't talk like that, and he's out. He dropped the
phone."

I was staying at the San Carlos Hotel, by the Black Angus.
Pretty soon half a dozen friends are there. They're all nervous,
but nobody knows what to do.

They called my brother. They told him they thought I was
dead, because they couldn't get any reaction out of me. But
Louie said, "Don't worry. He's not dead. He's made of iron."

They called the paramedics. They came by, and I was taken
to Bellevue Hospital emergency room, and finally they brought
me to. Apparently either in route or after I got to the hospital

I came up about six hundred dollars short out of my pockets. But I wasn't too worried about it. I was glad to be alive.

When I was out, what I really needed was a little orange juice. If somebody had got me to swallow a little orange juice, it might have brought me to, but nobody at the hotel understood the problem.

When you're diabetic, it's dangerous if you don't eat on time. I had an appointment. I went to sleep and figured I'd get up about six-thirty or so and go to dinner, but I overslept. So I was out, and if this guy hadn't called me from Florida, that'd be it. Probably nobody would have looked for me. I'd be that way the next day—they'd find me dead.

It was the first time my friend ever called me in New York, but his telephone call probably saved my life. I since told him that I was glad to hear from him.

In California, the Amalgamated had some of the same problems with the Clerks as we did in New York. This time it involved a vice-president of the international, in charge of the local in San Diego. So Max Oslow, a big guy, about six-foot-five and weighing maybe three hundred pounds, got into a problem.

A couple of Clerks got beat up, and supposedly Oslow was involved and he was held on it.

He could have walked away. Because I went out to California for a meeting and I got it set up with the Clerks that for twelve thousand dollars they'd drop the charges. Then I talked to Pat Gorman, and the Amalgamated was going to cover Oslow on it.

But for some reason, Emmett Kelly talked Oslow out of dealing with the Clerks. So Oslow wouldn't deal with them, and then the Clerks went ahead with the charges. Oslow was convicted on it, and spent over a year in a California Chain Gang. He lost about forty-five pounds. Because of Kelly, Oslow went into the Chain Gang. So I returned the check to Pat Gorman.

Emmett Kelly came to New York to an affair given by the Amalgamated. They had about a thousand people at the Waldorf-Astoria. And Emmett brought a couple of body-guards along, sitting next to him. He was the senior vice-president of the international. He could have become president any time he wanted now. but apparently he was satisfied with his own little racket in Chicago.

This was years after I retired, but of course, I was still in touch with everybody. I went up to the main table to say hello to the different people. He saw me, and we kind of nodded, but that was all, because we didn't have anything to say to each other.

So Kelly was staying on at the Waldorf, and they were having some meetings there. Then Kelly got a call. Someone came in to tell him there was a guy in the lobby with a gift for him. So Kelly went to the lobby by himself, he didn't bring his bodyguards, and he met this young guy, a tall, muscular fellow, and the guy told him he had a present from someone.

So the story is this fellow had a piece of carved wood. It was very hard, and apparently the guy told Kelly he was supposed to deliver this as a present to him for Christmas. Then, while they were talking, the guy gripped the hardwood—he belted Kelly over the head, in the forehead. Then he dropped the wood and rushed out, leaving Kelly lying there in the lobby of the Waldorf-Astoria.

Hilton Hanna, a black guy, a very sharp fellow who was an assistant to Pat Gorman a number of years, told me about it. Hanna came out of the men's room and discovered Kelly on the floor in a pool of blood, a gash in his forehead. Hanna ran into the meeting, to get help. So they wrapped Kelly up in tablecloths to try to stop the bleeding.

The police came with the ambulance. They took Kelly to the hospital. It took about fifteen stitches to close up the wound, and before Kelly would get through, he'd have to have skin grafting.

Now, when the police questioned him, who did he think did it, and so on, Kelly said there was only one person—"Max Block. Nobody else."

They asked him if he wanted to place charges. But he said, "No." Because, he claimed, "Max Block didn't do it himself—he had one of his men do it."

When I was told that by the cops, I said, "Gee, that son of a bitch must have done me a lot of harm, if he's so sure I did it." That's all I said.

But it showed what Kelly was. Apparently he figured I

315

wanted to get him killed. At the hospital, they wanted to keep him there, but he wouldn't stay. After he was treated, he left that night for his home in Florida, and not long after that, he retired from the Amalgamated.

Over the years Kelly knew he had done me a lot of harm. So he figured it was me who set the whole thing up and that I had made a mistake, because the guy didn't kill him. But Kelly was wrong. I wasn't looking to see him dead. However Kelly made a lot of enemies, and when you make enemies, you better worry about things.

But apparently Kelly wasn't too worried when his relations called up my house. His wife was screaming and they were yelling, "We're gonna kill him, we're gonna kill him," meaning me. A cousin of mine had answered the telephone and didn't know anything about what happened at the Waldorf, or what they were talking about. But finally, the cousin said, "Gee, it's the first time I heard that someone is going to kill someone that they call you up on the telephone and warn you about it."

No one came out to kill me, and I didn't send anyone out to kill Kelly. But then he didn't get much sympathy from me either.

By now I had learned a few things. I learned that with the labor movement there's always another angle, especially when you're not organizing, or if you're looking to make a dollar. I'd seen how it works.

Guys like Emmett Kelly gave the competition a hard time. Especially the chains. Emmett had become the power behind the throne of the Amalgamated in Chicago. So his father, originally in the syndicate with Capone, put him in. Then Emmett went to college and he came out, and pretty soon he became the head of the local union in Chicago, and also vice-president of the international. He should have been a big organizer, except that he didn't believe in organizing. He had an organization that he dealt with, independents, and so he made it hard on the competition.

From another angle, you can also make it too hard on the employer you've organized—you push up the union wages so high that the company can't compete with non-union companies in the industry. Then the organized shop gets put out of business, like the Safeway chain in New York went out of business because the A.C.T.U. got conditions that were not equal to the rest of the industry.

The Teamsters use equalized contracts, but not very many others do. Meanwhile, the unequalized contract can be a major cause of inflation. There's no control over the locals by the internationals, and no control of the locals by the AFL–CIO. The internationals and the AFL–CIO don't care about contracts being equalized. A local union pulls a strike, and you want to show you're getting improvements for the workers. The tendency is to always try to get a little bit more than the next guy.

So maybe a local will get a ten or fifteen-dollar raise when it's not entitled to it according to the industry standards. Maybe they should be getting an eight-dollar raise, if things were more equalized, in line with other union contracts. But because the contracts weren't equalized to start with, now the next guy wants a sixteen-dollar raise, and it continues like this, and there's no end to it.

And the boss has to push his prices up again, because his costs are higher. Soon it's harder for him to compete with others in the industry and more difficult to sell his product or services.

In the construction industry, for example, the electrican's salary may get out of line, and the same with the bricklayer and the carpenter, until the average man can't afford to buy a home. And at the same time, there's more unorganized workers than organized, so you got competition that kills the union shop because the locals are going too far out—instead of working and organizing the unorganized, they pressure the organized shop. In New York and Chicago and all the way down the line, from coast to coast, the organized shop keeps pushing and pushing and pushing, but still nothing is equalized and everyone feels entitled to a little bit more.

Meanwhile, the labor movement is not growing. There's all these people unorganized, maybe three quarters of the work force.

With as much power as the unions are supposed to have, the large unions have very few members, compared to all. About sixteen, seventeen million in the AFL–CIO, a little over two million in the Teamsters, and maybe four or five million in the independent unions. The established unions should be organizing everything—white-collar, blue-collar, the whole shop instead of part of the shop.

Now there are all the white-collar workers, and in every plant they've got a big staff, maybe fifty, one hundred, maybe forty or twenty—whatever the amount is—but with no union. With me, they didn't get away with it. If I organized a plant I wanted the inside, too.

I didn't ask about applications. I'd have the majority in the plant. So maybe it's just laziness. And maybe they get a few dollars paid off to stay away. Meanwhile, you got all these workers that could be organized. And when the workers are not organized by the established unions, they're picked up by the independents.

The independent union is not affiliated with an international —nobody. The state charters to the Teamsters or the AFL–CIO are all set up. These are the internationals and they have local affiliates. Here there are charters and laws, but, like I said, most of the independents are no good. The workers are concerned but they don't know what to do. The small independent union that has been set up, they give the workers things. They give them hospitalization, and so on. They give them these, but not as good as they should be getting.

You got a lot of organizers in the field for the more established groups, but they're laying back today. They don't go out to organize. So you have all these unorganized shops, and a lot of them are controlled by some of the wise guys. The organizers don't want to get hit in the head. They figure, what the hell. They get paid. They get the expenses. And they go to conventions. A home in Florida. And meetings in vacation areas where they can spend time with their wives. And so they wait for the time to retire. They make whatever they can this way, and they don't organize.

Since the Hoffas, the Reuthers, the Blocks are either dead or quiet, there's almost no organizing going on. Only conversation. So there are less people organized now than ten years ago, and yet the working population is increasing enormously and you got millions outside the unions.

I look back at my life and remember when I took a new apartment in Sunnyside, Queens, and my little boy was born already. He must have been about a year or less, and I went for a walk with my wife on Greenpoint Avenue.

318

"By the end of the month," I told her, "I'll have all these shops organized." I looked around and saw the buildings from all over New York. "One day," I said. "I'll have the whole city organized, and all the areas around New York.

"It'll take me a little time," I told Jean, "but I'll do it."

She said, "Max, please be careful."

"Look," I said, "Nobody gives me anything. You gotta be tough."

So that was my dream. I set it, and I did it—I believed you had to do something with your life and not just sleep through it, not just sit around.

So when you talk about the tough guys and the mob—in spite of all that, they made the most progress. The so-called peaceful ones are just collecting their money, their paychecks, waiting for their pensions.

Mine was a different story from theirs. It was like the old school had a fire going under it and the fire went out when the new guys came in. Yet I can understand how the changes came about, the new school you got today that goes along for the easy ride.

One day I was giving a little talk, when the labor people wanted me to go back into the movement. After listening to everybody and all the promises and everything else, I was reminded of a time when I was a young boy in Connecticut. I was not a very great swimmer. My cousin Joe and I had rented a cottage on the Shelton side of the Housatonic River, and we used to work hard with the cattle, and then we'd come home at night and we would strip and go swimming in the Housatonic.

We fixed up a diving board off a tree, and we used to get on the diving board and jump in. And I always felt like swimming across the river to Derby, but I didn't want to— I didn't have the guts.

Finally one day I jumped in, and I'm swimming, and now I feel like going all the way. Then I reach midway and I'm swimming not far from the dam, and the current is tough and you get a little scared. So I'm thinking, should I swim back, or should I continue? Then I said to myself, well, if I have to turn around and swim back it's just as far—I may as well continue. So I continued, and finally I made it to the other side. And I was glad for that. But then I stood up and

I looked over across the river and I said, "I'm not swimming that son of a bitch no more." I called up Joe. I told him, "Come pick me up with the truck."

So millions still lack decent working conditions. And maybe only twenty-five percent of the workers today are organized. But it's not up to me anymore to organize. I did the best I could, the only way I knew how. Maybe there are other ways. But I saw the challenge, and I met it. I swam across the river. I survived. Others can too.

We need to build a new fire. There ought to be a new labor federation, starting with the millions and millions of unorganized white-collar workers. We need another movement to spur things on, to wake up the sleeping AFL–CIO.

So maybe they'll wake up. The challenge is there. And there have always been those who, for whatever reason, have to buck the current and swim across to new ground. And they will see the need and meet the challenge. Because the labor movement has come too far, at too high a price, to let the worker slide back into the sweatshop.